PRAISE FOR

NOTHING MORE OF THIS LAND

"Lee brings his expansive journeys and conversations to life in this consistently thoughtful, accessible narrative that blends cultural history and memoir, research and reportage. Clear-eyed about both the destructive legacy of colonialism and the complications and contradictions often forced upon those working to challenge it, he positions himself as a curious and deeply engaged fellow learner, inviting readers to explore questions of community and identity along with him."

—Nicole Chung, 10 Best Memoirs, *Time*

"Through a diverse array of sources, Lee offers readers a valuable understanding of the many forms that twenty-first century Indigenous life can take and how they might evolve in the future. . . . It's clear how much Lee cherishes his connection to Martha's Vineyard, a place that's easy to love. And in these pages, he's crafted a must-read for anyone who seeks to know the island with depth that extends well beyond its superficial myths."

—Hannah Bae, *Boston Globe*

"Intimate and lively . . . Lee's reflections demand one contemplate not only the governments in Indian Country but the troubled experiment in government that is the United States of America."

—Philip J. Deloria, *The New York Times*

"A deeply personal account of Lee's search for identity and a forthright assessment of the modern-day effects of colonialism at home and abroad."

—Katy Abel, *The Provincetown Independent*

"A powerful, genre-crossing memoir that sparkles with clarity and perspective."

—*BookPage* (starred review)

"A searching and timely exploration of indigeneity and its many interpretations."

—*Kirkus* (starred review)

"A potent exploration of what it means to be Indigenous. . . . A deft combination of affective memoir and keen journalism, this profound examination on identity and place impresses."

—*Publishers Weekly* (starred review)

"*Nothing More of This Land* is written with scrupulous attention to nuance and ambiguity. It is an exploration of a complex heritage that is self-searching, deeply intelligent, and honest. But it is also a book about America, the public realm, what an Indigenous identity means in this country, and how this has molded the life of Joseph Lee, who is a brilliant and sensitive chronicler of his own destiny and that of his community."

—Colm Tóibín, bestselling author of *Brooklyn* and *Long Island*

"*Nothing More of This Land* is a moving meditation on the legacy of colonialism and what it means for the Indigenous to belong and find home on stolen land. I will never forget the personal and historical accounts Joseph Lee powerfully shares in this monumental debut."

—Qian Julie Wang, *New York Times* bestselling author of *Beautiful Country*

"*Nothing More of This Land* is a stark, beautifully rendered reminder of all that had to occur for the happening of our existences to take place, and all who lived and fought against their own erasure to maintain a semblance of a legacy. This is a profound, and moving book, a powerful indictment of the colonial mindset that firmly balances an ode to people, to place, to remaining."

—Hanif Abdurraqib, bestselling author of *There's Always This Year*

"A forcefully illuminating and utterly compelling blend of personal narrative and vivid reportage, Joseph Lee's *Nothing More of This Land* is a triumph of complexity and insight. We follow Lee from the red clay cliffs of Aquinnah to the halls of the UN, from the Klamath Basin to a feast of muktuk and tundra greens in Bethel, Alaska; and very early on I realized I'd follow him anywhere. Lee has given us a timely reckoning with Native sovereignty and community that is adroitly committed to the mess and nuance of lived experience, rather than sentimentalized accounts of victimhood or resilience. *Nothing More of This Land* is tender, ferocious, surprising, and tenaciously thoughtful; its existence makes the world a bigger and truer place."

—Leslie Jamison, bestselling author of *The Empathy Exams*

"With lucid intimacy, Lee traces the story of the Aquinnah Wampanoag across centuries and shorelines, anchoring sweeping histories in the particular texture of lived experience. The past is not background here—it presses forward, unresolved. At its core, this is a book about how to stay in relationship with a land, a people, and a culture that colonialism has scattered and strained. What begins as personal memoir opens into a broader reckoning with Indigenous identity in motion. Lee writes not to restore some lost purity, but to chart a map forward—one that embraces contradiction, survival, and the quiet force of continuity. Few books manage to feel this intimate and this expansive, this tender and this unflinching. It's not just beautifully told—it's deeply earned."

—Morgan Talty, nationally bestselling author of *Night of the Living Rez* and *Fire Exit*

"A wise meditation on belonging, Lee offers the reader a global perspective on what it means to be Indigenous. Lee's desire for reciprocity and community will move readers to think about our planetary future. A journalistic feat, heartfelt, well researched, and vital."

—Deborah Jackson Taffa, author of National Book Award finalist *Whiskey Tender*

NOTHING MORE OF THIS LAND

NOTHING MORE OF THIS LAND

Community, Power, and the Search for Indigenous Identity

JOSEPH LEE

ONE SIGNAL PUBLISHERS

ATRIA

New York Amsterdam/Antwerp London
Toronto Sydney/Melbourne New Delhi

ONE SIGNAL PUBLISHERS
ATRIA

An Imprint of Simon & Schuster, LLC
1230 Avenue of the Americas
New York, NY 10020

First One Signal Publishers/Atria Paperback edition July 2026

ONE SIGNAL PUBLISHERS/ATRIA PAPERBACK and colophon are registered trademarks of Simon & Schuster, LLC

Interior design by Jill Putorti

Map by Paul J. Pugliese

Manufactured in the United States of America

1 3 5 7 9 10 8 6 4 2

Library of Congress Cataloging-in-Publication Data has been applied for.

ISBN 978-1-6680-8725-1
ISBN 978-1-6680-8726-8 (pbk)
ISBN 978-1-6680-8727-5 (ebook)

For my family

CONTENTS

NOTHING MORE OF THIS LAND

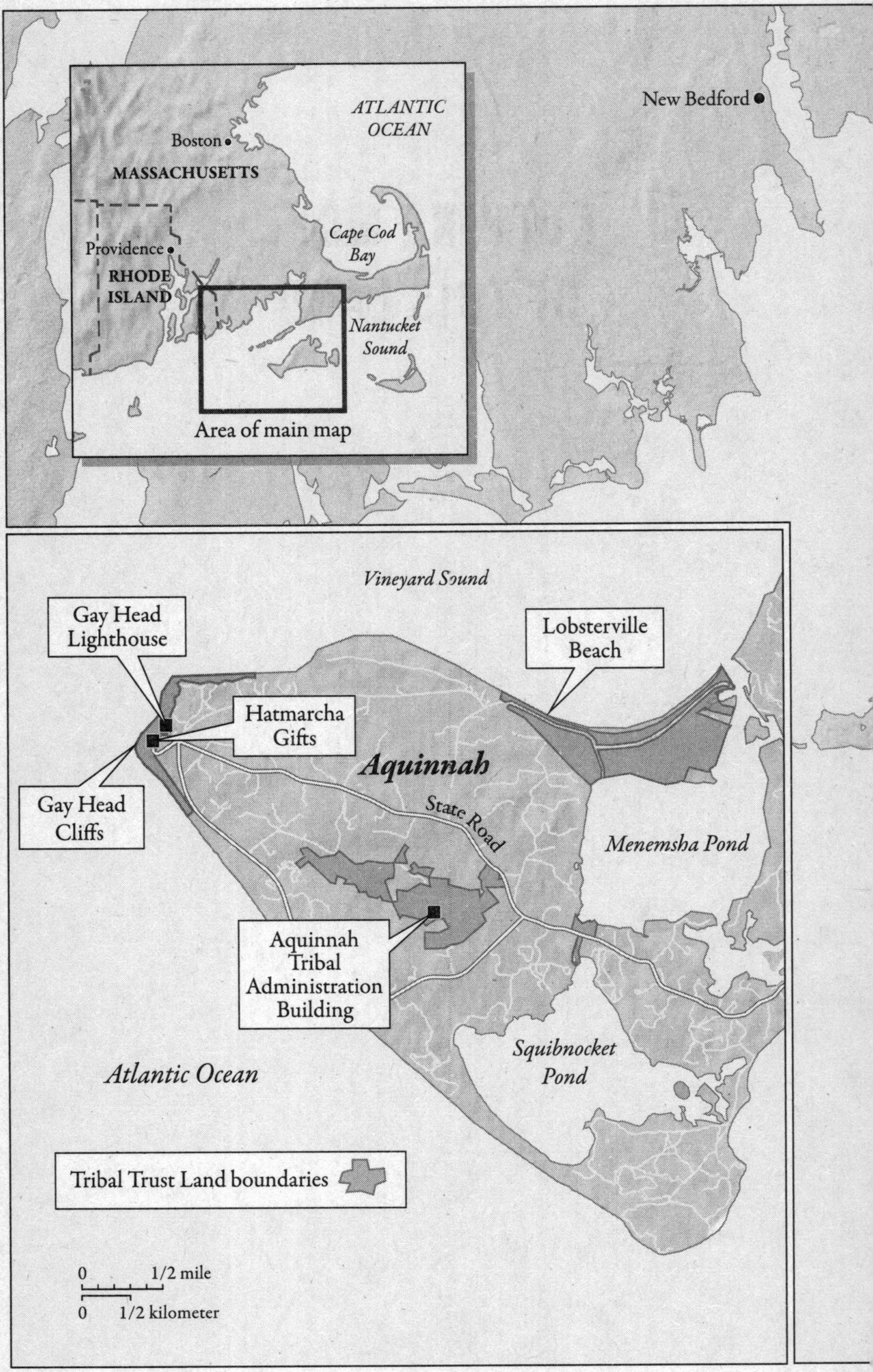

ATLANTIC OCEAN
Boston
MASSACHUSETTS
Providence
RHODE ISLAND
Cape Cod Bay
Nantucket Sound
Area of main map
New Bedford
Vineyard Sound
Gay Head Lighthouse
Lobsterville Beach
Hatmarcha Gifts
Aquinnah
Gay Head Cliffs
State Road
Menemsha Pond
Aquinnah Tribal Administration Building
Squibnocket Pond
Atlantic Ocean
Tribal Trust Land boundaries
0
1/2 mile
0
1/2 kilometer

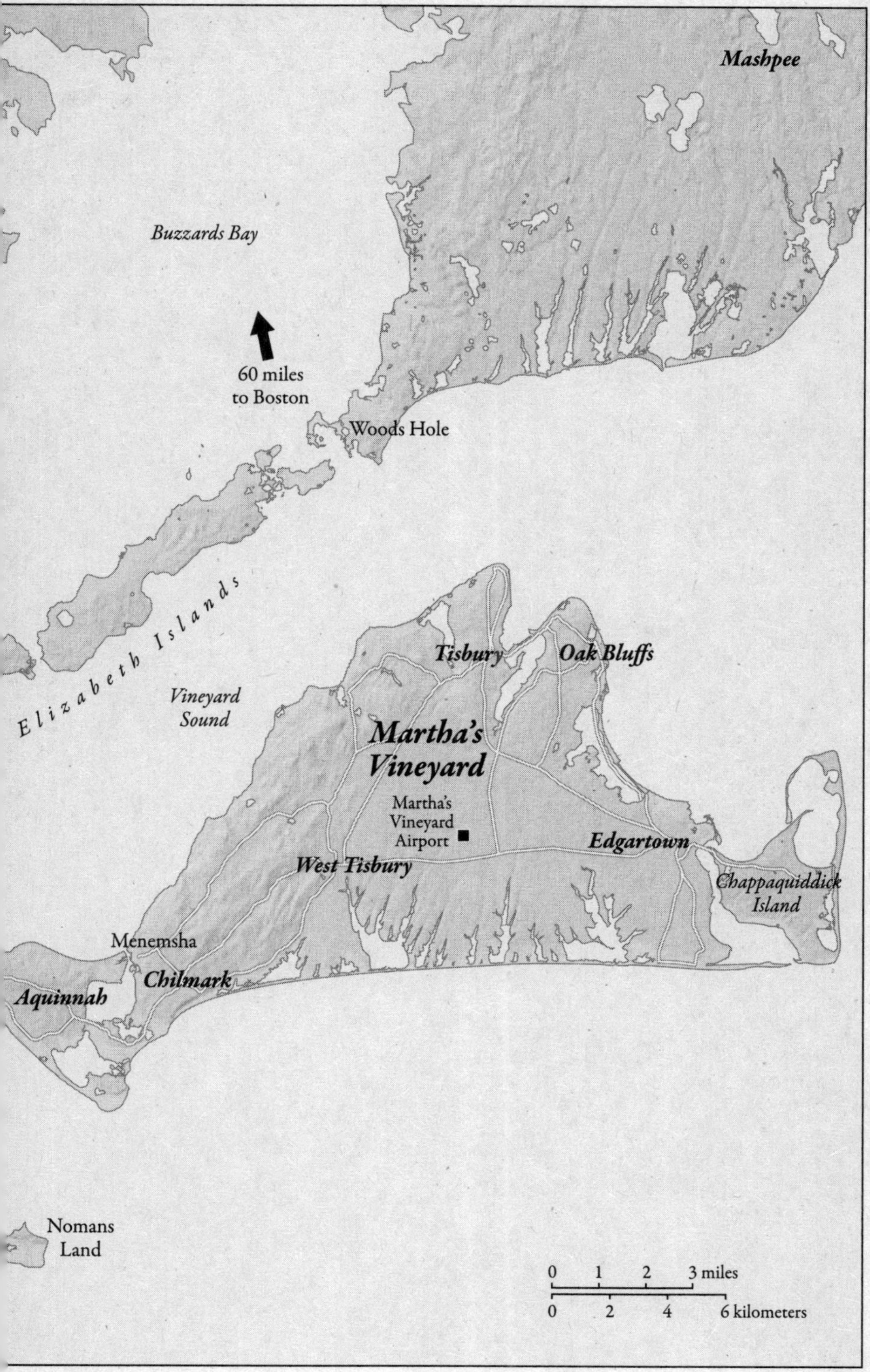
Mashpee
Buzzards Bay
60 miles
to Boston
Woods Hole
Elizabeth Islands
Vineyard
Sound
Tisbury
Oak Bluffs
Martha's
Vineyard
Martha's
Vineyard
Airport
Edgartown
West Tisbury
Chappaquiddick
Island
Menemsha
Chilmark
Aquinnah
Nomans
Land
0 1 2 3 miles
0 2 4 6 kilometers

INTRODUCTION: LAND AT THE END

According to Wampanoag legend, Martha's Vineyard wasn't always an island. In search of a new homeland for his people, the giant Moshup wandered the Massachusetts coastline. As he began to tire, Moshup's big toe dragged through the sand, leaving a deep trench. Cold seawater rushed in and eventually grew to become the Vineyard Sound. And so Moshup's weary foot inadvertently carved off a new home for the Wampanoag people: the island we call Noepe. A still place among the currents.

Over the long years of his rule, Moshup shaped other features of Noepe. To feed his people, the giant waded out into the cold ocean water to snatch whales from the depths. Back onshore, Moshup killed the whales by slamming them against the clay cliffs at the western tip of the island. Their blood stained the clay its distinctive red color. The Wampanoag people called this place Aquinnah—the land under the hill or land at the end.

Although their new life on Noepe was good, Moshup decided to build a bridge back to the mainland, so his people could trade with the mainlanders. While he tossed huge boulders into the sea, a giant crab snuck up and pinched his foot. Roaring in pain, the giant hurled the crab far out to sea, forming the small island we call Nomans. The bridge remained unfinished. To this day, the rocky area known as Devil's Bridge is treacherous for boats.

After a long, peaceful life, Moshup foresaw the arrival of a new people who would change Wampanoag life forever. He offered to turn the Wampanoag into whales and many accepted, preferring to live at sea rather than face the mysterious newcomers. Bidding farewell to those who remained, Moshup and his wife, Squant, walked into the southern dunes, never to be seen again. On foggy nights, Wampanoags say that Moshup is smoking his great pipe, still watching over us.

Every summer, my tribe reenacts these stories, "The Legends of Moshup," for a paying audience of summer tourists. Those are some of my earliest memories of the tribe—my moccasined feet squelching through the mud, the embarrassment of wearing a breechcloth, the familiar smell of citronella candles, and the echo of my cousin Adriana's narration in the summer night. As the performance moved toward its inevitable conclusion and the machine-made fog rolled in, I never wanted it to end, despite my mosquito bites and self-consciousness.

Acting out the familiar scenes, I always imagined a different ending, a Noepe without the invaders Moshup foresaw. In those moments, after a summer spent immersed in tribal community and exploring the same lands the giant shaped, it felt possible. I thought of him like a hero from my favorite cartoons, and I imagined new adventures he might have had. To me, Moshup wasn't an artifact from the past, but dynamic and alive. The real connection I felt to him, the land, and our ancestors made me believe that one day he might return. And when he did, the island would revert to the way it used to be. But once the performance was over, Moshup was gone again, the illusion was shattered, and we were all left to wonder if those he had turned into whales were better off. As I grew older, I spent less time imagining our tribal legends coming to life and more time dwelling on the sad finality of the story. I know now that Moshup is not coming back.

Today, we, the Aquinnah Wampanoag people, own only a small piece of the smallest town on the island home Moshup created for us, what is now Martha's Vineyard—one of the most expensive and exclusive vacation destinations in the country. But even as the island became best known for celebrity sightings and presidential vacations, we survived and we resisted.

As a kid, I blamed the tourists in the audience for driving Moshup away and changing Wampanoag life as he had predicted, but I was proud that we were still there telling the giant's story to—as I saw it—the descendants of the very people who tried to exterminate us.

I grew up off-island but spent every summer in Aquinnah at my grandparents' house. My brother and I spent those hot, sunny days carrying home piles of books from the local library and catching snakes we found under rocks and logs. I can still remember the day my cousin Eddie caught a ring snake, the first I had ever seen. We played stickball in our yard, salty and tan from a day at the beach. We rode our bikes up to the same cliffs Moshup had marked with whale blood, where there were then a half dozen gift stores and restaurants owned by our cousins. My grandfather told us our house used to be part of the Underground Railroad, and I imagined the big stone in the yard was a secret marker, signifying a safe house. We went to tribal summer camp, where my cousins and I learned the Wampanoag language and did Native arts and crafts. Our only worries were slicing a finger on a sharp clamshell while digging for a steamer or having a rainy day at camp.

I always knew how lucky I was to have a place like that, a place my family has lived for countless generations. But what I didn't know was what it took for me to have it, what fights happened just years before I was born. None of us realized at the time how remarkable it was that a group of Wampanoag kids was learning our language—a language that hadn't had a fluent speaker in generations. Even the building where we went to tribal camp was just a few years old when I was growing up in the 1990s. Many of my cousins lived nearby, in tribal housing, a few small clusters of affordable housing units on tribal land. I had no idea that just a generation before, none of this existed.

I assumed the tribal government had just naturally extended from Moshup's time to the present, when my cousins and I made moccasins and played tag outside the tribal administration building. I figured the building had somehow been the same headquarters that my tribe had used for generations and we simply updated the materials over the years. The first time I noticed the plaque commemorating the building's 1993 construction, I was shocked that I was older than the tribal building. I quickly realized that while I knew we had survived, I had no idea what that survival meant or looked like.

For most of my life, the three markers I had of our history were Moshup, colonization, and the tribe that I knew. I never knew what happened during the hundreds of years in between those moments, coasting along on vague assumptions about our history and what it means to be Indigenous.

It's hard for me to imagine Martha's Vineyard without the hordes of tourists. In fact, in the 1960s, my grandmother was one of the first people in Aquinnah to rent out the family house to summer tourists, a now common source of income on the island. And as Martha's Vineyard transitioned from remote locale to iconic vacation destination, my family's relationship with it also changed. For the tribe, the beautiful beaches, celebrities, and presidential vacations came with a price. Over the years, limited opportunity and constantly rising property taxes forced many Wampanoags off-island, but even those who managed to stay have been forced to confront the reality of relying on tourism—an industry that threatens to destroy our homeland year after year.

In time, I realized that Moshup's prophecy was more of a beginning than an end, but not necessarily in the way I had hoped for. Just as the invasion he had predicted was unceasing, taking new form with each passing generation, so too was the choice we faced to stay or go. I was proud of my tribe for refusing to leave our homeland, for choosing to stay, but that choice meant defending a home and a way of life constantly under threat. As Moshup's prophecy renews itself every summer, we have to fight harder to hold on to our land. I now understand the impossible choice he offered his people: to give up their home and live free as whales or to stay and live with the responsibility of protecting our land forever.

In tribal summer camp, I learned our versions of first contact between Wampanoags and the English and the First Thanksgiving. These stories, stripped of the usual patriotic flourishes, made me grow to resent the standard narrative of America's founding. I proudly announced to my first-grade class that I did not want to be friends with any "Europeans" since they were the ones responsible for the killing of my ancestors. But the contrast between my tribal experience and what my history textbooks said confused me.

Between learning about the first Thanksgiving and a unit on local Native Americans, Indigenous history—or at least a whitewashed version of it—was a relatively significant part of elementary school. And in the US history classes I took in middle and high school, tribes played a small but noticeable role during our colonial units. As the United States expanded, however, mention of Native people quickly decreased. After the War of 1812, the only mentions were a brief description of a forced removal here, a massacre there.

It was impossible not to grow up with a skewed sense of history. Aside from the Thanksgiving story, my tribal education had provided no alternative to the absence of history that I was taught in school. I was raised to be proud to be Wampanoag, proud to "still be here," a mantra I heard at countless tribal events, but I never knew what being here meant. Because my history classes taught me that tribes were powerless victims, I didn't understand what we had done to be proud of.

The only frames I had for understanding Native history were absence and genocide. Piecing together the limited information I had, I figured that my tribe had survived by staying under the radar. We suffered under colonialism, but once the American gaze turned westward, we were able to hang on to whatever pitiful existence was left for us.

Over time, I've learned that land is not something that is simply lost forever, but something that Indigenous people across the country have been fighting over—losing, regaining, losing again, and rebuilding—for as long as any of us can remember.

While I was researching my tribe's history, I came across a document known as Mittark's Will. Mittark was the leader of Aquinnah in the mid- to late seventeenth century. The will surfaced a few decades after his death, around the time of a proposed sale of Aquinnah to the State of New York. The will reads:

I am Muttaak, sachem of Gay Head and Nashaquitsa as far as Wanemessit. Know this all people. I Muttaak and my chief men and my children and my people, these are our lands. Forever we own them, and our posterity forever shall own them. I Muttaak and we the chief men, and with our children and all our common people present, have agreed that no one shall sell land. But if anyone larcenously sells land, you shall take back your land, because it is forever your possession. But if anyone does not keep this agreement, he shall fall and have nothing more of this land at Gay Head and Nashaquitsa at all forever. I Muttaak and we the chief men, and our posterity, say: And it shall be so forever.

There is some historical debate about the authorship and motivation behind the will, but I think that only speaks to how complexity and controversy have been woven into our land history since at least the colonial period. And either way, I couldn't help but read Mittark's words as a warning, still relevant hundreds of years later.

Even as I felt the haunting power of the will, I wondered what it meant for me. I didn't live in Aquinnah, but I still felt a strong connection to the community. In some ways, it was easier for me to understand the stakes of keeping Indigenous land in the seventeenth century than today. But I wanted to understand more about what protecting the land really means, and how relationships with land impact Indigenous identity and sovereignty. In the last few decades, the tribe has seen monumental changes—to our culture, politics, and community. I wanted to understand what caused those changes and what impact they were having on the tribe today.

To do that, I needed to unpack and overcome the assumptions I had about what it means to be Indigenous. The questions I was asking about our tribe and our history eventually led me to ask deeper questions about Indigenous history and experience more broadly. The more I learned about Wampanoag history, the more I wondered about similarities and differences for other Indigenous communities around the world. Part of the way I understood my own tribal experience was through the lens of what I had been told about what it means to be Native. But I realized that

I needed to create my own version of what it means to be Indigenous, and what a relationship with the land on our terms can look like.

Moshup may have given us this island, but we need to decide what to do with it. We can balance the challenge and the excitement of leaving with the joy and responsibility of returning. For years, that binary haunted me. I didn't want to be confined by this choice. I also wasn't sure I could live up to the standards set by my anonymous ancestors. Both those who stayed and those who left valued the land in a way I wasn't sure I ever could, either choosing to stay in the face of an unknown invasion or so saddened by the thought of the land changing that it was easier to leave it forever. My commitment to our land rarely feels that strong, but I have been learning to understand the little ways that it can permeate my life, whether I am on the island or not. And the more I meet other Indigenous people from around the world, the more I realize that I'm far from the only one struggling with these questions.

Seeking to answer the many questions I had about land, community, and identity took me from the beaches of Martha's Vineyard to the icy Alaskan tundra, the smoky forests of Northern California, the halls of the United Nations, and beyond. Along the way, I met Indigenous people on every step of their own journeys—to justice, to reclaiming land, to understanding who they are, to stronger communities.

Their stories include the complicated position of Freedmen—descendants of people enslaved by tribal members—who are often excluded by their own tribes, tribes deciding whether or not to keep their blood quantum requirements, international Indigenous advocacy, internal tribal tensions in Alaska, and deeply personal reflections from Indigenous people about what their identity means to them. In this way, this book is both a personal investigation into my tribe and an exploration of what it means to be Indigenous.

To begin, I knew I needed to learn more about my own community. I used to assume that my tribe once owned all of Martha's Vineyard and white greed slowly pushed us deeper and deeper in, until we barely had anything left and nowhere to go. But the reality was much more complicated.

1

A STILL PLACE AMONG THE CURRENTS

In May 1602, English colonizer Bartholomew Gosnold landed on what seemed to be an uninhabited island, which he named Martha's Vineyard. The island's namesake is still unknown, possibly one of Gosnold's daughters, or even his mother. One of his sailors, Gabriel Archer, wrote, "The place most pleasant [. . .] full of wood, vines, gooseberry bushes, whortleberries, raspberries, eglantines, etc. Here we had cranes, stearnes, shoulers, geese, and divers other birds." On the sailors' second day on the island, they encountered "thirteen savages, armed with bows and arrows without any fear." The Wampanoag party gave the Englishmen some fish, skins, and tobacco before parting ways. If this was the first contact that Moshup had predicted, it was far milder than I had imagined. But colonization can be like that, innocuous, until suddenly it isn't.

The year 1602 is etched in my memory, not because of this first contact, but because it was emblazoned on shot glasses, T-shirts, mugs, and magnets in my parents' gift store on the cliffs in Aquinnah. I always half wondered if that was a typo, since I had learned in school that the Pilgrims were the first settlers of America in 1620. That discrepancy should have been my first clue that our colonial history was not as straightforward as I had imagined. I always assumed that the change had happened suddenly—one day Wampanoag life was good, the next we were oppressed by colonial invaders. Moshup was right, of course, that the invaders would change

Wampanoag life forever, but he never specified how quickly the change would come about or what form it would take. Colonialism's slow poison is no less deadly than the sudden violence I had imagined. My parents eventually decided that 1602 products were too colonial and stopped selling them.

In the 1610s, a devastating plague hit Indigenous populations in the Northeast. From Maine to Massachusetts, tribal communities suffered from death rates between 75 and 90 percent. Many died within days of becoming sick and entire villages were wiped out. Before the plague, which has been called the Great Dying, there were sixty-nine Wampanoag villages with about a thousand people, each spread across what is now Eastern Massachusetts. Aquinnah was one of these communities. By 1618, tens of thousands of Wampanoag people were dead. When the Mayflower arrived two years later, land that had previously been full of Indigenous life was practically a graveyard. As colonization ramped up over the next decades, subsequent disease epidemics followed, continuing to decimate Indigenous communities while settler populations grew.

Although they were impacted by disease, the Aquinnah Wampanoag people remained relatively unaffected by events on the mainland, even throughout the colonial turmoil of the seventeenth century. On the island, there had historically been four separate Wampanoag villages, but most people from the other three were moved into the new Aquinnah Indian District after districts were established at the end of the seventeenth century. Today, Mashpee, on Cape Cod, and Aquinnah are the only federally recognized Wampanoag tribes.

Over the first hundred and fifty years of American history, the colonizers used a mix of theft, violence, trickery, and legal maneuvering to dispossess Indians of their land. Tribes negotiated in good faith only to see settlers openly violating treaty agreements just a few years later. Others were forced off their land to make way for American settlers. Although the removal of the Cherokee—also known as the Trail of Tears—is the most infamous example, dozens of other tribes were forced off their homelands onto foreign lands. This is the history I was taught in school about Native land.

I was confused how my tribe fit into this narrative. We hadn't been removed from our land, but we also didn't have very much of it. Perhaps because of this, I always found it hard to place the Wampanoag experience within the broader context of colonialism and Native history that I read about. I knew that we had suffered from colonialism, and that there's no way to measure who suffered the most. But because our history did not look like the more widely known stories of tribes like the Cherokee or the Lakota, I wondered how Native I really was, and what kind of legacy I could lay claim to.

In 1827, the lighthouse keeper in Aquinnah, a white man, wrote that, "there is no other Tribe of Indians within the Commonwealth that has kept the whole of its land as this Tribe has." While Indigenous land was quickly seized and settled by new settlers, Aquinnah remained a relative anomaly. And so Aquinnah remained a still place among the currents of the outside world. Today, as real estate prices skyrocket on Martha's Vineyard, it's strange to think that the island was once overlooked like that.

But like so many other previously undisturbed Indigenous lands, Aquinnah could not escape the American land-gobbling machine. This unstoppable force was driven, as always, by the promise of riches. Throughout the nineteenth century, a pattern emerged. The discovery of natural resources on Indian land would be quickly followed by American encroachment onto it. The government either turned a blind eye or actively helped settlers violate its own treaties. When gold was discovered in the Black Hills, Americans eagerly poured in, violating the recent Treaty of Laramie, which had declared the Sioux the sole owners of the land. When the Ojibwe refused to leave their timber-rich land, the government tried to legislate their land claims into thin air so that Americans would have unrestricted access to the billions of dollars to be made from Minnesota timber.

Tribal land that was home to valuable animals, oil, or other natural resources faced the same experience. In Aquinnah, whale meat had once provided food for Moshup's people and whale blood gave the land its defining feature, but it was the whales' oil that would deliver the irreversible change Moshup had foreseen.

A burgeoning industry before the Revolutionary War, American whaling continued to grow throughout the nineteenth century. Hundreds of ships left from ports like New Bedford and Nantucket, sailing as far as Peru and Japan in search of the fifty-plus-foot sperm whales that provided the oil for lamps and industrial-era machines across America. The spread of the whaling industry across the Cape and Islands region made once far-flung places like Martha's Vineyard newly relevant, bringing opportunity to Aquinnah Wampanoags. Although the island wouldn't see the seasonal residences that were popping up on less remote parts of the island for decades, it was suddenly part of the bustling comings and goings of industrial-era whaling.

My middle name, Vanderhoop, is a common name in the tribe, and I assumed it was because of the inexorable colonial influences from the seventeenth century, some white man on one of the first boats to land on our shores. I was wrong.

Drawn by the opportunity of adventure and riches aboard the whaling vessels, the booming industry drew immigrant men and freed slaves alongside opportunistic white men. My great-great-great-grandfather, William Vanderhoop, was one of those immigrants, arriving in the 1850s from the Dutch colony of Suriname. The son of a Dutch trader and a Surinamese woman, William landed in New Bedford, Massachusetts, at a time when the port city was one of the most diverse and exciting cities in the world. Herman Melville's *Moby-Dick*, published in 1851, was based on the city during those years. Abolitionist Frederick Douglass famously lived in New Bedford in the 1840s, and the city was well known to be friendly to escaped slaves, with a bell sounding whenever a slave catcher came into town, openly violating the 1850 Fugitive Slave Act.

Only in this time and place could the South American–born Black son of a Dutch man fall in love with a half-English, half-Indian woman from an unknown island. My great-great-great-grandmother, Beulah Occooch Salisbury, had left Aquinnah to seek work in New Bedford, like many other Wampanoag men and women. There, William and Beulah met and married before she convinced him to return to Aquinnah with her. Each new piece of information I learned complicated the simple story I had been told about colonization.

Once they were married, William traveled back to the Netherlands to get money from his father to build a house. With this money, William built a small homestead in Aquinnah, where he and Beulah started a family. My mom once pointed out where this land is. It's less than a half mile up the road from our house. She said a nontribal person owns the land now. Of course, back then, what was considered a small homestead would occupy a piece of land that is worth millions of dollars today, not to mention subdivided into a half dozen individual lots.

Land ownership was simple back then: if you lived on it, it was yours. It's almost impossible for me to imagine. Land in Aquinnah is so loaded with history and financial implications now that a more informal system seems impossible. The rolling hills and scrubby grass were divided only by the rough stone walls residents constructed to mark boundaries. Many of these stone walls remain across the island, but otherwise, the island would be almost unrecognizable to William Vanderhoop and his contemporaries. There were few tall trees then, and the beaches that draw summer crowds today were used primarily for fishing, a crucial source of supplemental income and food for many families.

A few years after William and Beulah moved to Aquinnah, however, the land situation changed. In 1862, Aquinnah was designated an official Indian district and renamed Gay Head after the colorful clay cliffs Moshup had marked with whale blood. This was the first step toward Massachusetts making our land into an incorporated town, a legal part of the state. To me, Indian district sounded like Indian Territory in what is now Oklahoma, or any of the various other schemes that happened to Indians out west.

After the Civil War, as the country began to rebuild, Aquinnah could no longer hide from the next phase of settler colonialism. While I had learned in school that nineteenth-century American expansion was purely westward, the Antebellum period also saw the consolidation of American land holdings along the East Coast. Land, however, was not the only issue standing in the way of making Aquinnah an official town of the United States. Throughout the first half of the nineteenth century, Aquinnah Wampanoag Indians were under state guardianship and not granted American citizenship. They were not allowed to vote and did not have full control over their land and money, which added another wrinkle to the process of incorporation. This uncertain legal status plagued Indians across the country, many who were trapped in a system that devalued their sovereign rights while also barring them from full rights as American citizens.

While I knew, growing up, that there must have been a complicated history between when Gosnold's men encountered Wampanoags and when I grew up in Aquinnah, I had never paused to think about what it might have looked like. I had always assumed that Wampanoag identity, and more broadly, Indigenous identity, was forged in those early years of colonization. Somehow, I figured, it settled then, leaving generations of Wampanoags to deal with it. But the truth is that the choices each generation made defined and shaped what it meant to be Wampanoag. And with choices comes disagreement. I underestimated the internal tension these changes caused in the tribe. Assuming that past generations were united is making the same mistake non-Natives make when they assume that all Native communities want the same thing.

On April 30, 1870, the town of Gay Head was officially incorporated and the Wampanoags were given US citizenship, despite strong resistance from many of them. Incorporation would not be the only time the tribe would be forced to sacrifice sovereignty for economic survival.

That August, there was a town meeting to figure out how the town would run. One of the most important questions was what would be done with the land. Being an incorporated town meant that traditionally informal land practices would have to be modified to match contemporary American law. The state also conducted a census of the Gay Head Indians, often resorting to guesswork to list their residence and percentage of Indian blood. I've heard from elders that census takers would peer down a dirt road and guess how many people lived at the end of it. From the very beginning, this new legally recognized form of Wampanoag identity was led by the same people trying to exterminate us. The more I learned about other Indigenous communities, the more I saw that pattern repeated—regulating our identity was one of many tactics used to steal our land and violate our rights.

In 1871, the state commissioned an assessment of land titles and determined that there were 227 Indian residents in Gay Head living on about two thousand acres. Today, there are about a hundred Wampanoags in Aquinnah and we own even less land. This land was divided into plots falling into three categories: farming, woodland, or beach. Most residents were allowed to keep the land they lived on. Common land, however, was still shared for planting, hunting, fishing, pasturing, or fruit picking. These lands included the cranberry bogs, clay cliffs, and herring creek. Because this unclaimed land was shared by most residents, they all assumed that it was shared property, belonging to the Gay Head Indians as a collective group. No one told them that incorporation meant this land belonged to the state, that the introduction of private land ownership meant the end of collectively owned land. It would take over a hundred years to get it back.

But the Gay Headers had more pressing concerns. As many had feared, the newly instated property taxes proved impossible for many Wampanoags to pay. Their largely subsistence-based lifestyles left little room for extra money to put toward property taxes. Even if they could afford the taxes, the Wampanoags wondered why they should pay for land their families had been living on for thousands of years. After Gay Head's incorporation, many quickly sold their land for the payout and to avoid having to pay to live there.

The rapid decline of Wampanoag land ownership after incorporation mirrored the national loss of Indian land during this time, which was the result of the colonizers' latest scheme. Instead of using war or disease, Americans began to use the nuances of private ownership to separate Indians from their land. Like in Gay Head, many tribes across the country found their homes suddenly part of an incorporated town, subject to taxes they couldn't possibly afford.

This was all part of a disastrous federal policy known as allotment, which was codified by the 1887 General Allotment Act. Allotment removed Indian land from collective, sovereign ownership and made it privately owned by individual people. Like they did in Gay Head, many immediately sold their land to avoid paying impossibly high taxes or were swindled out of it by opportunistic settlers. Before allotment, tribes lost land to war and theft. Allotment made Indians victims of a rigged capitalist system no one bothered to explain.

By the time the allotment period ended in 1934, Indians had lost about one hundred million acres—roughly the size of the entire state of California—totaling around two-thirds of their preallotment land holdings. And yet, across the country, they adapted, finding ways to live within the white man's system. In Gay Head, Indians learned how to buy and sell land, often acquiring from family members who couldn't afford to keep it.

Although many members of my family pursued careers off-island, most held on to their land in Gay Head. When I was young, I knew my family had land on the island, but I didn't realize how lucky that made us. Not only did the land provide financial security for generations, but it also provided a home for us, and a physical tie to the tribe and the island when we left.

Of course, not all Wampanoags sold land to fellow tribal members. Many ended up selling to white outsiders. Land that had never really been available for purchase was suddenly on the market. And like they did on Indian land across the country, white Americans quickly took advantage. And so the land that had once been our refuge from the outside world, land given to us by Moshup thousands of years ago, land that had been completely occupied by Wampanoag people just a few years prior, slowly began to fade from our control. But like Gosnold's arrival, this latest version of colonial land grabbing was the beginning of a fight rather than its conclusion.

Life had always been hard in Gay Head, but the additional burden of taxes made it impossible for many to remain. Today, many of my tribal cousins talk about the high property taxes we have to pay. Combined with the high cost of living and lack of affordable housing, this is a major barrier to Wampanoag people living on Martha's Vineyard. This hardship, as well as the lure of opportunity on the mainland or aboard whaling vessels, led to the departure of many young Wampanoag men.

During the first half of the twentieth century, traditional lifestyles, farming, and stock raising began to disappear from Gay Head. As these practices faded, the collective sense of Indian identity suffered too. The breaking of cultural and community ties was no accident. A group of federal laws known as Termination Policy began in the 1940s with the goal of completely eradicating tribes. Indians, it had been decided, had lived on the periphery of American civilization for long enough. The government's effort to eliminate Native nations once and for all was bad enough, but it was exacerbated by its unwillingness to present any alternative ways to live. It was the same story on Indian lands across the country—as traditional ways of life were suppressed, new opportunities were slow to fill the gaps, leaving many Indians grasping at any chance to survive.

I don't know if Moshup ever thought the whales would make their way home, but my family has, generation after generation. And each time we return, we bring something back with us. Keeping, protecting, and honoring the land means more than simply living on it—sometimes that means looking beyond the island's shores. The island Moshup created for the Wampanoag may have once been a still place among the currents, but Martha's Vineyard is increasingly influenced by the outside world.

The parts of my family's story that extend beyond Martha's Vineyard are also an essential part of the Wampanoag story. As my own life changes and I see my relationship to the island changing with it—I am learning what Moshup already knew: The land is not some abstract, unchanging ideal. It has value as long as we call it home, but what that means is up to us.

2

OFF-ISLAND

Growing up, Martha's Vineyard and being Wampanoag went hand in hand. On the island, I was surrounded by tribal family, culture, and community. I knew I was exploring land my family had lived on for generations, filled with endless layers of history and memory. But when I left the island at the end of each summer, that feeling was hard to hold on to.

Back in the Boston suburb where I spent the rest of the year, my Wampanoag identity always seemed more like a fun fact, a distant summer memory, than a core part of who I was. It wasn't relevant in the way that other parts of my life were, like going to soccer practice or playing computer games with my friends. And so, my sense of being Wampanoag ebbed and flowed.

As I grew older, I spent less and less time on the island each year and I could feel that sense fading. Being Wampanoag in the way I knew it as a kid—going to tribal summer camp, picking cranberries at our annual harvest festival, and learning our language—quickly became a smaller and smaller part of my life. And for years, I felt like that was something I had to accept, that I could choose between the life I was growing into away from the island or recommit to it. But I didn't want to be forced into that choice. I wanted to find a way to be Wampanoag and live where and how I chose. I just had no idea how to do it. I had no understanding of what Wampanoag identity or culture could look like separated from the island.

Those feelings were grounded in my childhood experiences of the tribe, but they were also rooted in a stereotypical, narrow understanding of what it means to be Native. Based on what I was taught in school and saw on TV, Native identity was inherently tied to a mystical conception of land and our connection to it. But since I didn't have that kind of connection, I wondered how I could really be Wampanoag. These feelings were heightened by the fact that I don't look like what most people think of when they think of Native people. My mom's mother is from Japan and both of my dad's parents were born in China. I know I look Asian to most people and I always struggled to reconcile that with my experiences with the tribe.

Even when I overcame those stereotypical assumptions, I wasn't sure what was left. I understood that being Native didn't mean looking a certain way or being some sort of spiritual caricature, but I wasn't sure how I could embody it when most of my life took place away from the island.

For a long time, I was always thinking about what my Wampanoag identity was not. It was not, for example, something that involved fluent speaking of our language. It did not involve living on a reservation. It did not involve going to powwows. But in always looking for what it was not, I realized that I had overlooked so many of the things that identity was, the things that actually made up what being Wampanoag meant to me.

My childhood experiences on the island—cool mornings in the cranberry bogs, sticky summer afternoons at camp with my cousins, foggy evenings up at the cliffs—all those moments were part of being Wampanoag. Talking to other Indigenous people also helped me realize that our parents had worked to give my brother and me those experiences, to help us have a foundation on the island and in the tribal community.

During those summers on the island, the stories we grew up on were part of the fabric and magic of Aquinnah. When we drove past the thick trickle of water pouring from the small pipe at Cook's Spring, I thought about my grandfather and his family taking an oxcart to fill up barrels of water. Standing at the top of the lighthouse with my brother, our baggy sweatshirts like flags in the wind, I imagined my great-grandfather looking out at the same ocean view, a hundred years before. Digging through the coarse red and black sand at Menemsha Pond, I liked to imagine Wampanoag ancestors getting clams in the same place for countless generations. Exploring Aquinnah with my brother and our cousins, I found it easy to see the connection between Moshup and the island that I grew up with.

I don't think I fully realized it at the time, but the physical connection I felt to the place was intertwined with the emotional connections I was also forging. Family history didn't feel like something from the past; it felt like it was happening all around me, all the time. From the rusty tools in my grandfather's barn to landmarks that Moshup had shaped, the stories I was told became part of that world.

My grandfather passed away when I was eight years old, so I never really got to know him. But with the time I've spent exploring Aquinnah, learning about our family history, listening to my mother tell his stories, and talking to relatives and customers at the store who remember him, I feel like I do know him. And the more I learn about Aquinnah, the closer I feel to him.

But for my three other grandparents, I didn't have that. I didn't get to know them or grow up steeped in their stories and history. I didn't grow up immersed in their land, community, and culture in China and Japan. For a long time, it was hard not to compare what I had with my Wampanoag identity with those other parts of my family history.

My dad's father passed away years before I was born, but growing up, we saw both of my grandmothers quite often. My paternal grandmother didn't speak much English, and I didn't speak any Cantonese, but I remember calling her every year so my brother and I could wish her happy Chinese new year, before passing the phone back to my dad so they could talk. My brother and I took Chinese lessons twice a week, but we were learning Mandarin. Later, my mom told me they had looked for a Cantonese school, but couldn't find one near our house. Sometimes I wonder what our relationship would have been like if I spoke Cantonese or if she had lived longer, or both.

My paternal grandmother had picked out Chinese names for my brother and me, and I remember writing out the characters on every piece of paper I could get my hands on. We visited her in her apartment in Boston's Chinatown and went out to big family dinners. I remember being proud when I learned that gunpowder was discovered by the Chinese. I bragged to my classmates that the Chinese system of counting made much more sense than the English one.

On one of my first days of elementary school, I was playing outside at recess, when an older white student ran up to me and asked how to say something in Chinese. I didn't know what to say, so I just told him how to say the number one. He ran off, calling out to his friends that he could speak Chinese. That was far from the worst thing that happened to me because of how I looked, but it was one of the first times that I can remember feeling like I was different. Over the years, those little moments added up, until I felt like being Asian was the bad kind of other.

Looking Asian made me stand out to white people for racist jokes and comments. It also encouraged other Asian people to talk to me, which made me feel bad because I had to admit that I couldn't speak Chinese or Japanese. Sometimes I almost felt relief when Koreans asked me if I was Korean, because I could at least be honest and say sorry, I'm Chinese. It was easier to be something else than inadequate.

On the other hand, being Wampanoag was always a choice because I didn't look like what people assume a Native person looked like. I chose to learn more about our history, to take language classes, and to write this book. I chose to make Indigenous affairs my beat when I became a journalist. I made other choices too. I moved away to New York and stayed there. I did other things instead of signing up for another language class. I missed general membership meetings. But I keep returning to the tribe. Although I was initially fixated on how questions about identity affected me, I've since wondered more about how they are impacting the tribe as a whole. Living away from Aquinnah and having a mixed identity doesn't make me unique in the tribe; in fact, those who still live there are the minority.

Today, only about a quarter of the tribe lives on Martha's Vineyard, and an even smaller percentage actually lives in Aquinnah. The rest of us are scattered around the world, with a few clusters in places like New Bedford and Boston. Many, like me, still have close family on the island that we go back and visit. Others stay with cousins or friends. Some rent houses when they visit in the summer. Others make day trips from the Cape for meetings and elections. Many rarely, or never, come back. Several members of the tribal council live off-island and take the ferry over for council meetings. I've come to think that as we transitioned from a tribe where practically everyone lived in the same place to one much more spread out, we never took the time to consider what that means.

In an attempt to examine how that transition affected the tribe as a whole, I began to investigate how my family has navigated their relationship with the tribe and the island over the years. The more I learn, the more I realize that our history has been shaped just as much by what happened to us away from the island. My relationship with the tribe and with the island was greatly influenced by my family's choices to leave it. I misunderstood the link between Indigenous land and Indigenous identity for an absolute relationship with no space for anything else. I've also realized that the way I understand Wampanoag identity and heritage cannot be separated from my attempt to reckon with my Chinese and Japanese backgrounds.

My grandfather Charles Vanderhoop Jr. always seemed like the paragon of Gay Head and Wampanoag identity. Charlie, as everyone called him, was born in Gay Head in 1921. He grew up in the house behind the Gay Head Lighthouse, where his father was the first Wampanoag keeper. My great-grandfather, Charles Sr., was stern and proud. He loved being photographed in his keeper's uniform and enjoyed the prestige that came with the position. For my grandfather, the benefits of his father's success came with the price of growing up in a long shadow. He spent years trying unsuccessfully to impress his father—the remote town of Gay Head offered little inspiration for a young man looking to prove himself.

Gay Head was one of six towns on Martha's Vineyard and was by far the most secluded, which it still is today. Even though Gay Head was less than fifty square miles, trips outside of town were rare. My grandfather spent his childhood running over the fields and hills with his cousins and siblings, playing imaginary games in the woods. The family had a large garden and cold cellar to store their food. The five siblings spent long hours preparing barrels of salted fish and canned vegetables. Getting fresh water meant a trip down to Cook's Spring with a horse and a couple of barrels. As a boy, my grandfather had loved the freedom of Gay Head, but as he grew older, he felt increasingly trapped by the small town. When Charlie was fourteen, his father sent him to live with family friends in Connecticut. When he was eighteen, he joined the merchant marines as a deckhand.

My grandfather joined an accelerated officer training program at the start of World War II. After scoring at an extremely high level in the program's IQ test, my grandfather was shocked. He had always been told he wasn't smart enough to succeed; now he had proof that he was. He'd tell the story of his IQ test for the rest of his life. This confidence carried him through the academy and into service in the merchant marines during the war, where he served in the dangerous North Atlantic convoys. He eventually achieved the level of master mariner, the highest level of seafaring qualification.

My grandfather was one of many Native men who served abroad during the war. Around 12 percent of Native Americans served in the US military, the highest rate of any group. Most famously, the Navajo Code Talkers and men from other tribes used their Indigenous languages to send coded messages. And then there was Ira Hayes, an enrolled member of the Gila River Indian Community, who was one of the six men to raise the American flag at Iwo Jima.

These high rates of service changed not just the men themselves, but their communities. Of course, the world was also changing during those years after the war. Cities were growing throughout the US, and many Americans were moving to urban areas. The highway system was rapidly expanding, connecting once distant places. And Native people were leaving their lands more than ever before. In the middle of the twentieth century, less than 10 percent of Natives lived in cities, but by 2000 the number was over 60 percent.

For my grandfather, the story was a little different. After the war, he ended up in Yokohama, Japan, where he met my grandmother, Hatsuko Sugita, in 1950. After they met, my grandfather took a job as a port captain, so he could stay ashore with her. They soon married. As a condition of their marriage, Charlie promised Hatsuko's father that he would never leave Japan. It was an easy choice. Everything he had ever accomplished had been away from Gay Head, and he loved exploring the world. He felt no urgency to return to the place where he had been told he was nothing.

When my mom first told me this story, I was surprised that my grandfather had intended to stay in Japan. I always figured that was just meant to be temporary. When I thought about my grandfather, I thought about the cliffs, the lighthouse, the tribe, and other elders. And when I thought about the island, he was the first person who came to mind. It's strange to think that as a young man he was ready to give all that up. Maybe, by idolizing his relationship with the island, I was setting an impossible standard for myself, one that not even he could live up to. I wish I could ask my grandparents about these things, but by the time I was old and curious enough to start asking questions, they had all passed away.

For Hatsuko, marrying my grandfather was a natural step in an already unconventional life. Charlie—the boat captain—had always seemed like the great adventurer, but the more I learn about Hatsuko, the more I admire her.

An independent woman during a time of rapid change in Japan, Hatsuko dreamed of someday opening a hat shop. The first time she wore pants was during World War II, when women were instructed to wear kimono trousers to help them run faster to bomb shelters. Like many Japanese women, she continued wearing Western-style clothes even once the hostilities had ended.

Hatsuko's grandparents had no sons and planned to adopt their oldest daughter's husband—my grandmother's father—as the heir to their large farm outside of Tokyo. When a surprise pregnancy resulted in a baby boy and natural heir, the plan changed and my grandmother's parents were left to fend for themselves. Hatsuko's father was a calligrapher, a line of work that did not pay well.

By the time she was a teenager, my grandmother was forced to drop out of school to help provide for her four younger siblings. Thrust into responsibility at a young age, Hatsuko knew that she could not expect anything free or easy in life. By the time she met my grandfather after the war, she was ready for something different from what traditional Japanese society could offer her.

I always knew that my mother had been born in Japan, but I saw that fact as little more than an interesting detail in the intertwined story of my family and Martha's Vineyard. I never thought that much about the four years the small family spent there before moving back to Martha's Vineyard. If in some alternate universe my family had stayed in Japan, and I had been born there, too, I wonder if I would have considered myself Wampanoag at all or what kind of relationship I might have had with the tribe and the island.

When I was a kid, I had a picture book called *How My Parents Learned to Eat*. The book was about the narrator's grandparents—an American sailor and a Japanese woman—who met in Japan. For their first date they went out to dinner. Each of them, nervous about the meal, practiced how to eat according to the other's customs. The Japanese woman consulted her uncle for advice on how to eat Western food while the American man practiced with chopsticks. At the end of the book, the narrator revealed that she grew up eating with both chopsticks and forks and knives. I used to flip through those pages, wondering if that was how my grandparents met. I read and reread the book, hoping to understand more about their lives and what it meant to have more than one background. I knew the differences couldn't have been as simple as eating implements, but the book didn't offer further answers. When I think about that book now, I realize that even then I was trying to make sense of a mixed identity.

During the war, Hatsuko had worked for a Japanese railroad company to help support the family. Fiercely independent and proud that her earnings had sustained them, my grandmother refused two arranged marriages. By the time she was thirty, she had already accepted that she would never marry, or at least not have a conventional Japanese marriage. But she had never expected to meet anyone like my grandfather. A compulsive storyteller who already had a lifetime of experiences around the world, Charlie represented such a contrast to the rigid constraints my grandmother felt from Japanese tradition that she was immediately drawn to him.

And as long as she stayed in Japan, Hatsuko's father, who had worried his eldest daughter would never marry, was satisfied. My grandfather loved the new life he had made for himself. The new couple spent their free time collecting Japanese art and enjoying Japanese food that neither of them knew how to cook. My grandmother could enjoy her own culture from an outsider's perspective, finally free from the overwhelming expectations she felt.

But within five years of their marriage, my grandfather would change his mind. When my mom was born in Yokohama on November 11, 1954, he named her Martha, after the home he missed. He began to realize he didn't want to spend the rest of his life in Japan. When his mother died back in Gay Head in 1958, Charlie decided it was time to go home.

After the war, Hatsuko had begun watching American television and was fascinated by the strange culture she saw on her favorite show, *I Love Lucy*. Lucy's exploits made Hatsuko feel like anything was possible in America. This kind of exposure to foreign culture would never have been possible in the Japan of her childhood. Entertaining visions of a country free of Japanese tradition and expectation, she was excited to start a new life on the other side of the world. Although Japan was increasingly accepting, my grandmother was worried about raising a biracial child there. Enticed by the freedoms she had heard American women enjoyed, she agreed to move to Martha's Vineyard.

While boxes full of their possessions—including hundreds of pieces of Japanese artwork my grandparents had collected—slowly made their way by boat to the United States, the family of three embarked on the multiday journey to Gay Head—my grandmother's first time on a plane. As the plane flew over the island, she peered out the window for her first glimpse of her new home. Astounded by how green and undeveloped it was, she thought it looked like a jungle. I had spent so many hours imagining what it must have meant for my grandfather and my mother to come back to Martha's Vineyard in the 1950s, but I hadn't thought that much about what it was like for my grandmother to move from Japan to the island.

For Hatsuko, life on the ground was as remote as it had looked from the air. In 1950, the Greater Tokyo Area, where she had spent her entire life, had a population of around thirteen million. In the same year, Gay Head had a population of eighty-eight. Life in tiny, rural Gay Head was nothing like *I Love Lucy*, and Hatsuko quickly became miserably homesick. She missed her family, the food, and the bustle of Yokohama.

In Gay Head, Hatsuko never really had the freedom she had imagined back in Japan. Handcuffed by her limited English and surrounded by her husband's close-knit extended family, my grandmother found life in Gay Head nearly unbearable, often sneaking out of the house to cry in private. My grandmother had finally left Japan and its pressures behind, but found herself feeling even more trapped in Gay Head. She soon discovered that she was pregnant, constraining her to even more time alone at home. My uncle, Charles the third, was soon born in Gay Head. The family called him Charlie Boy.

Sympathetic to her plight and curious about Charlie's foreign wife, his cousins threw her a baby shower a few months after they arrived. Hatsuko was touched by the gesture, but it did little to alleviate her homesickness. Calling Japan was far too expensive in the 1950s, and telegrams were impractical. In fact, Gay Head had only acquired electricity a few years earlier—one of the last towns in the state to do so.

As a reprieve from country life, Charlie had tried taking the family on shopping trips to New Bedford in his boat, but Hatsuko got seasick and stopped going. With nowhere to go and no one to talk to while my grandfather was on his boat, she dedicated herself to raising her children. Home alone, my grandmother had plenty of time to reflect on her life. She was determined that her children would never be as trapped as she felt. She wanted them to go everywhere and do everything they wanted. Instead of feeling bitter and regretful, she took her experiences and turned them into lessons for her children. I never realized how much of my grandmother's early experiences had influenced the way she raised my mother. Anxious about her daughter's educational development, Hatsuko asked a doctor for tips on raising a bilingual child. She knew that education, especially in America, was important. He told her that two languages would be too difficult for my mom to learn, so my grandmother forced her to learn English and forget Japanese. For Hatsuko, the decision to sacrifice her own language to give her daughter the best chance to succeed was clear, though it broke her heart. Raising two children mostly by herself, my grandmother had no time to waste dwelling on such losses.

When my mom wanted a swing set, my grandmother spent weeks picking beach plums from the sandy dunes down the road. Turning the plums into jelly, she used the money to grant her daughter's wish. Decades later, my mother told me these stories, using her own happy memories to cheer me up when I felt sad. As I think now about my grandmother's life, those sweet stories seem like tiny revolutions.

Fortunately for my grandmother, my grandfather's return to Gay Head wasn't exactly what he had hoped for either. Although he appreciated being back home, surrounded by his extended family, making a living in Gay Head had only gotten harder over the years. Just as he had left in search of opportunity before the war, in the early 1960s Charlie departed again with his family. They moved to New Bedford, just a short boat ride away from Gay Head, and where my great-great-great-grandparents William Vanderhoop and Beulah Occooch Salisbury had met about a hundred years earlier. Learning these cyclical waves of coming and going helped me realize how foolish it was to think that leaving was a permanent choice that defined us.

In New Bedford, Charlie bought a boat and started a fishing business that was part of the then-booming industry that had replaced the whaling trade. Hatsuko soon discovered a small community of Japanese women, which helped her to feel more comfortable in America. Even as the family settled into a suburban life, Charlie made sure that Gay Head was still a part of their lives. New Bedford's proximity allowed for the kind of double life that had been impossible from Japan. My grandfather never wanted to experience the suffocating feeling he felt as a boy in Gay Head, but he wanted his family to stay connected to the island. In the summers, Hatsuko and the two kids spent the summer there while Charlie was away on fishing trips. It's strange to think now that my grandfather, the person I thought exemplified Gay Head, wasn't even there most of the time my mom spent on the island.

Gay Head was a difficult place to live, but it was just as hard to leave. New Bedford was a sort of compromise: close enough to conveniently visit the island, but far enough away to make their own way. Decades later, my parents would make a similar choice when they began running the family business on the island, but we kept living off-island while they commuted back and forth. And so I grew up like my mother, going to school off-island, but spending summers back in Aquinnah. This routine gave our relationship with the island the seasonal pattern that, in time, would make me feel like I had more in common with summer tourists than my cousins who lived on the island.

My grandfather wasn't the only Wampanoag who saw the appeal of New Bedford. In fact, the whole south coast of Massachusetts quickly became home to a mini-diaspora of Gay Headers, most of whom had also left the island for opportunity, whether that was a job, education, or marriage. The mainland could simply offer more than the island could. Some went farther, moving to Boston, New York, and beyond. And though many, like my grandfather, remained tied to the island via family and land, some found that their connection to Aquinnah was increasingly tenuous.

My family was fortunate that they were able to leave the island for better opportunities without sacrificing their land on the island. Sometimes I wonder how my relationship with the tribe and island would be different if my family had sold our land before I was born. In some ways the defining aspect of our relationship with the island isn't when we left it, but the fact that we were always able to keep land. Many other families ended up selling their land as they left, making it much more difficult to come back and maintain ties.

After the family moved to New Bedford in the 1960s, my grandmother met Toshi, a Japanese woman who was also married to an American fisherman, and the two quickly bonded over their shared challenges. Hatsuko, unusually tall for a Japanese woman, towered over her smaller friend. They found the size difference hilarious, switching between Japanese and English as they laughed. With Toshi's help, my grandmother learned how to navigate American supermarkets, cook American food, and understand her husband's transient life. Toshi also helped fill in details of Japanese life that my grandmother had missed out on as a working teenager. My grandmother had never learned to cook Japanese food because she was always out working. When my mother's schoolteacher invited my grandmother in to demonstrate Japanese cooking, Toshi taught her how to cook a few recipes.

Although New Bedford had always been a relatively diverse city, given its busy port, my mother and uncle were among a tiny handful of Asian students in a high school with thousands of students. My father and his siblings were three of the other Asian faces in the school.

My dad, Marshall, was born and raised in New Bedford, where his family ran a laundry business. Even though I knew the role that New Bedford played in my family and Wampanoag history, I never really thought that much about how my father's family, like so many other immigrant families, ended up in New Bedford. It wasn't until I was in grad school that I really became curious about it all and began to ask questions about my father's family history.

My great-grandfather, Wing Lee, was born in Southern China. As a young man, he left to find work in the US, arriving in California with thousands of other Chinese men looking for work. The first Chinese immigrants to the US were mostly men, many brought over to help in the feverish search for gold in the mid-nineteenth century and build the railroads that would connect the East and West Coasts.

Although most of those first Chinese immigrants arrived in California, the desire for cheap labor quickly brought them to the East Coast. In 1870, a shoe factory in North Adams, Massachusetts, brought in seventy Chinese "strikebreakers" from California. Many of these families eventually moved to Boston, where a small Chinatown began to grow. In 1921, when my grandfather George was five years old, he followed his father to Boston. Through friends in Boston's Chinatown, my great-grandfather heard of a Chinese laundry for sale in New Bedford. At that time, many white Americans did not want to hire Chinese workers. Owning a laundry was a rare path to stability. Although he was nervous to leave the comfort of Chinatown, Wing knew that greater risk offered greater rewards. In 1928, the two founded Wing Lee and Son laundry in New Bedford.

While his father worked long hours to build the laundry into a successful business, George received an American education, soon losing almost all traces of an accent. Despite his American life, he remained proudly Chinese, making a point to learn how to read and write in Chinese too. Education had become a priority for the family, which grew every year with new arrivals from China. In China, most family members never went to high school and few could read and write. For my grandfather, being literate in English and Chinese was a point of immense pride. Education, he believed, was the key to success in America. Growing up, people always told my dad that his father was the smartest boy in New Bedford. But he never finished high school, dropping out to help support the family.

When he was seventeen, George had to go back to China because business was so bad during the Great Depression. While there, he married my grandmother, Mee Lee. The marriage, set up by their two families, was seen as a silver lining to my grandfather's forced departure from America. When he returned to New Bedford in 1935, his new wife was forced to stay behind because of American immigration laws. Both families, when they arranged the marriage, knew that the new couple would be forced to separate, but the match was worth it. George, an educated man living in America, had a good chance of financial security. For his family, a strong match with a local bride was an important part of securing his bond with his homeland. For many Chinese families, America was seen as a place to make money, not a permanent place to live. American immigration laws helped to reinforce that attitude. Although the way that American businesses used cheap Chinese labor enabled immigrants to find work across the country, it also spawned widespread anti-Chinese racism. This reaction eventually led to legislation that specifically targeted Chinese immigration to the United States. These laws culminated in the Chinese Exclusion Act of 1882, which banned all new Chinese immigration to the country until it was repealed in 1943. As a man, my grandfather could return, but he was not permitted to bring his new wife. The government was happy to have Chinese labor but had no desire to have Chinese families.

After the Great Depression, business picked up. The location, so close to the docks, was a huge asset for the business. Sailors and fishermen could walk straight off their boats and drop off their laundry at Lee and Son. Unfortunately, competition with larger cities and regulation designed to prevent overfishing limited the industry in New Bedford.

Despite the challenging economy, the loosening of immigration restrictions allowed my grandmother to come to the US, where they soon had three children. All three received American names: Warren, Sue, and Marshall. My father, the youngest, was born in July 1954. Less than four months later, my mother would be born on the other side of the world.

Even though the connection to China remained strong, George had no plans to return to the family village. He raised his children as Chinese Americans and shared the love he had for America with them. Mee Lee, however, remained solidly Chinese and preferred to use the Chinese names she had chosen. As an adult immigrant who had lived in China her whole life, my grandmother found her new home strange and uncomfortable. Every day when the kids left for school, they entered a world she did not understand.

Every night, the family had dinner around a big table in the back of the shop. Surrounded by towering stacks of brown paper laundry parcels, they enjoyed my grandmother's cooking. Years later, she would cook some of the same foods for my family. My mom still talks about what a great cook she was. After school, the kids ran over to the laundry on Second Street, where their grandfather often gave them a dollar or two to spend on comic books. On Sundays, they went to the Methodist church, where my grandfather George was a lay leader and my dad proudly served as an acolyte, lighting and extinguishing the candles.

By the middle of the twentieth century, New Bedford was one of many American cities left with few options after deindustrialization. In an attempt to revitalize such places, the government passed policies as part of a nationwide effort that came to be called urban renewal. Like in many places across the country, urban renewal was a false promise that ended up destroying communities. In 1967, Lee and Son was forced from its Second Street location by urban renewal projects. The new location on 47 Foster Street was only half a mile away from its original location, but the financial difference was significant.

One year after the business moved, my great-grandfather died and the family moved above the new laundry. They lived there until the business closed for good in the late 1970s. Urban renewal had not only pushed the business out of its prime location by the docks, but it was also responsible for the new highways that cut through the city, making the new location noisy and more difficult to get to. An article from the *Standard-Times* described it as "a special kind of place, and not just because it's the last Chinese laundry in the city [. . .] because you can't get there from here or from anywhere. Not legally anyway." Street reconstruction had put the business on the wrong end of a one-way street, quickly putting a dent in profits.

The article's title, "Last Chinese Laundry Has Problems," reflects the financial difficulties the business faced in its later years. In the article, my grandfather said that he was kept in business by a handful of loyal customers. By this time, the business had evolved from the archetypal Chinese hand laundry and had heavy pressing and cleaning machinery in the back. The article ends by talking about my father and his siblings, all three of whom went to college. "The children don't want the business, they have an education," my grandfather said. "When they were going to school they helped out every chance they got, but it's really hard work, very hot in the summer."

I had always wondered about the framed picture on our piano of my grandfather standing in front of the Wing Lee and Son sign. I had assumed that my grandfather started the business, but eventually learned that my great-grandfather had. A year or two after I finished grad school, I visited the location of Lee and Son with my dad. Today, there is a YMCA and a Santander Bank around where the original Second Street location stood. Among all Massachusetts's cities, New Bedford currently ranks in the bottom five for categories like income per capita and median income per household. Tourism—centered on the city's whaling history and several annual festivals—shows signs of bringing life back to New Bedford. In 2010, a Fairfield Inn and Suites opened on MacArthur Drive by the harbor. It was the first new hotel to open in forty years.

Learning about the ways that places like New Bedford shaped the tribe and my family just as much as Aquinnah helped me embrace a more nuanced version of Indigenous identity. For as long as our collective memory goes back, tribal members have always left the island, but the twentieth century saw an exodus unlike any before. This has led to irrevocable shifts in the way our community works. We were already a small tribe, but this exodus has created a situation where a small number of people in Aquinnah can have a larger impact on tribal culture and politics. There are some who think that this is the way it should be, that those who still live in Aquinnah should have the biggest say over the tribe, since they will be affected most directly. I don't know if that's right or wrong, but I think it overlooks the way that Wampanoag identity has evolved over the years. Moving from the island in search of opportunity is not a deviation or departure from Wampanoag identity, it is a part of it.

And we aren't alone. Since World War II there's been a steady flow of Native people from their homelands across the country. Today, about 75 percent of Native people live off their reservations, with a similar percentage living in cities and suburbs.

Indigenous people like to use this statistic to remind white people that we aren't all living in teepees on the reservation. But for me it speaks to something different than just a challenge to the way white people perceive us—it questions the way we perceive ourselves. It also raises the question of whether people leaving their home is good, bad, or just the way things are. We do need to do more to create opportunities, namely jobs, housing, and education, so people can stay in their tribal communities, should they want to. But we also need to adapt to the reality that Indigenous people have been leaving their homelands for generations now.

For so many people I talk to, they know that being away from home doesn't make them any less Indigenous, but it does limit their ability to engage with certain aspects of Indigenous life, like ceremony, community events, tribal politics, and so on. And that's not to say that Indigenous community cannot or does not exist outside of reservations. Many cities have diverse and vibrant Indigenous communities, even those relatively far from reservations, like New York City or Los Angeles. For a long time, I've struggled to reconcile the fact that Wampanoag identity can and perhaps must exist off-island with the reality that Martha's Vineyard is still the home of the Wampanoag people, even as it, and we, evolve.

For many of my cousins, moving back home to the island, whether they grew up there or not, signifies a commitment to the tribe and the island. They come home to work for the tribe, to get closer with family, and to learn more about our culture. I have never felt ready to make that commitment and sometimes wondered if my belief that I could both live off-island and be an active member of the tribe was little more than wishful thinking. But I could always go home. Although the frequency and duration of my visits to the island fluctuated over the years, I always went home at least once or twice a year. So in some ways, I put the question on hold. I went back to the island just enough to maintain ties and feel connected to what was happening in Aquinnah. I kept up-to-date on major changes, like who was running for council or renovations on the lighthouse.

As I got older, I realized that my Wampanoag identity was only limited to my relationship with the land if I let it. Spending summer vacation on the island as a kid might have been the clearest way for me to connect to the tribe back then, but there was nothing stopping me from finding different ways as an adult.

As much as I sometimes felt insecure about my Wampanoag identity, my tribal cousins and I were all just figuring it out. No one was fluent in our language, but there were plenty of people fluent in Japanese or Chinese. In some ways it was easier to identify as Wampanoag because it felt like a lower bar in terms of cultural and language expertise. We are all mixed, all reconnecting, all trying to learn our language, while there are literally millions of people speaking Japanese, not to mention more than a billion who speak Chinese. But the older I get, the more I realize that just like there is no one way to be Wampanoag, there is no one way to be Chinese or Japanese or Asian.

Through talking to so many Indigenous people around the world, I've come to see that even if people aren't dealing with the same specific questions, so many of us are trying to figure out how we can embody all the disparate parts of our identities. I've never known how to balance honoring my family and where I come from with making my own way, but talking to other people working through the same issues has helped.

3

BRINGING OUR PEOPLE HOME

Once I turned five, my brother and I started attending the tribe's summer camp in Aquinnah. After eating our cereal, we would skip across the dew-covered grass to the car. Our mother dropped us off at the tribal administration building, where we joined a dozen or so of our Wampanoag cousins. Although the camp became a steady feature of our summers, there was no consistency to the camp itself. Every year there were new counselors and our activities varied with the changes in staff. Some years we went on a lot of trips to island farms or spent most of our time playing tag around the tribal building, while other years we focused on Wampanoag culture and language. In this way, we picked up a scattered education on being Wampanoag and the island itself.

Although the group of campers also shifted from year to year, there was a core group of us who went regularly. We all called one another cousins. We never really knew exactly how most of us were related, but it didn't matter. The other kids at camp were mostly island kids, but occasionally fellow off-islanders would show up for a few weeks. My brother and I usually played with our favorite cousin, Mikey, who often came home with us after camp to look for snakes and watch *Pokémon* on TV.

Those were the kinds of things we wanted to spend our summer days doing, not the cultural activities we were forced to do at camp. Every year, we used rolls of deerskin to make moccasins and pouches, and we all hated the leather needles we used. Instead of the usual cylindrical shape, these needles had a pyramid shape halfway down, where each edge was razor-sharp. I never figured out how to use those needles without cutting myself, and my moccasins were inevitably smeared with specks of blood.

Gladys Widdiss, a tribal elder, occasionally came to show us her pottery made from clay from the cliffs. Gladys talked about the different colors of clay she took from the cliffs—red, yellow, black, and white—as she showed us how to make pinch pots. I wanted to learn from Gladys, but I also wished we could just play with the clay. Unlike the Sculpey clay my brother and I used at home to make monsters and funny figures, the clay from the cliffs felt precious. I revered the clay but was annoyed that everything at camp had to be some special tribal thing. I just wanted to have fun.

Every morning, we sat in a circle in the Big Room—what we called the council meeting room at tribal headquarters—and practiced Wampanoag phrases. As my cousins introduced themselves in Wampanoag, I felt the same self-conscious dread I felt in music class when we had to sing in front of the whole class. I resented having to feel that way over the summer. It reminded me of the Mandarin lessons my brother and I went to twice a week during the school year, something extra that I had to do because of who I was. Even worse, learning Wampanoag came with the pressure of saving a language, unlike Chinese, which I knew would continue being spoken by a billion people whether I learned it or not.

We learned how to tread silently through the woods and dunes. At home, I practiced scanning the ground for any leaves or sticks that might make a noise before gently setting my heel on the ground and slowly rolling my weight forward onto my toes. Learning outdoor skills felt more concrete than learning a few phrases in Wampanoag that I knew I'd forget by the next summer. I can see now that what was so special about those experiences was developing a relationship with and understanding of the land, not to mention doing it with my tribal cousins, not for some misguided belief I had that Natives should be good at walking and hunting in the forest.

Every year, the tribal camp took a trip to Water Wizz, a water park on Cape Cod. Most of the other kids looked forward to the trip all summer, but my brother and I preferred to stay home and do something with our parents, appreciating a break from the chaos of camp. One year, however, we went to camp anyway, where we spent the day with Tobias Vanderhoop. Tobias—a cousin we called Toby—worked in the Education Department, but normally wasn't involved in the camp.

For years, I looked up to Tobias as someone who knew what it meant to be a Wampanoag person. Tobias knew so much about our language and culture and seemed committed to working in tribal government. My earliest memories of Tobias are when he came to my elementary school class to give a presentation on Wampanoag culture during our unit on Native Americans. Back then, he was participating in the national circuit of powwow dancing competitions and had an impressive set of regalia.

We sat outside and spent the day making wooden stick toys, bending a green stick into a loop, which we secured to a longer, straight stick with bark. The game was to flip the loop so that it landed on the straight stick; the difficulty depended on the length of the connecting bark. We had made the same toys in camp year after year, hardly ever playing with them after we made them. While we worked, Tobias asked us about ourselves and our lives. That day, working quietly in the morning sun, something felt different. We were no longer just campers, but real members of the tribe talking with a tribal adult. And suddenly, for one day, being Wampanoag didn't feel like a burden or a quirk; it felt like something I was lucky to have.

For most of my childhood, my only conception of Wampanoag identity oscillated between these rare moments of connection and the vague frustration I usually felt. Most of the time, I was never able to make sense of my heritage. In school we drew pie charts showing our family backgrounds, with most of my classmates sketching circles divided into even slices of English, Irish, or German. After drawing a straight line down the middle of the circle to create one half—labeled Chinese—I painstakingly drew slivers of Wampanoag, Japanese, Dutch, English, African. Someday, I imagined, I would know exactly how big—or small—to make each one.

Looking down at my pie chart, I would try to figure out what color I would be. My friends helped me to puzzle out my strange background—if Asian was yellow, Native was red, and the black and white slivers balanced each other out, then I must be some sort of orange. The unique color felt briefly exciting, until I realized that I was no closer to figuring out what that meant.

I knew that Native identity was not about blood. Nobody in Aquinnah ever seemed to care about it. The only people who ever did were those who didn't know anything about our community. But I still wasn't quite sure what it actually was about or how to respond when classmates asked me how Native I was.

When I left the island, the blurry jumble of experiences and feelings reduced my Wampanoag identity to little more than a unique fact about my family. On the island, being Wampanoag may have meant having to go to a camp that I didn't love, but it also came with summer adventures with my cousin, long days at the beach, and countless memories.

But as I grew older, I spent my summers working or at soccer practice, and those kinds of shared experiences became less and less frequent. Sometimes it felt like those childhood experiences were lost in the past, but now, when I look back at those summer days, I don't think that's true at all. That childhood foundation helped shape the way I think about tribal and Wampanoag identity today. It's just taken a bit of time and work to uncover and sort through all of those experiences and emotions. I eventually realized that the questions I was trying to work out for myself are much bigger questions that have been fought and debated over for generations.

Thinking and learning about the complicated history of tribal land in Aquinnah made me reflect more deeply on my family's land than I ever did before. My family's house in Aquinnah is relatively new. My grandfather built it in the 1970s as a rental property on a piece of land next to the main family house. Today, the house, a small two-bedroom ranch, sits on about three acres of land, most of which is covered by the short trees and tall grass you find all over the island. It's just a few hundred feet off the road and up a sandy driveway, but like many houses on the island, you can't see the house from the road.

The house has an open deck, weathered by decades of island wind, rain, and sun. Weeds constantly sprout up through the cracks in the wood. There are some white Adirondack chairs scattered around, but we rarely sit out on the deck. Mostly we use its rails to hang laundry and beach towels. In front of the house is my dad's garden, which is surrounded by eight-foot wood and chicken wire fences that have grown higher each year to keep out deer. Every summer, he fights to keep deer and rabbits from eating his crop of tomatoes, squash, and cucumbers before he can pick them.

There's a thin layer of crushed shells in the driveway where we toss clamshells after shucking them. It's surprising to me how long it is taking to transform the driveway from sand to crushed shell. Each summer, we toss hundreds of clamshells onto the sandy driveway, where they are soon crunched into pieces by car tires. But in the years we've been doing that, it seems like we've barely made a dent. In some ways, it's reassuring to know how little impact we can make on the land, even after years.

Then there's the small, two-story house that I built with my father and cousin when I was in college. Today, my parents use it to keep inventory for the store, but someday, when they retire, my dad plans to redo the interior to make it livable. On the far side are the shingles I put in that my father said were too close together. As the individual shingles have shrunk over the years, I like to point out how nicely spaced out they are now.

A few hundred feet away is my uncle's house, separated by a low stone wall and overgrown bushes. This is the house I grew up spending my summers in when my maternal grandparents were still alive. Filled with old books, strange artifacts, and hidden stairways, I always felt the house reflected our family history, even if I didn't know what that meant. We call it the "big house." My family's house is the "new house." The big house is so old, it is older than the main road in town. The house had been moved by oxen from the previous road once the new, modern road was built. A few years after my grandparents died, my family started spending our summers in the new house. So most of my younger memories from the island are in the big house, while teenage memories and beyond are in the new house.

The layout of the big house was perfect for exploring and making up adventures. The indoor, wraparound porch was filled with rows and rows of dusty books. I wondered if my grandfather had read them all. At one end of the porch was an enormous safe the size of a refrigerator—I liked to imagine the treasures my grandfather hid inside. My mom later told me that my grandfather had gotten it from the bank in Chilmark when they upgraded to a newer safe.

My grandparents' bedroom was above the kitchen and had a narrow, winding staircase that led down into the laundry room. In my imagination, that staircase was a secret passageway, a hidden escape route. The house felt like a museum, except instead of strangers' stuff, it was filled with family history. I liked knowing that this place had been in our family for generations, that over the years the house had filled up with signs that we had been there.

In a glass cabinet in my grandfather's office was the crumbling top tier of his and my grandmother's wedding cake—they had mailed it back from Japan when they were married fifty years earlier. I liked to stare through the dusty glass, imagining what it would be like to eat the fossilized dessert. I knew it was from my grandparents' wedding, but the cake just seemed so ancient, I couldn't imagine people I knew had once eaten it.

Like the house itself, its three-acre property has accumulated signs of my family's presence over the generations. A white split-rail fence stands between our yard and State Road, ending at our sandy driveway. The faintly orange earth always seemed unique to me—not quite sand, but not dirt either. The driveway cuts straight through the tough grass, a barren path with a narrow strip of sprouting weeds in the middle. After a few hundred feet it curls sharply left, swinging up a brief incline before meeting the small concrete patch where my grandfather parked his car. The sand in the curving incline up to the parking spot is deeper and looser than the rest of the driveway, making it treacherous for my bike. For me and my brother, the little rectangle of concrete was a skatepark, a highway, a fortress, and the base for our games.

On cool evenings we would ride circles on our bikes, pretending to be a motorcycle gang, making pit stops to snack on the ziplock bags of Goldfish and green grapes our mom had packed. From the corner of the patch that faced the yard, we set up mini jumps for our scooters, daring each other to leap higher and farther out over the grass our grandfather had just cut on his John Deere riding mower.

Next to the concrete parking spot in front of the house was the shop—a cluttered workshop filled with tools, cans of paint, bikes, boogie boards, and garden equipment. My mother's story about stepping on a loose nail when she was young never stopped me from going into the shop barefoot. On the floor was a strange green carpet that seemed halfway through the process of melting into the wooden floor. Scattered across it were buckets and bins filled with tools and piles of tennis balls.

Halfway up the hill behind the shop stood the chicken house, a former chicken coop that had been converted into a one-bedroom home. When my mother was young, she had spent summers in the tiny space while summer renters were in the big house. On one side of the building was a huge bush of mysterious plants that sprouted strange seedlings and flowers. We stayed away from there, afraid of what might be lurking inside.

Past the chicken house, in the far corner of the yard, was the trailer, the only other occupied structure on the property. The trailer had a path down the east side of the property that led to the road through an opening in the white fence. My brother and I stayed away from the trailer, too, scared of the unknown renter. Facing the house and the shop was the barn, the second-largest structure after the big house and the only other one with two floors. The barn was a classic barn, with a small garage on the side. My grandfather kept a dinghy in the garage and I imagined that this tiny vessel was the boat he had used for his fishing trips. Other than the John Deere lawn mower, both floors of the barn were filled with ancient and mysterious objects—rusted tools and piles of crumbling devices—relics of my family's history.

The shop, trailer, barn, and chicken house were more than just buildings to us, they were landmarks, deeply familiar but strangely foreign, as if they were from another time. They were also the defining features of our games, most of which we made up and modified each summer. Some, like stickball, we inherited. Using an old wooden closet rod and tennis balls, our uncle explained the rules he had invented when he was our age. The pitcher stood at the edge of the driveway and lobbed the ball toward the batter, who stood in the shadow of the barn, right on the bottom of the small, concrete ramp that led up into the barn. A grounder or a caught ball was an out. A ball hit into the trees or off the roof of the shop was a double. Off the roof of the house was a triple. Over the house, trees, or shop was a home run. The chimney and the big flat rock on the far side of the shop were the foul lines.

I loved knowing how permanent these landmarks were, that my uncle used them to play the same game when he was my age. He used an old leather baseball glove that my grandfather had bought for him when he was a teenager. Charlie, who didn't know that the glove goes on the non-throwing hand, bought the wrong hand glove for my uncle, who soon learned to throw with his opposite hand. When we weren't playing, the glove hung from an old nail in the shop. I imagined that when I was his age my weathered glove would hang below it, although I wished my glove had its own origin story.

When I think about our land, I think about all this family history and memory. Sometimes I wonder if this land is important to me because it is Wampanoag land or just because it is my family's land. To me, my family's land is Indigenous because it is surrounded by my cousins' homes and tribal land, and because the town itself feels Indigenous, because of the people and the history. It's hard to think of it as Indigenous on its own, as anything more than the place where my family has lived for generations.

Sometimes I find it hard to connect the land my family owns and has lived on for generations to the abstract ideal of Indigenous land that I've built up in my head. I realized I never really thought about what it might mean to own Indigenous land and what kind of responsibility comes with that ownership. When I think about Indigenous land as an ideal, I think about living on it and protecting it, but not so much paying taxes or inheriting it. I began to wonder about the differences between private and collectively owned Indigenous land and if protecting them looked different.

For as long as I can remember, I have believed that it was important to hold on to our family land. Today, my mom owns several pieces of property in Aquinnah that my grandfather left to her. My mom says her dream was always to be able to leave one house to me and one to my brother, but they never got around to building a second house. Our house needs work too. I've told her that I don't mind sharing with my brother. We can figure it out. My mom has also warned us about the high property taxes that we will someday have to take over paying. Because of that, when I think about what it will take to keep the land, my first thought is about financial stability. I worry I won't make enough money to afford the taxes, and then I wonder if simply doing enough to keep the land can be considered a victory. I also wonder what we might be able to do with the land if we could move beyond struggling to simply keep it.

Most of the land my family owns today was once owned by other family members. My grandfather, for example, bought land from his siblings. His father did the same. Sometimes, I feel the weight of a responsibility, like we are now carrying the torch for those who weren't able to stay. But I'm not sure what to do with that responsibility. I don't know what it will take to keep our land in the family, or what I am willing to do to ensure that we do. I'm also not sure if I value my family's private land differently than tribally owned land. The very idea of owning Indigenous land can feel a little abstract to me, especially when Indigenous land is so tied to collective, rather than individual, ownership.

It is one thing to know that this land has been Wampanoag land for thousands of years. It is another to build a history with it, to have personal memories and experiences on it. Getting land back isn't just logistical, it's a gradual, grinding process of rebuilding a relationship with the land. Much of the land that I now consider indisputably tribal, like tribal housing, was completely different just a few decades ago. I grew up in a time when I was able to form those relationships and develop that connection with it.

As my tribe confronts existential questions over land, housing, and membership, my privilege has in some ways allowed me to avoid tough questions about what role the land should serve and how to best connect with it. I've always had the best of both worlds—the life I wanted away from the island and a family home and land that we were never under any pressure to sell. I can come and go from the island when I want. As much as I've struggled with my relationship with the tribe and the island, I've always had the luxury of going back to my family's house summer after summer.

In many ways, the big question the tribe has been wrestling with for the past few decades is what to do with the land and what purpose it serves. And even if I can't quite wrap my head around the idea of Indigenous land and what it means to me, the concept of Indigenous land that I have come to know is under constant threat. And although the shape of that threat has evolved over the years, the desire to separate Indigenous people from our land has remained just as strong as ever.

Like most aspects of colonialism, I always saw land allotments, where Indigenous land was divided into individual pieces of private property, as a onetime action. And it's true that nineteenth-century land allotment policies were almost immediately disastrous, that the years after incorporation saw some of the biggest losses of Wampanoag land in our history. I never thought about the long game, but colonialism is both—the sudden onslaught and the slow poison. Even as my family's land feels secure now, I see how quickly we can lose it. One catastrophic event or financial loss and we might be forced to sell.

My mom owns what is a relatively large amount of land, enough to leave chunks for both me and my brother. But if each of us has a couple of kids, the land will have to be split up even more, and some of them may decide to sell. When I think even one or two generations ahead, it's easy to see how land that has been in my family for generations, that has been Wampanoag for thousands of years, could just slip away. And that's a best-case scenario in a family privileged to own multiple plots of land. It has happened countless times before in our history and it will continue to happen until we find a way to stop it. Collectively owned land that can't be sold or lost depending on one family's whims or fortunes is one solution, but not the only one.

The more I learn about our history, the more I see parallels with the present and lessons for the future. At the turn of the nineteenth century, Gay Head was a place in flux. It was still over sixty years away from being an incorporated town, but it had already experienced over two hundred years of colonial incursions. Most people lived in contemporary American houses, but there were still a few wetus, traditional homes made out of tree bark.

Its people were not yet American citizens, but they all spoke English rather than the Wampanoag language. And so, despite the uncertain legal status of the town and its residents, Gay Head was beginning to transform into a nineteenth-century American town with regular town meetings and elections.

But despite this and their long history of contact and trade with white people, two hundred years after the Wampanoag first encountered Bartholomew Gosnold, nearly everyone in town was still Wampanoag. In 1792, Moses Howwassawee, a Wampanoag man, took a census of the area's residents and found that there were 251 people living in Gay Head, including just 15 non-Wampanoags. But about a hundred of those people, mostly children, did not actually live in Gay Head. Wampanoag children were forced into indentured servitude to repay their families' debts.

For most Wampanoags, there was little opportunity to make a living beyond fishing and farming. Many lived in poverty. The fledgling town government did what it could to help struggling families, buying quilts and coffins for those who could not afford them. Even with help from the town, families sold their land to help pay their debts, left with no choice but to sacrifice the one thing they had a right to in order to survive. It was this period when the loss of Wampanoag land in Aquinnah began in earnest. A few decades later, town incorporation accelerated the loss.

When I think about these families, living in poverty and forced to sell their land, I wonder what Aquinnah would look like today if more of us had been able to hang on to our land. I can only assume that back then, like now, some people wished they had more options to stay in Aquinnah while others would have done anything to leave, whether that was because of a lack of opportunity or merely a desire to live somewhere new. There's no way we can go back and somehow help them keep their land, but maybe we can find a better way now. Back then the tribe had few options—virtually no money or power. Now we have at least some land and more resources.

The land is our home, but sometimes I'm not sure what that means. It is literally the home of Wampanoags who live in Aquinnah year-round. It is my home a few weeks out of the year. It is also the home of our government, culture, and history. But increasingly, it is not the home of our people. Less than a quarter of the tribe lives in Aquinnah today, and less than half are on the island overall.

I don't know how many Wampanoags would move back to Aquinnah if they could. I could, but choose not to. In an ideal world, the tribe would do what it can to support people who want to move back and those who choose to stay away, for whatever reason. There are so many ways to facilitate people's connection with the tribe and even the island itself without them living there.

I know I was able to have that through tribal summer camp, our annual cranberry harvest festival, and other events. But for me, most of that was made possible by the fact that it's easy for me to drop by the island. Many tribal members are not so lucky, and with real estate prices sky-high on the island, there are few good options. The tribe has some affordable housing, but there is always a waiting list. People find it hard to even visit for a weekend in the summer or for one of our important events. Some people have floated the idea of the tribe setting up temporary housing for off-island members to stay when they come over for powwow, meetings, and cranberry day.

I like that idea because it gives people the option to engage with the island in a way that makes sense for them. You don't have to live on the island to be a part of the community. But we as a people do need more options than we have now. And that's been true for generations. The more I learned about tribal history, the more I realized how central the housing question is to our story.

After securing federal recognition and nearly five hundred acres of land in the late 1980s, the tribe had land and status for the first time in centuries but lacked the material resources to do much with either. And so the tribe had two priorities: making money and providing housing for members to live in Aquinnah. Both were seen as equally essential projects toward securing the tribe's future. Although federal recognition meant that the tribe could now take advantage of various federal grants and programs, the goal was always to establish an independent income stream. Other tribes had begun to see astonishing returns from casino gambling, and so the new tribal government began pursuing a casino of our own. But even dreams of mountains of casino money meant little if the tribe could not protect its home and people.

The rapid decline of Wampanoag land ownership on Martha's Vineyard over the previous hundred years meant that Wampanoag people had fewer and fewer places to live. Even without land, some Wampanoag stayed on the island but were forced to share homes with family or rent homes on land that, until recently, had belonged to them. Even more left the island entirely.

"More than half the tribe lives off-island," Beverly Wright, our tribal chairperson, told the *Boston Globe* in 1994. "Bringing our people home is one of our highest priorities. There is a sense of belonging here that we can find nowhere else." With federal recognition, the tribe finally had the organization and legal status to begin to reverse the flood of Wampanoag people away from Aquinnah. Looking back on this quote, it's telling that one of the very first things the tribe did after federal recognition was to create affordable housing, not just to reduce living expenses for people in Aquinnah, but with the explicit goal of bringing Wampanoags back home.

And so, a year after federal recognition, the tribe began work on a thirty-home affordable housing development on the newly acquired tribal land. The project, which cost $6.2 million in federal funding, took years to complete and features homes with curved roofs designed to echo our traditional wetus. The homes would be leased to tribal members at no more than 30 percent of their annual income and included either three or four bedrooms. Before the project was completed, seventy-two families had applied for the thirty units.

Of course, building any new housing development—let alone one on Martha's Vineyard that required millions of dollars in federal money—is far from simple. Beyond the logistical details and hurdles, the biggest thing the new tribal government needed to overcome was a growing desire among nontribal town residents to restrict the tribe's influence. As the tribe's land base and power had steadily decreased over the years, nontribal members had gotten comfortable doing what they wanted on the island. A new thirty-unit housing block threatened to upset that.

In 1993, the town's zoning board tried to limit the number of homes in tribal housing that could be occupied by families, in an attempt to reduce the potential impact on the town's school budget. The fact that the town had any control over the tribe's plans was the legacy of a compromise the tribe had made with the town just a few years earlier. The resistance from the zoning committee was a check on the tribe's newly acquired sovereignty that showed regaining land and power was not just a fight against the past, but part of an evolving campaign against Indigenous sovereignty.

Both the tribe and the federal government pushed back against the zoning board, with the DOJ opening an investigation. Eventually, the town voted in favor of the project, clearing the way for it to be completed. According to the *Boston Globe*, the town meeting where the project was approved was firmly in support of the tribe, giving the episode a relatively happy ending.

But despite the amicable resolution, it was an early sign that even though the tribe was newly empowered by federal recognition, competing interests in town wouldn't just let it do whatever it wanted. While the tribe had been fighting for its very existence, nontribal landowners and residents had been consolidating both their land and power. For as long as I can remember, virtually every major action taken by the tribe has been opposed by white town residents and landowners, and often by the (primarily white) town government itself.

The tribal housing homes were built in small clusters of five or six homes that were connected by paved roads that wound their way through the shrubby hills. Each cluster was given a name in the Wampanoag language, but most people just refer to them by single-letter initials—"I live in 'E,'" someone might say. Suddenly, families who hadn't had land in Aquinnah for generations and didn't have millions of dollars to buy it back could afford to live in Aquinnah.

When my brother and I were going to tribal summer camp in the late 1990s, most of our cousins lived in tribal housing. After camp we would roam around tribal housing, playing basketball or hunting for snakes in the tall grass. If the goal was to help strengthen and grow the tribal community in Aquinnah, tribal housing worked.

It's strange to think now that most of those homes were only a few years old, that before then, there had been no affordable housing option for tribal members. Almost overnight, the tribe had created a community of tribal homes and families, a small neighborhood within Aquinnah. According to tribal plans at the time, this was just the first phase of a multistage effort to create more housing for tribal members.

But in the twenty-plus years since the project was completed, the tribe has been slow to build more new homes. And some of the existing homes are in need of repairs and maintenance. For years, many tribal members have been calling on the tribe to put more effort into building more affordable housing, which includes constructing new homes, but also acquiring more land to build them on. As real estate prices and taxes continue to skyrocket, there is also an island-wide affordable housing crisis that is impacting non-Indigenous island residents too.

In 2021, the median home sale price on the island was around $1.2 million, a number that continues to rise. Empty plots of land regularly sell for millions of dollars. According to the Dukes County Regional Housing Authority, over a thousand islanders were on affordable housing waitlists in early 2023. Meanwhile, around 20 percent of the houses on the island are used for short-term rentals, rather than as year-round homes. And this is all without considering the high cost of living and limited job opportunities on the island.

In the summer of 2023, I looked at the website of one island real estate company and found eleven listings for Aquinnah homes. The average was over $3.5 million, with one over $8 million. I perked up a bit when I noticed a listing that was just under a million dollars ($975,000), but I quickly realized that it was just an empty piece of land. Every year these numbers get worse. I know that if my family did not already have a home in Aquinnah, I almost certainly would never be able to buy one.

These are the challenges we face. I don't think providing housing is the end goal, but more of a beginning that can help to heal the harms of the past, erasing hundreds of years of trauma and loss of land. Indigenous land is Indigenous because the people make it so, whether they live there full time or not.

Part of what Indigenous land means is fighting for it, but I'm slowly starting to realize that just because we choose to fight for it does not mean that's all there is to it. Fighting is something we need to do to achieve the freedom to decide who we are. Focusing on the struggle for land can cause us to lose sight of what we are really fighting for, which is the community and its people. That means fighting for the land and fighting to assert who we are, even as the rest of the world is increasingly eager to erase our existence on the island.

4

THE SETTLEMENT

After I graduated from college in 2015, I spent the whole summer on the island. For just over three months, I worked nearly every day at my parents' store, saving up money for when I went back to New York for grad school in September. That summer was, and still is, the longest I've ever spent on the island without leaving. It was also the first time I had really thought about the complex political and cultural factors that shaped the Aquinnah I knew. I grew curious about the tribe's recent political history after hearing some cousins discussing a settlement agreement with the town that I had never heard about. They also kept alluding to bitter fights among tribal members that had taken place during the settlement negotiations.

Slowly, I pieced together the basics: In the late 1980s, when the tribe was granted federal recognition and about five hundred acres of land, it also signed an agreement that it would follow all town and state laws. The settlement raised the question of what the tribe was allowed to do on our own land and who gets to make those decisions. And increasingly, I began to wonder what had happened in our recent past to create the current land dynamic, especially those mysterious internal fights. The idea that tribal members were fighting over land decisions contradicted my simplistic assumption that Natives always united to protect their land from colonizers.

Learning about the settlement made me realize how little I actually knew about the land history of the tribe. For example, many of the crucial land decisions that shaped the Aquinnah I knew had been made just a few years before I was born. I also started to understand that if I really wanted to understand tribal dynamics, I would have to learn more about the last fifty years of our history, and that I might find more answers there than by picking apart Moshup's story looking for metaphors and messages.

The first thing that I had to learn was that in the 1960s, when my mom was growing up, the tribe was very different. The island's popularity with summer tourists had begun to grow, but Gay Head remained pretty isolated. The tribe that I knew—the administration building, the tribal council, tribal summer camp, language classes—did not exist yet.

For the most part, traditional tribal structures had been replaced by American small-town dynamics and systems, but the Gay Headers didn't feel a significant loss of control. The town government, led by a board of three selectmen, had always been controlled by Wampanoags, and the vast majority of residents were Wampanoag.

Across the country, dozens of other tribes were in a similar situation. For decades, the federal government had pushed policies designed to take Indian land, rights, and sovereignty. But by the 1960s, a new era of self-determination was beginning. Tribes had more freedom to structure their own governments and operate as sovereign entities. But for tribes like mine, that had no legally recognized government or land, what that meant was unclear.

Many tribes quickly realized that the key to getting anything done was taking back as much of their land as they could. Of course, local governments and private landowners were not happy about that. But with each passing year, tribes were finding more ways to reclaim their land.

In the 1970s, a young white lawyer named Tom Tureen was working with tribes in Maine when he discovered a loophole in the 1790 federal Nonintercourse Act, which states that only the federal government can transfer ownership of Indian land. According to Tureen, that meant that millions of acres of land up and down the East Coast had been improperly transferred, since towns and states had done much of that work. This opened the door for nearly every East Coast tribe to claim that they were entitled to get their land back.

In Maine, Tureen helped the Passamaquoddy Tribe gain thousands of acres of land in a settlement with the state, which feared that allowing the case to go to federal court might allow tribes to reclaim the entire state. After this success, Tureen began reaching out to more tribes, including the Aquinnah Wampanoag, who he said could hope for such a positive settlement. Using Tureen's strategy, the tribe moved to get back the cliffs and cranberry bogs. The town government, which was run by Wampanoags, immediately approved the transfer. The problem was that there was no official tribal entity to receive the land.

So the Gay Headers organized under the new banner of the Wampanoag Tribal Council of Gay Head, Incorporated, a nonprofit organization that was not recognized as a sovereign tribal nation by the US or the state. In 1978, the council elected Gladys Widdiss, a sixty-four-year-old tribal matriarch, president. My grandfather was elected vice president.

While the tribe was getting organized, so too was a rapidly growing number of nontribal homeowners. Early pioneers of "summering" on Martha's Vineyard grew concerned that the island would quickly change from the undisturbed idyll they had grown to love. Bob Stutz, a labor arbitrator who worked for the US Department of Labor, organized a group of summer residents to fight the tribe's efforts to reclaim land in Gay Head. They called themselves the Gay Head Taxpayers' Association, a name based on the racist assumption that Indians don't pay taxes. But my grandfather and other Wampanoags who owned land all paid the same taxes as non-Indians. On the other hand, many Wampanoags became members of the Taxpayers' Association, a fact that shows how tangled small-town politics can be.

The Taxpayers' Association feared that their private property would be threatened unless they challenged the tribe on every land claim. Led by Gladys, the new tribal council pushed for a land settlement that would return a chunk of land to the tribe and leave the majority of Gay Head land to private ownership. As much as that sounds like a compromise, the more I think about it, the more impressed I am by the audacity to demand any amount of land back. This was not the Land Back efforts of today, where campaigns to reclaim Indigenous land are boosted by major grants, hashtags, and stickers. This was a time when Indian identity was still deeply stigmatized and tribal land holdings had been rapidly shrinking for three hundred years, with no end in sight.

But for some Wampanoags, the idea of a settlement was simply not acceptable. As the tribal council negotiated the details of this settlement, a dissident wing of the tribe organized itself. This more radical group, led by my grandfather's cousin Thelma Weissberg and other members of our extended Vanderhoop family, believed that a land settlement was an unnecessary compromise. They wanted all our land back.

Thelma quickly rallied most of the Vanderhoops against Gladys and the council. She and her seven siblings had always been close, but the land crisis united them even more. My grandfather stayed out of it, believing that his cousins' goals were unrealistic. He felt it was better to get something than nothing at all.

The tribal council and the Taxpayers' Association eventually came to an agreement, despite the strong opposition from the dissident side. The settlement gave 238 acres of land to the tribe along with $1.5 million to buy 175 more acres, and, in exchange, the tribe agreed to follow all town laws. The settlement also stated that all Indian claims to land in Gay Head would be erased moving forward. Sometimes I wonder if that clause will come to be questioned, too, and what that will mean for the island.

Once the settlement agreement was signed by both sides and made into federal law, the tribe also received federal recognition as a sovereign nation. Federal recognition came with a host of benefits, including access to federal grants and resources. It also meant that we had a new tribal government, the one that I know today. In 1987, Gladys's son Donald was elected as the first chairperson. In an attempt to reassure dissidents and other tribal members about the compromise, Gladys promised that Gay

Head would remain under tribal control. Within ten years, Gladys would be proven wrong.

Despite the relative successes of the 1980s for the Wampanoag—federal recognition and land settlement, all of which meant more money and influence—the tribe was ill-set up to confront its future on a rapidly developing and changing island. Always a popular vacation spot for national celebrities, the Vineyard saw an explosion of wealthy visitors in the 1980s and 1990s.

Although the Vineyard's pristine beaches and isolation from the rest of the world had always appealed to national celebrities like Walter Cronkite, Art Buchwald, and Thomas Hart Benton, Martha's Vineyard had little cultural resonance for most Americans. The combination of the proliferation of national media coverage of celebrities and a new wave of the nation's biggest names moving to the Vineyard quickly changed the island from a little-known getaway to one of the most iconic vacation spots in the country.

The enormous popularity of the 1975 blockbuster film *Jaws*, which was filmed on Martha's Vineyard, helped to propel the island into the national consciousness as a perfect American vacation spot. To this day, *Jaws* fans flock to filming locations. I used to be proud that such a famous movie was filmed on the island. I never thought about how it was part of the machine that took our land.

But this was just a prelude to the explosion of national interest that would fall on the island when one of the country's most famous figures bought a piece of land on Moshup's rumored final resting place. In the summer of 1978, the same year Gladys Widdiss was elected president of the incorporated council, rumors flew across the island that former First Lady Jacqueline Kennedy Onassis had acquired property in Gay Head.

Although Onassis had done her best to keep a low profile since her husband's assassination, her fame and mystique had only increased. On August 22, 1978, the *Vineyard Gazette* published a statement from Alexander Forger, Onassis's lawyer, declaring that the rumors were true. In January of that year, Forger had purchased a 375-acre piece of this land from the Hornblowers—a wealthy family known for its successful New York brokerage firm—on her behalf for just over a million dollars. With just a drop in the bucket of the family fortune, Onassis was able to acquire a chunk of land almost as big as the one the tribe had fought ten years to get.

In the statement, Forger told the *Gazette* that "announcement of her ownership has not previously been made in the hope that the tranquility of the island might be spared the intrusions and publicity that so frequently accompany her life." Once it became apparent that the secret was out, Forger explained that he was making the announcement in the hopes that it would end "the unwanted attention to the Island brought on by rumor and speculation." This statement, her first public foray into Vineyard life, carefully crafted and magnanimous, assumed that any attention to the Island risked spoiling its "tranquility," an attribute that summer residents were increasingly protective of.

In the statement, Forger also explained that conservation was one of the primary reasons Onassis had wanted to purchase the property: "The moment she saw its moors, dunes, ponds, and marshes she determined that its unique beauty and wild state should be preserved. Because of the size and value of the parcel, its development by a purchaser or a group of purchasers, even if only with a dozen or so houses, seemed inevitable." Then and now, "only" a dozen houses for tribal members would be a monumental shift in housing availability in Aquinnah.

Like Moshup thousands of years before, Onassis sought sanctuary in the quiet dunes and ponds on the south side of Gay Head. Red Gate Farm, as the property was known, offered both comfort and privacy—exactly what the former First Lady was looking for. But even someone with as much money and power as Onassis could not avoid the effects of the complicated land history in Gay Head. When the Hornblower family originally bought the land, they had been unable to buy a tiny stretch of beach land in the middle of the property since it was owned by a different family—mine, as it turned out.

This acre-and-a-half piece of beach in the middle of Onassis's new sanctuary, officially designated as Lot 615 on the town's property map, was collectively owned by over two dozen Vanderhoops, including my grandfather and his cousins. Years later, I found a box in our attic filled with newspaper clippings, property maps, and correspondence my grandfather had labeled "615." I used these materials and conversations with my mom and other cousins to piece together the details of the dispute. As I read through the pages, I marveled at the level of detail my grandfather needed to protect just one piece of relatively inconsequential land.

By the 1970s, less than two hundred Wampanoags remained in Gay Head, and Lot 615 was one of the last Indian-owned beach plots. As they slowly lost land, most Wampanoags preferred to hold on to farmland, which had always been more valuable to them. The beach was never really something they considered property. It was just a place to fish and launch boats. Plus, back then, there were no fences or even clear property boundaries in Gay Head, especially on the beach.

Onassis, however, brought an unprecedented need for privacy and security. After her brother-in-law Robert Kennedy's assassination in 1968, she famously said, "If they're killing Kennedys, then my children are targets. I want to get out of this country." Months later, she married Greek shipping magnate Aristotle Onassis and moved to his private Greek island. This marriage led to some public criticism of the once beloved First Lady and further inflamed the press surrounding the Kennedy family. In 1972, Onassis obtained a restraining order against controversial photographer Ron Galella. After Aristotle Onassis's death in 1975 and her return to the United States, Onassis's desire for privacy remained high.

I've seen two presidents—Clinton and Obama—spend their summer vacations on the island, accompanied by SUVs full of Secret Service agents. So for me, the idea of security guards enforcing a private beach doesn't seem all that strange, but back then, it was completely unheard of. Bristling at the new restrictions, Wampanoags began pushing for access to the beach, threatening to disrupt the peace Onassis sought in Gay Head.

In an attempt to solve the problem of the pesky acre and a half, Alexander Forger, the attorney, bought a share of Lot 615 from one of the Vanderhoop descendants—an elderly woman named Julia Andrada—for $1,000 in 1979, one year after the purchase of the Hornblower land. Now a partial owner of Lot 615, Forger could petition for a partition auction of the land, a mechanism designed to consolidate land ownership. From Forger's point of view, it must have seemed like a fairly straightforward land proceeding. The auction would be called, and the current owners would be bought out at a fair price.

From the Vanderhoop family's perspective, Forger had taken advantage of a tribal elder in yet another case of rich whites stealing land from them. Everyone knew who would win an auction if it came to that. Thelma Weissberg and the other Vanderhoops felt that losing a culturally important piece of land simply because they couldn't match Onassis's wealth was deeply unfair. In the hundred years since the 1870 land division, Wampanoags had seen their land holdings shrink by the year. This time, they resolved to fight back.

Unable to afford an elite team of attorneys like those working for Onassis and lacking the contacts to sign on any pro bono lawyers, the Vanderhoops turned to Paul Sulla, a Boston-based lawyer who spent summers in Gay Head. Sulla agreed to work on the case for a promise of a share of any settlement won. The first problem Sulla and the Vanderhoops encountered was that Forger believed that Lot 615 was virtually worthless. Some family members were told that the property had completely eroded into the sea. But if that was the case, why was Forger working so hard to buy them out?

Early in the negotiations, Forger offered to swap another piece of land for Lot 615. The proposed swap would give the Vanderhoop family a piece of beach land on the edge of the Onassis property, making it more convenient to access for everyone. Forger also stated that this new land was more valuable and requested that the Vanderhoops also pay $150,000 as part of the deal. Sulla and the family quickly rejected this deal. Why should they pay such a wealthy woman? At this point, the goal became getting a new, accessible piece of beach in exchange for Lot 615, plus some cash.

Knowing the key to getting a favorable settlement was proving Lot 615's value, Sulla adopted a two-pronged strategy. The first part was a counterattack: suing for access to Lot 615, which would immediately raise the property value and undermine Red Gate Farm's isolation. Sulla's second tactic was waging a publicity campaign against Onassis's attempt to acquire the Vanderhoops' land.

Knowing that Onassis's ultimate goal was privacy, Sulla planned to bring as much media attention to Gay Head as possible. Eventually, he reasoned, this pressure would wear her down and force a settlement. Privately, Sulla also believed that Lot 615 was worthless on its own, since half of it was "underwater," and the rest was likely to erode soon. The beach itself was small and had no place to park.

Forger and his team of attorneys made the same argument, offering to compensate the owners for what they believed to be a fair price—$30,000–$50,000. Forger may have also believed that the Vanderhoops were trying to capitalize on his client's wealth to get more than they would from any other person. In truth, Onassis simply had the bad luck to encounter a tenacious Vanderhoop family sick of seeing their land disappear. For his part, Sulla was willing to resort to any tactics he felt would work.

In the summer of 1987, Sulla organized a sit-in on the contested beach and made sure that several news cameras would be there to witness it. Parking at Sulla's house across the street, the group, which consisted of Sulla and around ten family members, made the long walk through the dunes down to the beach. The Onassis security team was instructed to let them cross through, and so the small group made their way down to Lot 615. Pinpointing exactly where to stage the protest was tricky, since lot boundaries aren't drawn on the sand, so the group made their best guess. Instead of signs or angry chants, they brought a picnic lunch.

For the older members of the group like Weissberg, relaxing on the beach was a strange way to spend an afternoon. The beach had always been important to Wampanoags, but the water was for fishing, not swimming. Grand beach parties like the ones that Onassis threw were a foreign concept. When they were done for the day, Onassis's caretaker drove the group back off the estate. Thelma felt that the fancy lawyers were complicating the whole matter and it would best be resolved by sitting down with Onassis and talking it out.

But things had gone too far for that. Onassis was hardly seen in town during the whole affair. Meanwhile, Sulla's press strategy was working. All the local papers and TV stations were covering the situation. Onassis had especially hoped to avoid any kind of toxic coverage. She wanted to be seen as a gracious neighbor, one who respected the land as much as the Wampanoags. This desire to avoid public conflict with the Indians was likely the reason Onassis had stayed out of the settlement fight, despite her clear interest to prevent any Wampanoag seizure of private lands.

Although Onassis did her best to avoid taking sides in the settlement fight, the weight of the Kennedy name could not be avoided. During a 1986 Senate hearing on the settlement, moderator Peter Taylor stopped a Vanderhoop dissident named Roland James in the middle of his statement to ask a question about the group's intentions. James had been explaining that the Indians were entitled to reclaim all land in Gay Head, which was a dramatic but real possibility. Instead of talking about acreage or the sheer impracticality of changing ownership of an entire town, Taylor focused on the specific example of Onassis's land: "Are you saying that Jackie Kennedy's estate, as well as the other properties that are within these 3,400 acres, the title has been currently issued to by the State of Massachusetts, that that land should be taken from the current owners and returned to the tribe? Is that what you are recommending?" Confronted by the most prominent name in the country, James demurred—"No, I never said that"—even though what Taylor had asked was exactly what the dissidents had been suggesting all along.

If the settlement discussions had been haunted by the looming presence of the Kennedy name, the dispute over Lot 615 was equally affected by the invocation of Moshup's name. Publicly, Thelma and the others made sure to stress the cultural importance of the land as Moshup's final resting place, and that story played well in the papers. This cultural significance, however, was little more than a rhetorical strategy for the Vanderhoops: They wanted to hold on to *any* land in Gay Head, whether or not Moshup may have settled there. Even then, they knew that Native culture was a powerful card to play, whether or not they believed in it.

At the same time, Sulla warned Forger and his team that an auction might not be as simple as outbidding a handful of poor Indians. In Massachusetts, such auctions must take place on-site, so Sulla threatened advertising the auction to a wide range of bidders eager for a front-seat view of Jackie O. The Vanderhoops, he presented as an alternative, simply wanted a fair exchange. They were not trying to gawk or exploit.

About thirty years later, I called Sulla at his office in Hawaii, where he eagerly launched in to the story as soon as I said who I was. He told me that around this time, he felt like his aggressive strategy was really getting into his adversaries' heads. On the phone, Sulla told me that the real problem was getting all the Vanderhoops, including my grandfather, on board.

Pinpointing why some family members were hesitant to join the efforts is tough. Sulla told me he suspected that some were so used to being ripped off in land deals that they would only believe it when they saw a profit or new piece of equally valuable land in their hands. In this way, the settlement and the long history of land issues in Gay Head were the unspoken subtext of the whole situation. What this meant for Sulla was that the closer he got to achieving results, the more people he felt he could convince. As resolution seemed to be getting closer, Sulla finally got my grandfather and enough others on board to move forward.

Worn down by the publicity tactics and lack of progress, Forger came up from New York to make a deal in the spring of 1990. Onassis was anxious to resolve the issue before the summer crowds and attention descended on the Vineyard once again. Finally the two sides came to an agreement: They would swap the parcels of land and Onassis would pay the Vanderhoop group $100,000. Both sides were reasonably happy with the final deal: Onassis's estate was complete and the Vanderhoops were rewarded for their tenacious fight to hold on to their land with a piece of beachfront property that they could actually access and enjoy.

As the details of the settlement were hammered out, Paul Sulla named his price: In addition to the percentage of cash they had agreed to, Sulla would also acquire a share of the new land. Sulla felt he deserved more than just monetary compensation for his efforts. For the Vanderhoops, a tiny share of a piece of land already owned by over two dozen people seemed like a small price to pay.

Over the phone, I asked Sulla why he wanted a piece of land, rather than payment. He felt it was fair, he told me, that he would get a share of the winnings too.

Today, that piece of land is a "family" beach. I've been there a few times, but it's rockier and less convenient than other beaches in the area, so I normally go to other beaches in town. A few cousins regularly use it, but many of the descendants live off-island. There are probably some who barely know it exists. It feels somehow fitting that my access to a private beach, supposedly the pinnacle of Vineyard living, comes with such a dark and complex history.

In 2019, the Kennedy-Schlossberg family put over three hundred acres of the land on the market for $65 million. Even though I'm used to seeing high real estate prices on the island, the number still shocked me. Not surprisingly, no one bit at that price. I remember fantasizing about the tribe buying the land even though I knew $65 million was far beyond the tribe's resources.

In two purchases made in 2020 and 2021, the Martha's Vineyard Land Bank Commission bought 350 acres of land from the family for roughly $37 million. The Land Bank is a nonprofit agency that owns 7 percent of the island's land today. The Land Bank uses its land for a variety of purposes, including conservation areas and public beaches. The Land Bank does not pay property taxes on the land, meaning the town lost the tax income the family had been paying. The Land Bank is funded by a percentage taken from most land sales on the island. In other words, the model for a program to fund Wampanoag land reclamation exists, but it is the Land Bank who benefits, not us. In a press release, the Land Bank announced that they planned to open much of the Kennedy property to the public and that the lands would generally be for conservation purposes. The family is going to keep roughly the rest of the property, including the house and its surrounding buildings.

The word on the island was that the family didn't want the land anymore, that it was too much work to maintain, and that few of them actually took advantage of it. It hurts that less than fifty years after they bought such a huge chunk of land, they are already done with it. In the meantime, prices on the island have skyrocketed. If the tribe had gotten that land back in the 1970s or 1980s, everything could have been different. We could have used the land to build more affordable housing, to increase the influence of the tribe's environmental programs, and to generate income.

While the Kennedy-Schlossberg family gets to keep their house and a $37 million payout, my family has a tiny sliver of beach on which we have to pay rapidly increasing property taxes. When I take all this into account, I wonder how much of a victory it really was.

Across Aquinnah, dozens of plots of land are owned by tribal members who share ownership with a group of cousins. One acre of land can have literally dozens of owners, a status that is far more confusing than beneficial. Typically, in these situations, one family member buys the others out, or, more often, an outsider comes in and buys everyone out. Over the years, I've seen my mom sell pieces of land that way, and every time she's relieved when it's over. It feels as though we're just being slowly ground down by rising costs and the burden of bureaucracy and logistics until we have nothing left.

And I'm not sure what the solution to that is, other than somehow getting a lot more money. In theory, land that is privately owned by multiple generations of Wampanoag cousins could be something like the collective land ownership we used to have, but the reality is different. Much of that land is wedged between other private properties. A lot of it is not buildable, meaning we could never put anything on it, unless town laws change (unlikely).

The settlement, on the other hand, led to another version of collectively owned land—tribal land that is used for mutual benefit, like tribal housing and the community center. As a tribe, we have to figure out how we want to use that land. But those decisions will never be easy. We'll always argue about what to do with our collective resources, especially as limited as they are. The benefit of private land is that it isn't subject to the fluctuations of tribal politics.

The real difference between the two is that private land can be sold at any time, but the tribal land can never be sold. The land we got in the settlement is a safeguard. Even if every tribal family is forced to sell their land, at least the tribe will always have that land. But it's simply not enough. It also makes me question what our land—both private and tribal—should really be doing. I always thought the goal was to get as much land as possible, to return as much as possible to some sort of original state, but I've realized that simply having the land—whether tribal or privately owned—doesn't mean much. We need to find new ways forward, new ways to make the most of the land we have before it's too late.

5

HATMARCHA GIFTS

Wampanoag people are often overlooked on Martha's Vineyard. Many customers who come into our store are surprised to learn that there are any Indigenous people at all on the island. I think this is partly because Indigenous people, especially on the East Coast, are often forgotten entirely. The other reason is the way that Martha's Vineyard is perceived by most people.

Whenever I tell people my family is from Martha's Vineyard, they almost always say *wow* and look at me as if they are trying to figure out exactly how rich my family is. Then they usually say something like *Wait, I didn't know people actually lived there . . .* before trailing off, probably trying to figure out if I'm a poor townie or ultrarich landed gentry.

I grew up in Newton, a wealthy Boston suburb where families tended to divide themselves into Cape and Islands people or Maine people based on if their vacation home was on the beach or the ski slopes. In a way, I fit in because I also went somewhere fancy each summer. I knew that what I had was different, that my grandparents' house wasn't the same as a ski cabin in Maine, but I had no framework to help me understand it.

I always want to correct people's assumptions when I say I'm from the island, but hesitate because I'm worried that they might be right. In a lot of ways, my personal experiences are not that different from the stereotypical Vineyard tourist. I rarely spend any time there outside of the summer months. I go to the beach every day and complain when I have to share the beach with more than a few people. I grew up looking forward to the same summer traditions as the tourists, like the rides and games at the annual agricultural fair. I wondered how I could claim Martha's Vineyard as my Indigenous home when I barely knew more about it than the average summer renter.

Explaining that my family is Wampanoag brings on a whole new wave of shock. *I had no idea*, they often say. *I thought the Vineyard was just rich white people.* Their surprise says as much about Martha's Vineyard as it does about the way this country sees Indigenous people. To them, the island is a place for rich white people, and such a place surely cannot have any Natives. In fact, I think encountering any Natives at all on the East Coast is surprising to many people. Very few people ever say it, but I can always feel an unspoken *but I thought you were all dead* in those moments. Most people, I think, expect to encounter Natives on rural land out west, not in Massachusetts, and certainly not in one of the most exclusive beach communities in the country.

And to be honest, that threw me off a little too. My tribe's land and community did not look like what I imagined other Native lands did and so those assumptions clashed with the Martha's Vineyard that I knew.

For a long time, I never fully realized how limiting the lens was that I was using to understand both my Wampanoag identity and the island it was based on. To unpack those and develop a more nuanced view of both, I needed to understand more about exactly what Martha's Vineyard represents in American culture and how it became such an extreme cultural symbol.

In the same way that I had looked for the one moment of colonization where everything changed for the Wampanoag, I wanted to find the one key moment in history when Martha's Vineyard transformed from a remote island to what it is today. But just as I've had to learn about the slow, undulating process of colonization, I've also had to come to terms with the complex way that Martha's Vineyard has evolved.

There's no way to pinpoint one specific moment or celebrity who catapulted the island into national consciousness. Since at least the early twentieth century, the island, and particularly Oak Bluffs, has been a popular vacation spot for Black families looking for a safe space to enjoy the beach. Shearer Cottage, the island's first Black-owned inn, opened in 1912 and was featured in *The Negro Motorist Green Book*. And by the mid-twentieth century, white celebrities like news anchor Walter Cronkite and columnist Art Buchwald had vacation homes on the Vineyard, but the island still wasn't really on the country's radar as a whole. As I researched, I felt like I was gathering breadcrumbs but not finding the answer I had been looking for. I wish I could ask my grandfather more about the changes he saw on the island throughout his life. Without that, I've had to make do by asking other relatives, looking up history, and reading old newspaper articles.

In 1969, Senator Ted Kennedy drove off a bridge on Chappaquiddick, the small island at the eastern tip of the Vineyard. Kennedy's passenger, Mary Jo Kopechne, drowned, while Kennedy fled the scene and waited until the next morning to report the incident to the police. The incident, for which Kennedy only ever received mild punishment, became a national scandal that jeopardized the young senator's presidential ambitions and helped solidify the image of Martha's Vineyard as a playground for the country's elite.

Although the Chappaquiddick incident may have been the first time that the Kennedy name and Martha's Vineyard were entangled in national headlines, it was far from the last. Since Onassis bought Red Gate Farm, most Americans have thought of the island as an exclusive place where the country's elite spent their summers. The list of artists, musicians, movie stars, writers, and politicians who have spent their summers on the Vineyard is seemingly endless, although some attract more attention than others. I can remember people at my family's store asking me where comedian John Belushi's grave was before I knew who he was. I grew up knowing these names and figures were part of Vineyard history, but I never really drew the connection between them and the tribe or my family. I viewed them more as fun facts or quirks about the island, but when I look at them all together, it starts to become clear how a gradual trickle eventually became the unstoppable flood I know today.

Although Onassis may have set the tone for what the island was quickly becoming, it was Ted Kennedy who most actively worked to shape the island. Throughout the 1970s, Senator Kennedy pushed for a bill known as the Nantucket Sound Island Trust bill, which was designed to protect the beaches and wilderness of Cape Cod, Nantucket, Martha's Vineyard, and the Elizabeth Islands. As the island grew more popular and development increased, Kennedy and other environmental allies wanted to put federal protections in place. These protections, among other provisions, would have restricted development and transferred beach land to federal ownership.

On the island, the response was mixed. In Gay Head, tribal members quickly realized that the bill would have taken beach land that they hoped to reclaim and given it to the federal government. Fear of this was one of the catalysts for the tribe's organizing efforts in the 1970s. Other nontribal islanders resented the idea of the federal government stepping in to control their lands or had questions about how the bill would be implemented.

But many islanders welcomed the idea of federal resources and protection for the island's environment. The specter of development threatened private homeowners as well as business owners who worried about chains and big corporations threatening their livelihoods. A federal bill to limit development was seen by many as a crucial way to stem the increasingly overwhelming tide of new visitors.

Despite Senator Kennedy's efforts, the bill never passed, but it helped pave the way for a movement on the island to protect the environment and restrict development. But just like the original bill, these efforts often prioritized a particular vision of conservation, one that suited wealthy white landowners, at the expense of the tribe. This would soon become a core dispute on the island. As it turns out, the fight between white-driven conservation and Indigenous land management is one of the fiercest conflicts around the world.

The conversation around conservation and development was becoming increasingly urgent in the 1970s because while the island had always been popular for elites, it was quickly gaining more traction as a vacation spot for the masses.

In June 1975, Steven Spielberg's *Jaws*, which was filmed largely on Martha's Vineyard, hit theaters across the country and was an instant, record-breaking success. *Jaws*, which famously used Vineyard locals as extras in the film, set a number of firsts. It was the first major movie to be filmed on the ocean, the first film to gross over $100 million at the box office, the first to take advantage of TV advertising, and was widely regarded as the movie that set the trend for decades of summer blockbusters. I was surprised to learn that before *Jaws* and a few other hits, the summer was considered the quiet season for movie releases. The Vineyard was picked as a filming location in part because of its relatively shallow beaches, but also because of the isolated, almost eerie feeling that producers felt on the island. Ironically, the movie would help to change that.

Jaws helped to catapult Martha's Vineyard into a place that thousands of people wanted to visit every summer. The film's impact has not faded with the years. Today, nearly fifty years after *Jaws* first premiered, there are tours on the island of filming locations. A bridge that featured in the movie is still known as "the *Jaws* bridge." Every local saying they were an extra has become a running joke. I remember watching *Jaws* as a kid and thinking how cool it was that such a famous movie was filmed on the Vineyard. I liked recognizing places I knew in the movie. It never occurred to me how much *Jaws* had shaped the island, rather than the other way around.

All these people and events—*Jaws*, the Kennedys, and the rest—shaped the island before I was born in the 1990s. By the time I can remember taking the ferry from Woods Hole to Vineyard Haven each summer, Martha's Vineyard's status was firmly established. But even during my life, things continued to change. Presidents Bill Clinton and Barack Obama vacationed on the island while they were in office. Both returned to the island multiple times, bringing SUVs full of Secret Service, throngs of photographers, and even bigger crowds than the usual summer rush.

I remember one day Clinton came up to the cliffs, where he was immediately swarmed by crowds. I stood on the steps to our store, peering out of the crowd as if I was at a concert. My dad fought his way through the crowd to shake the president's hand, but when he tried to go back so someone could take a picture of the moment, Secret Service shoved him away. We still joke about that. My uncle's friend told us a story that she was hanging out in her apartment down-island one quiet evening with the window open when police stormed in, saying that President Clinton was out for a run and she had been flagged for watching out her window.

And when John F. Kennedy Jr., his wife, and sister-in law died in a plane crash off the Vineyard coast in 1999, it felt like the country's most powerful people and the island were even more inextricably linked. We sell a T-shirt that has the longitude and latitude of the island on it under some crossed oars or something like that. Once a woman came up to me and asked in a hushed voice if that's where JFK Jr.'s plane went down. I didn't know what to say. So while it was hard to escape the Vineyard's celebrity reputation, it was difficult to see exactly how it impacted me beyond those kinds of questions.

When Barack Obama came to the island early in his first term, it felt like the perfect combination of the Vineyard's features. Obama was not just a president, he had a kind of rock star, celebrity presence, not to mention the enormous attention he got as the first Black president. That summer, it seemed all anyone could talk about was Obama and what he was up to. My parents made special T-shirts with his name and the year. We quickly sold out.

One day during one of Obama's later trips to the island, a woman came and asked me what the president's plans were while on the island. I told her I had no idea. She patted me on the shoulder and said it was okay, she knew the Secret Service told the locals not to say anything to tourists.

In September 2022, Florida Governor Ron DeSantis sent a plane with around fifty asylum seekers from Texas to Martha's Vineyard. The men, women, and children were mostly from Venezuela and had been told they were being sent to Boston, where there were jobs available. Instead, their plane landed in the middle of the night at Martha's Vineyard's tiny airport, where local officials and volunteers scrambled to find somewhere for them to stay.

The stunt was part of DeSantis's campaign to send asylum seekers from Florida and Texas up to liberal cities in the Northeast, to make immigration advocates confront their supposed hypocrisy. "The minute even a small fraction of what those border towns deal with every day is brought to their front door, they go berserk, and they're so upset that this is happening," DeSantis said of sanctuary cities. "And it just shows you that their virtue-signaling is a fraud."

Of course, very few people on the island did go "berserk." The group was quickly placed at a local church, where camp beds had been set up and donations of clothes, food, and supplies poured in. The next day, videos floated around the internet of children from asylum-seeking families playing soccer and speaking Spanish with students at the local high school. The initial outpouring of support was so great that the church had to put out a call that they did not need any more food or clothing donations.

Even though the stunt didn't play out exactly how DeSantis may have envisioned it, he still got the media coverage he wanted. "The posh liberal enclave of Martha's Vineyard has been thrown into chaos by the arrival of two planeloads of migrants sent there by Florida Gov. Ron DeSantis," read a *New York Post* article. "Martha's Vineyard has long been a favored vacation spot for left-leaning celebrities and Democratic pols including former President Barack Obama, who owns an $11.75 million estate where he celebrated his 60th birthday with a blow-out party last year."

In DeSantis's mission to target supposedly elite liberal enclaves, Martha's Vineyard was perfect. There is no other reason to send a plane full of people to a small island airport in the middle of the night. Most Americans, if they've heard of Martha's Vineyard, think of it as a fancy vacation place where celebrities and presidents eat oysters and clam chowder on private beaches. And they're not wrong.

But in September, even though the weather is still good and the island's beaches are perfect for swimming, most of the summer elite that DeSantis targeted had already left the island for the year. In the flurry of reaction, one of the points that many local residents stressed was that year-round Martha's Vineyard was not the same as summer vacation Martha's Vineyard. Namely, that most year-round residents are middle-class people struggling with high costs of living and an affordable housing crisis that gets worse every year.

Of course, the most important thing about this story was the way that these vulnerable people were taken advantage of and used in a political game, not whether or not right-wing characterizations of Martha's Vineyard were accurate. Most of the asylum seekers were eventually taken to a military base on the mainland, where more complete and official resources were provided to them. A few stayed on the island, eventually finding work and housing. Like many asylum seekers, their journey to security and stability is ongoing.

And while I don't think it's worth reading too much into the decision to pick Martha's Vineyard as the latest destination for a plane full of asylum seekers, I wonder if they considered sending the plane to Nantucket or the Hamptons, but even if they did, I'm sure the Vineyard's history of Democratic presidential vacations pushed it over the edge. I doubt DeSantis knows about the Wampanoag tribe or any of the island's complex history. To him, both the island and the asylum seekers were pawns in his political game.

Even as Republicans and right-wing media crowed over DeSantis's supposed coup, much of the country was outraged. An op-ed in the *Los Angeles Times* bore the headline "Ron DeSantis' Cruel Political Theater Falls Flat on Martha's Vineyard." But even if they disagreed with the governor's politics or actions, they probably agreed with his assessment of the island as a luxury vacation spot.

The thing about Martha's Vineyard is that it is more complicated than people think. There is a Martha's Vineyard where politicians and wealthy Democratic donors have private parties with catering and security guards. There is a Martha's Vineyard that is filled with Vineyard Vines polos, private beaches, and sailboats. There's another for families who come over for the day to buy ice cream and keychains. There are those who own a summer house, those who rent one, and those who might stay at a hotel or the youth hostel. It has been home to fishermen, hippies, tribal members, Brazilian immigrants, working families, and so much more.

It may also be that people simply don't realize how big Martha's Vineyard is. Unlike Nantucket, which is smaller and has only one town, Martha's Vineyard has six distinct towns, each with its own characteristics and town governments. The island is divided into up-island and down-island, each with three towns. The terminology comes from longitude, with the up-island towns—Aquinnah, Chilmark, and West Tisbury—on the western side of the island with its higher longitudinal coordinates. The three down-island towns are Oak Bluffs, Tisbury, and Edgartown. Up-island is much more rural, and while the up-island towns do have smatterings of stores and businesses, we go down-island to get groceries, pick visitors up from the airport or ferry, and go shopping.

Edgartown has a rich whaling history and today has a preppy feel with quaint shopping streets, sailing clubs, and stately houses. Edgartown also includes Katama and Chappaquiddick, both of which are more sparsely populated. Tisbury includes Vineyard Haven, the island's main harbor, and a small shopping center. Oak Bluffs is the town with the most lively nightlife, as well as many tourist attractions like its colorful gingerbread houses and iconic carousel. Circuit Avenue in Oak Bluffs is one of the island's busiest commercial streets. Oak Bluffs also has a long history as a vacation destination for Black Americans.

West Tisbury is right in the middle of the island and is known for its farms and the annual agricultural fair held each year in August. Chilmark, the next town over, is considered one of the toniest places on the island. The Chilmark Store is a popular market where summer residents like to hang out on the front porch in a see-and-be-seen kind of way. Chilmark is also home to Menemsha, a fishing village famous for seafood restaurants and fish markets.

And finally, at the western tip of the island, Aquinnah is the smallest and most remote town. Sometimes, when tourists make it to Aquinnah, they say they can't believe how long it took to get there. If they biked, usually they are exhausted and desperate for another option to go back down-island. Unlike other towns, we don't really have a town center. Our only stores are the ones at the cliffs, which are only open seasonally. We are also the only town without our own school.

Many people who visit the island spend their entire time in a single town. While it's true that each town has its own unique characteristics, I also think that it's a little game people play, as if to distinguish themselves from the other rich white people.

But even as these identities solidified throughout the 1970s and 1980s, the one consistent thing in each town was the rapidly increasing numbers of summer tourists. Down-island towns like Oak Bluffs and Edgartown, with their shops and ferry connections to the mainland, quickly grew to accommodate the new crowds. But word about the idyllic beaches in Gay Head was spreading, and the people soon followed.

As tourism became a bigger and bigger industry, lease lots for shops at the cliffs attracted interest from tribal members who had previously thought the only way to make a living was to leave the island, as my grandfather had. A few cousins were already operating successful summer businesses at the cliffs. At the advice of an uncle, my grandfather leased one and opened a souvenir store that my grandmother planned to run. Hatmarcha Gifts—named for my grandmother (Hatsuko), my mother (Martha), and my grandfather and uncle (both Charles)—opened in 1974, while my mom was in college. Decades later, people still ask if the name has some sort of mystical Native meaning. I wonder if my Japanese grandmother knew people would think that when she came up with the name.

Nestled against the high grass that covered the sandy earth, the store stood just a few hundred feet away from the cliff edge. The wind, salt, and water that blew up from the beach year-round soon stained the wood-shingled building a dark, weathered brown. My grandfather helped my grandmother haul in display cases and shelves for their new merchandise. Behind the counter, she placed a maneki-neko, the Japanese beckoning cat that is said to bring good luck to businesses, that her family had sent from Japan. With its back to the cliffs, Hatmarcha Gifts faced the smooth coastline of the island's south shore. From the store, Hatsuko could make out the colorful dots of beach umbrellas and sunbathers through the front double doors. Nomans Land, the uninhabited island, was the only interruption in the dark blue water's steady rise toward the horizon.

Other cousins were also operating increasingly profitable businesses on the cliffs. As the tourist-heavy seasons got busier and busier, my grandparents expected my mom to come home every summer throughout college to help with the store. And yet the same thing that offered these opportunities—the allure of the island's pristine beaches and raw landscape—also made it increasingly difficult for tribal families to stay on the island.

The first eight years of my life followed a familiar pattern. From September to June, my brother and I went to school in Newton. Our mom worked at our preschool and our dad worked as a civil engineer in Boston. Every night we'd wait for my dad to come home on the train, known as the T, which stopped right behind our house. Sometimes we would take the T into Boston to meet my dad at work or visit my grandmother in her apartment in Chinatown. On the weekends, we played soccer and went to Chinese school, where my dad also taught martial arts.

This comfortable suburban routine ended each summer, when we'd say goodbye to our friends and head down to Martha's Vineyard, where we stayed with our maternal grandparents. My dad would come down on weekends while he kept working in Boston.

Back then, there were seven stores on the cliffs, including three take-out restaurants and one sit-down restaurant, all of them owned by tribal cousins. The stores sat on either side of a dirt path that led up to an overlook area with a view of the cliffs and the lighthouse. On a clear evening you could see all the way to Rhode Island. Back then, I remember huge crowds would gather to watch the sunset on clear summer nights, cheering and clapping as the last sliver of sun dipped under the deep blue horizon.

The clay cliffs themselves are owned by the tribe, but the land on top, where the shops sit, is owned by the town. The tribe has an agreement with the town that only tribal members can lease the lots for stores on the cliffs, and most stores have been run by the same families for decades. As my grandparents grew older, they hired nontribal people to run their souvenir shop. I felt no special attachment to the store, and the couple who ran it always seemed like strangers. In fact, I felt more comfortable at my cousin's store where we got special prizes for the library's summer reading competition or the restaurant where we got free french fries.

But when I was in the second grade, our parents told us that my father was going to leave his job in Boston. They were going to take over the store that summer. I had never seen my grandparents run the store, so I had no idea what was involved. I didn't understand how much our lives would change.

During our school's spring break a few months later, the four of us went down to Martha's Vineyard to open up the store. My parents gave me small tasks like wiping down the metal hooks that bracelets and necklaces would soon hang from. I sat on the dusty wooden floor and impatiently wiped a rag around the curves of each hook. My favorite job was pricing. The satisfying click of the blue plastic pricing gun echoed around the small store until a long tail of empty sticker paper hung out the back of the gun. My brother and I carefully removed it and taped it over the entrance to the store, like the finish banner at a marathon for our first customer.

The store is small, no more than a couple hundred square feet that we soon filled to the brim with T-shirts, hats, garden decorations, magnets, and jewelry. That week, the store felt like a new playground, but over the next twenty years, it would become like a third home, a place that felt familiar even as the T-shirt designs and other merchandise changed.

During that first week, the store felt like a family project. Another adventure. As soon as the week was over, however, our family split. My parents, like my grandparents, decided to run the store without moving to the island. Even though they wanted us to have a closer connection to the island, they were hesitant about raising us there full-time. The island, they worried, would be too insular. My father already worried that we were growing up sheltered by Newton's privileged bubble. The island, he thought, would be even worse. To keep the store open in the spring and fall shoulder months while my brother and I were in school in Newton, one parent stayed on the island and the other stayed with us. We began to spend our entire summers on the island, along with long weekends and school breaks.

And so we settled into a strange new routine during the spring and fall. Once or twice a week my parents switched, meeting in the parking lot of the ferry terminal before heading in opposite directions. We called the commuting days "switch days." I hated this new schedule. When my mom was on the island, I missed her. When she was in Newton, I was constantly stressed about the time, knowing that in a few days she would have to leave. Every night, one of us called the parent on the island, chatting about our day for a few minutes before passing the phone off to the next person.

Back then I was too young to really work at the store, but I would hear my parents talking about "tourists" and I knew those were the faceless adults who came to buy things from us. Eventually I realized if no one wanted to come to Martha's Vineyard and buy things, then my mom would still be at home all the time. I felt guilty for telling her I hated tourists, because I knew that's how my parents made a living, but I just wanted those tourists to go away.

Before the store, I'm not sure I even knew the word *tourists*. I knew they were there, of course, but they never affected my life beyond a long line for ice cream or a ride on the carousel. I had never thought of Martha's Vineyard as just a vacation destination. It was my vacation destination because my grandparents and the tribe were there. But once my parents took over the store, the reality of Martha's Vineyard's tourism economy bullied its way into our lives. I now understand how privileged I was to be shielded from the impact of tourism. The cliffs, which had been little more than a place to collect our library prizes and occasional treats, were now the center of our lives on the island.

But the store didn't just change the circumstances of my life, it also transformed my relationship with Martha's Vineyard. The island had been a relaxing, special place for me to spend my summers, but when my parents took over the store, it became a place of work, tension, and stress. And even though I never thought of it this way at the time, my perspective had completely flipped. I had been experiencing the island as a consumer, as a visitor, but suddenly my family members were the ones catering to, and relying on, the visitors. Now, it's almost impossible to remember a time when I thought about the island unencumbered by the demands of the tourism economy.

What's even more surprising to me is realizing how much my experiences with the store have also shaped the way I think about what it means to be Wampanoag. The island was the foundation of my Wampanoag identity, and so the store, as the place I spent the most time on the island, quickly became a key part of shaping that identity. It's strange to say, but working at the store was often the time when I felt most Wampanoag. There was no other part of my life where I talked about being Wampanoag as much and no place where I reflected more on what that meant.

When I wasn't at the store, I spent the summers reading at home, going to the beach, or going on bike rides. Just like it was hard to think of my family's land as Indigenous land, it was sometimes hard to think of my summer experiences as anything other than typical summer activities. But at the store, whether it was by my choice, or a customer's questions, my Wampanoag identity was always near the surface. We are proud that all the shops are run by tribal members, but that doesn't mean it is always easy.

Over the years, countless interactions have shown the assumptions and expectations that most people have about Indigenous people. I have always known about the stereotypes most Americans have about Indigenous people, but it's different encountering them day after day, year after year, especially in a situation where I need to make customers happy.

Looking back, it was practically an education in determining what Native identity is not. Countless offhand comments as well as ignorant and offensive questions gave me something to resist. But it only occurred to me much later that by focusing on pushing back, I had been sealing myself off from figuring out what Indigenous and Wampanoag identity might actually be. And as much as I rejected what I heard from customers, their opinions inevitably began to shape my understanding of what it meant to be Native.

At the store, I learned that most people believe that Natives can only exist in some sort of eternal precolonial state. I assume these people imagine warriors in headdresses on horseback, galloping and whooping across the plains. Sometimes these people push back, saying that we may technically be Wampanoag, but since we don't live the way we did five hundred years ago, we aren't real Indians. I've had people ask if we live in houses and use iPhones, and when I say yes, they seem satisfied, as if I've confirmed that I'm not an authentic Indian.

And then there are the people who get incredibly excited about meeting an Indian. They might say they have a Native ancestor or have always felt a kinship with Indigenous people. Multiple people have told me that they think they were Native in a previous life and that's why they are so spiritual. Some ask to take a picture with me. Or, even worse, of me. Sometimes they ask if we have a reservation and if they can go look at it.

Whether they think Indigenous people are long gone or beautiful, spiritual beings, we are a fascinating relic to them, something completely foreign to the world they live in. Working at the store and confronting people's expectations of Native people was a constant exercise in balancing the urge to push back, apathy in the face of seemingly endless stereotypes, and the ever-present knowledge that I needed these people to like me in order to make a sale. And that's just one of the many sacrifices that tourism and colonialism demand of us.

At the store, I also became acutely aware of Indigenous identity as something that could be performed, and something that could exist differently in different places. It also helped me think about being Indigenous away from the island for the first time because whenever I talked to people, they always were surprised to hear that I lived somewhere else during the offseason. And later, when I went away to college in New York, they were even more surprised to learn that this Native kid from an isolated island town might live in the country's biggest city.

While I was trying to work out what my Wampanoag identity meant to me, the island's tourism machine rolled along. I was never hidden away at home, ruminating on what Native identity meant or looked like; I was behind the showcase in the store, trying to figure out what it means to rely on an economy that is slowly but surely destroying our homeland, who tourism actually benefits, and what it all says about how we think about Native identity.

In the early years of the store, when I was too young to help out much, being there was something to do—and an excuse for my mom to buy me ice cream and french fries from one of the restaurants. I would help my parents make change, restock magnets, and close the windows at the end of the day. I preferred these simple tasks that did not involve interacting with customers, but most of the work of the store meant being friendly and helpful to the steady stream of people that came through our store every day. In particular, my mom encouraged me to practice selling wampum and scrimshaw, two specialty items that required explanation.

Scrimshaw is etching or carving done on bone or ivory. The term usually refers to work done on whale bones and teeth, traditionally by whalers out on long voyages. The carved images are often nautically themed: elaborate sailboats, lighthouses, whales, etc. We sell a range of scrimshaw knives and a few other items like cribbage boards. Because the sale of ivory is now illegal, most of our scrimshaw is done on deer antler or fossilized pieces of bone. We do have on display a few whale teeth left from before the sale of them was illegal. Some were carved by my grandfather. In the showcase next to the teeth there are rusty dentist picks that he used to carve scrimshaw. If we saw someone peering into the showcase at the knives, we were supposed to ask them if they knew about scrimshaw and, if not, explain the full story. The scrimshaw knives were some of the most expensive items in the store. I can still remember the night that my parents sold a knife for over a thousand dollars, late one summer evening. My mom was great at telling people about scrimshaw, while I was usually too shy even to speak.

And then there is the wampum. Wampum jewelry is made from hardshell clams that we call quahogs. In the waters around the Vineyard, quahog shells turn a deep purple color. Our tribe has made jewelry and ceremonial pieces from these beautiful shells for thousands of years. Huge belts with hundreds of hand-carved beads were used to tell stories or mark treaties. King Philip, our seventeenth-century leader, famously had an eight-foot wampum belt that went missing after he was executed by English settlers. Many Wampanoags believe the belt is hidden away in a private collection in England.

In the middle of my wampum spiel, sometimes tourists interrupt to say that wampum is like Indian money, right? My mom trained me to correct them, to say that it only had value once we made it into something beautiful, like a beaded belt or bracelet. Today, Wampanoag artisans make the shells into bracelets, earrings, and necklaces.

When customers ask if we sell anything local, I always show them the wampum. We have a whole quahog shell in the showcase to help show people where the purple beads come from. Most of the time, people are impressed by the wampum and say that it is very beautiful. But because wampum is relatively expensive, these people rarely buy anything. Sometimes, they might pick out one of the cheaper pendants or bracelets. Selling a beaded wampum bracelet has always been a guarantee that we had a good day of business.

Recently, I was selling a pair of wampum earrings to a woman and I told her that they had been made by one of my cousins. She asked his name, and when I told her it was Jason, she scoffed. "That's not an Indian name," she exclaimed. "What's his Indian name?" Sometimes I'm still stunned into silence. Jason, I said, after I recovered, that's his name.

I've learned to try to sell myself as much as the products. Most people want their shopping experience enhanced by talking to locals, and over the years I've gotten better at playing that role. This isn't always so easy. I like to think that I find ways to make people feel they are getting an authentic experience without indulging their stereotypes, but being Wampanoag at the cliffs doesn't always just mean posing for photos or explaining that Indians still exist.

The cliffs are made from different colored clay and form an impressive vista over the pristine water below. At high tide, the water laps at the base of the cliffs, dislodging small chunks of clay that often end up embedded in the sand. The tribe's Natural Resources Department posts signs that warn it's illegal to touch the clay even if it's detached from the cliffs. Still, I always see kids coming up with faces painted with red and white clay. I know it's not the kids' fault, so sometimes I tell off their parents, who usually reply that it's just a bit of clay, so what's the big deal.

Every year more of the cliffs erode into the ocean. Even in the years since my parents first took over the store, I can see gaping voids where colorful red, yellow, white, and black clay once was. The last time my mom and I looked at the cliffs together, she gasped and said that she couldn't believe how little was left. Of course, a couple of kids smearing clay on their faces isn't going to make the difference in a thousands-of-years-long geological process, not to mention climate change and rising sea levels, but I can't help being upset at how little they care.

So even though working at the store is made up of thousands of individual moments and interactions, it's hard to ignore the bigger picture. In this way, the store, the cliffs, and the tourism economy at large have also become the prism through which I understand bigger issues facing the tribe.

Because Aquinnah is so far from the other main attractions on the island, tour buses are the cliffs' lifeline. In the early days of the store, I can remember a line of ten or twelve buses parked up at the cliffs. When I used to call my mom every night I would ask her about the buses and she'd tell me that they had twelve at a time or something like that. In recent years, however, more and more tour buses have started doing down-island-only routes. Now we're lucky to get two or three at a time.

One reason we've seen decreased bus traffic is because residents of one of the three roads in town complained about all the loud traffic disturbing their peaceful seaside homes. The emissions from the tour buses, they claimed, were also an environmental hazard to dune plants along the coast. I don't know if that's true or not, but it was hard to not see it as a group of privileged people fortunate enough to buy homes in Aquinnah early on simply trying to preserve the tranquil place they had grown to love.

For most of my life, I thought these challenges were unique to the island. As much as I protested against tourists' stereotypical assumptions, I also found it difficult to understand that Indigenous people could exist in a place like Martha's Vineyard. I wanted to connect our situation to other

Indigenous communities that I read about, but fights over tour buses and small clumps of clay seemed so trivial compared to the generational fights over land, language, and rights that I imagined or believed other Indigenous people were dealing with. But the more I learn about other Indigenous communities, from Alaska to Kenya and Indonesia to Brazil, the more I see how common these issues around tourism are.

In my late twenties, I started working as a journalist covering international Indigenous environmental and climate issues. I took the job because I enjoyed learning about other Indigenous communities and sharing their stories, which were so often under covered by most media outlets. I didn't really expect to be able to make that many connections between what I was reporting on and my own experiences. But the more I learned about what other Indigenous peoples around the world were facing, the more familiar those fights sounded.

Much of my reporting focused on conflicts about conservation projects on Indigenous land. In particular, many Indigenous communities are resisting a colonial form of conservation that takes land from Indigenous people to "protect" it. The climate, biodiversity, and environment are meant to benefit from this practice, but the reality is that it often means violently removing Indigenous people from land they have successfully stewarded for generations. This practice is known as "fortress conservation" and can be found around the world. It is especially popular in places like Kenya and Tanzania, where tourists come from around the world to go on safaris.

Just like I had always imagined that crucial land agreements between my tribe and the town, state, and federal governments had been made in long-ago colonial days, I assumed most Indigenous people in Africa were in the same situation, that hundreds of years ago white Europeans had arrived and carved up their land and lives. But when I asked a Maasai leader in Tanzania to help me understand their current legal struggle, he texted me pictures of documents from just a few decades earlier. I was surprised to discover land agreements from the 1970s and 1980s that were pivotal in their current, ongoing land disputes. The same time my tribe was fighting for federal recognition and the return of our land in Aquinnah, the Maasai in Tanzania were fighting the latest iteration of a colonial land grab.

Today, the Maasai are still fighting for their land, much of which is now part of the Ngorongoro Conservation Area, an internationally regarded wildlife park in an ancient volcano crater. While reporting the story, I read through a UNESCO report on Maasai presence in the park. UNESCO was concerned that the Maasai's growing tendency to construct modern homes, rather than traditional ones, would compromise the aesthetic integrity of the park. I couldn't help but think of the tourists who asked if we lived in American houses and if they could drive through tribal housing to take pictures. The report also urged the Tanzanian government to develop a plan to limit population growth in the park, including family planning. All these recommendations were made to limit the Maasai's presence in the park to an amount that would enhance, rather than encroach upon, tourists' safaris.

The government is also trying to compel the Maasai to move to "relocation sites" by restricting or cutting off their access to essential services like water, schools, and health care. This isn't exactly the same as what's happening on the island, but the lack of affordable housing, reliable year-round job opportunities, higher education, and other services feels like a gentler, more passive version of the same mission.

Later, while working on a story that tracked over a century of colonial conservation, I read a Belgian report from one of the first colonial wildlife parks established in Africa. After they violently removed thousands of Indigenous people from their land to create the park, they left "300 or so, whom we like to preserve" to help add to the exotic character of the park. With each passing year, as Aquinnah becomes more and more unaffordable, and the tourism industry becomes increasingly all-consuming, I wonder if this is what they want for us, too, just enough Wampanoags still around to give the town some of its flavor and to sell things at the cliffs, but not to interfere with the otherwise idyllic summer experience on the island.

Although the scale of what I was reporting on in Tanzania and other countries was far more violent and extreme than anything that I had seen in Aquinnah, I saw the same underlying belief behind it all: We can take care of the land better than you. The Land Bank, the island nonprofit that had bought the Kennedy-Onassis land, has a mission of environmental protection and preservation. The summer residents who fought against tour bus traffic claim to be concerned about the dune grasses and wildlife. For a long time, I thought this made the antitribe actions I saw in Aquinnah unique. But the more I learn about other Indigenous conflicts around the world, the more I can see that this is simply another version of the same problem, and one that most, if not all, Indigenous communities and nations are dealing with.

In Tanzania and other countries I reported on, nonprofits partnered with local governments to evict Indigenous people, often saying that traditional hunting or pastoralism harmed the environment, or that Indigenous people were guilty of poaching endangered species. In these articles, I found myself repeating the same lines about how Indigenous land management has been proven to be most effective at preserving the environment and its biodiversity, linking to scientific studies that supported what Indigenous people have been saying all along.

The people behind fortress conservation policies are not the sneering, evil oil tycoons or slave masters of the old colonial period. In fact, most of them are liberal environmentalists. They run or donate to major environmental NGOs and nonprofits. Some of them probably have summer homes on Martha's Vineyard. But if they really cared about protecting the land and environment, they would entrust it to the people who have been taking care of it for generations. This is the same ideology that drove Ted Kennedy's bill. What they really cared about, I learned, was control, the same thing I had seen the tribe struggle to regain for years. The white colonial land-gobbling machine evolved from brutal, genocidal men to refined nonprofit executives, but that shift has only benefited those trying to separate us from our land, not us or the land. We too need to find ways to evolve.

The more I looked, the more I saw connections between my own experiences and those of other Indigenous people around the world, and not just in generational fights over land. In that same job, I reviewed a novel about a young Indigenous Sámi woman in Sweden, written by a Sámi journalist. In one scene, tourists come to her rural town for a winter festival, where they stare at the traditional Sámi clothing and ask for photos. Elsa, the main character, tolerates these people for a bit before storming out into the cold. It was just a small moment, and far from the most serious example of anti-Sámi racism in the novel, but it struck a chord with me, perhaps because the context of the winter market, where Sámi gathered to sell traditional goods, reminded me of working at the store.

In the novel, and the real-life events it is based on, Sámi reindeer herding is a nuisance worthy of violent retribution—namely, butchered reindeer and threats against their owners—but Sámi markets are an attraction. Sometimes that's how it feels to be Wampanoag in Aquinnah. I know, of course, that the character in the book and I aren't the only Indigenous people in the world dealing with annoying tourists, but I had never seen my own experience reflected so perfectly in a book, let alone one about people halfway across the world.

Just like the cliffs steadily, inevitably eroding is something I have to watch every year, sometimes losing our land feels the same way. Victories like a family land purchase or the tribe buying an occasional plot of land feel like drops in a bucket of the enormous and rapid loss of Wampanoag land. Fighting for land on the same terms as those that have caused us to lose almost all of it in the last hundred and fifty years is never going to work, but that doesn't mean we can't find other ways. To do that, it means finding new ways to grow, within our government and outside of it, as a community. It also means thinking of my Wampanoag identity beyond the four walls of the family store. And as I get older, I've worked on this, finding opportunities to get involved in the tribe beyond working at the store or going to tribal summer camp—working with our tribal youth, participating in tribal politics, learning our language, and forming adult relationships with my cousins and tribal family. Part of that work has also been understanding the connections between the Wampanoag and other Indigenous people around the world.

6

THE PEOPLE AND THE PANDEMIC

The summer after I graduated from college in 2015, I went to my first tribal general membership meeting on the island. At general membership meetings, which are held quarterly, the council updates the membership on tribal business and initiatives. They are also a chance for individual tribal members to put forward resolutions for membership to vote on. I had grown up going to informal and cultural events like our annual cranberry harvest festival or drumming practice, but tribal meetings are official government meetings for adults only.

Although I was twenty-two at the time and had been able to attend general membership and tribal council meetings since I was eighteen, my time on the island had never seemed to align with the meeting schedule. The few times that it did, I always preferred to do something else, like go to the beach or work at the store. But that year, I had spent the entire summer on the island and wasn't carefully rationing my time like I had the past few years. That was also the same summer that I had learned about the settlement and the tribe's political history, and I was eager to see what I had learned in action.

Our tribal council meets twice a month—on the first Saturday and the third Wednesday of each month. Any adult tribal member can attend council meetings simply by showing up and signing in with their tribal ID, an official card issued by the tribe that looks a bit like a driver's license. At council meetings, tribal members can ask questions or raise issues with the council. Council members who live off-island often have to rush to catch the ferry home after meetings end. For decades, both council and general membership meetings were held exclusively in person. Council members and tribal members alike had to show up in person to listen and speak at meetings.

At the first meetings I attended, I began to learn how some of the departments—like Housing and Education—that I had been dimly aware of as a kid actually worked and what the tribal government did. And the more I learned, the more I wanted to know. But as my interest in tribal government grew, the distance I felt between myself and the tribe did too. Even though I felt like I was finally starting to understand some of the nuances and history of our tribal government, I was increasingly focusing on my life in New York.

It was around that time that I began wondering why there was no remote option for council and general membership meetings. Until then, I had never really thought about it, but I became frustrated that there was no way for me to stay up-to-date on tribal politics from New York. I would attend a meeting or two when I went home in the summer, but once I was back in New York, it was nearly impossible to keep up with what the council was doing for the rest of the year. If most of the tribe lives off-island, it seemed to make sense that we should be doing whatever we could to make our government accessible. My brother, who is three years older and had recently moved to New York, was feeling the same way.

A few years after my first meeting, my brother and I began speaking up at meetings in support of remote access for tribal council and general membership meetings. The issue had popped up a few times in the past, but it had never really gotten any momentum. Now, we argued, there was no reason not to take advantage of conference call and videoconferencing technology to expand access to meetings. Thinking back, I realize that those were the first times I ever spoke in tribal meetings. I wasn't weighing in on a particular side of an issue, but simply trying to find a way to participate.

I remember one general membership meeting that my mother, brother, and I all attended. We sat near the front and raised our hands multiple times to speak in favor of a remote meeting option. Cheryl Andrews-Maltais, the chairperson, expressed some interest in the idea but was concerned about privacy and security. What if we held a virtual meeting and a nontribal member somehow got access to it? Andrews-Maltais pointed out that there was no way for tribal administration to confirm who was listening. One possibility, she suggested, would be for the tribe to set up official meeting live streams at off-site locations in places where there were large populations of tribal members like New Bedford, Boston, and New York. Council would appoint someone to check tribal IDs of everyone who came to attend the meeting to ensure that only tribal members could listen.

It seemed like a lot of hassle just for people to watch a meeting live stream, and I wasn't really sure what the privacy concern was, but it seemed like somewhere to start. I wondered if I should volunteer my apartment as a potential location. I felt weird about opening up my tiny New York apartment to tribal members who I might not know, but I also liked the idea of being a key part of a new initiative.

After our exchange went back and forth a few times, someone got up to say that they could imagine tribal elders rolling in their graves hearing about remote meeting options. The whole point of the tribe was that people needed to maintain their connection to our community and our land by coming back to participate in meetings and other gatherings. My mom stood up right away to defend me and my brother, saying she thought it was ridiculous to talk about tribal elders rolling in their graves. Times change, she said, and we have to change with them.

While I was glad that my mom was so quick to defend us, I wondered who was right. Maybe I was lying to myself that I could really stay connected to the tribe while living off-island. For years, I told myself that as long as I tried, that was enough, but maybe it wasn't. Or maybe I needed to try harder. Those questions were at the heart of my insecurity since childhood that I wasn't Wampanoag enough, and that maybe I never could be.

The conversation eventually moved on to another topic, and we left the meeting without any concrete plan or resolution. No one on the council seemed to be willing to make it a priority. People who went to meetings and voted regularly had no real reason to push for a change. The people who would most benefit from remote access were hardly ever there to advocate for themselves. Now, I wonder how much better prepared we would have been for what was to come if we had found a solution back then.

A few years later, at the beginning of 2020, I had finished graduate school and was teaching writing classes at a state university in New Jersey. I took the train out to New Jersey in the morning and headed to the Upper West Side in the afternoon, where I tutored a middle-school student from China. In January, I stayed at her apartment while her mom spent a few weeks at home in China. Watching the news, as cases of this terrifying new disease seemed to spread unchecked through the country, she began to panic. Everything would be fine, I assured her. On the train home from her apartment one night, a woman started talking about how Chinese people were disgusting and that's why we all had the virus. I was the only Chinese person on the train. I wanted to buy some face masks, but I was afraid wearing them would make me even more of a target.

By March, the whole world was on edge. Everyone I knew was compulsively washing their hands and wondering if they should get face masks. Grocery store shelves quickly grew sparse. Things like toilet paper became hard to find in stores. Before spring break, my students asked me what I thought was going to happen. I told them I had no idea. A week later, the university announced that we'd be shifting to a fully online class model. Our spring break was extended by a week to give faculty time to adjust to and plan online classes. I started teaching and tutoring online, spending entire weeks inside except for my biweekly trips to the grocery store, where I waited in line outside for the store to open in the morning.

Like many people, my family started having weekly Zoom calls to stay in touch and pass the time. My dad enjoyed picking a new background photo that was relevant to the week's news (like a bottle of bleach after Trump suggested drinking it might help fight COVID-19). I also suddenly had more time on my hands, since I wasn't spending hours every day commuting.

That year, during the height of the COVID-19 pandemic, I took an online Wampanoag language class over Zoom. It was the first time our language had ever been taught in an online forum. Like most aspects of

Wampanoag culture, my only experience with it had come in person and on Martha's Vineyard.

In one of our first lessons, we learned how to introduce ourselves and say where we lived. Most of us were spread around the Northeast, with just one person actually in Aquinnah. But we all learned how to say the same phrase. *I am from Aquinnah.* Camille, our teacher, explained to us that the phrase refers to where our bones, our DNA, is from, even if we live somewhere else. It was a poignant reminder that Aquinnah was something we all shared, but it also showed me that even when we weren't there, weren't even in the same place, we could still connect and learn together. Those moments helped me unpack and complicate the way I thought about my own Wampanoag identity.

It was just a weekly, one-hour Zoom, but it was unlike anything I had ever experienced. I had always thought that Wampanoag culture and community were tied so firmly to the island because of some sort of inherent fact of Native identity, that Wampanoag gatherings and conversations simply had to take place on our ancestral land. Taking that Zoom class made me realize that the barriers were logistics and habit more than anything else. I don't know if the ability to stay in touch online would have stopped my grandfather from leaving Japan, but I do know that he would have had a much easier time staying in touch with the tribe today. Thanks to the language class, I suddenly had a way to connect with tribal language, culture, and community from my apartment in New York.

And it really was the community aspect that made the language class such a powerful experience for me. Through the class, I met tribal members I never knew, reconnected with cousins I used to be closer with, and got to know people I hardly knew a little better. My mom was taking the class, too, but her section met at a different time than mine, so we called each other to practice the phrases we were learning. Even as social media, FaceTime, and other digital tools became a bigger part of the way I communicated with friends and family, I had never really taken advantage of them to stay in touch with tribal cousins. I saw them when I went home and then we'd catch up the next summer when I saw them again. But you can only build so much of a relationship when you see people only once a year.

I began texting with Amira Madison, one of my cousins who was taking the class with me. We had grown up going to tribal summer camp together. In high school, she worked at my parents' store, but we hadn't stayed in touch regularly. Once we started, it was almost embarrassing how easy it was to catch up and before long, we started to talk about some of the issues we saw in the tribe. Why, we wondered, could we have online language classes, but not online tribal council meetings?

We had heard that the tribal council had been meeting privately since the beginning of the pandemic. Normally, tribal council meetings are held twice a month at the tribal administration building in Aquinnah and are open to any tribal members. But during the pandemic, council meetings had shifted to conference call, with no option for tribal members to join. As the rest of the world was quickly adapting to remote communications, the tribal government seemed to be contracting. A group of us started reaching out to council members, asking why they weren't making meetings public, and when they planned to do so.

After months of pushing and complaining, the tribal council announced that our next quarterly meeting, in August, would be done virtually. Until then, the tribe had never had virtual or remote participation in meetings. We had also never done mail-in or absentee voting, which we would do for that November's election. Membership meetings had always taken place behind closed doors at the tribal building, where you had to sign in with your tribal ID.

Although the new system was far from perfect—and we spent that first virtual meeting in August arguing about the details of how the meeting should work—it was by far the most accessible tribal meeting ever. I sat at my kitchen table in New York and heard cousins chime in from Aquinnah, Boston, Brooklyn, California, New Bedford, and more.

So in a strange way, the restrictions from the pandemic led to the best access for off-island tribal members in our history. In the couple years since then we've seen not just the predictable increase in participation from off-island members, but also from those on the island. Even people who live on the island used to have to drive up to forty-five minutes to get to a council meeting. Now, they can tune in to a meeting while they cook dinner. Once again, we still don't fully know how these changes are going to affect the tribe going forward. But they showed both me and the tribe that we don't have to live on our land to be part of major decisions. That's both exciting and a little scary—Wampanoags who live off-island have always been able to influence what happens on the island, but these new developments are increasing that ability.

Amira and I started organizing informal meetings with a few other cousins around our age. We spent evenings on Zoom, catching up and brainstorming ways that we could change the tribe or create structures outside of the tribal government to help benefit the community. We tossed around ideas like a book club, regular cultural meetings, and putting forward a slate of candidates for tribal council in the next election with a unified platform of transparency and community development.

Of course, political engagement is just one part of Native identity. As much as I enjoyed those conversations, what I liked the most about our little meetings was the chance to catch up and develop new relationships with cousins I had grown up with but lost touch with over the years. A year or two later, Amira and her partner visited New York and we all got dinner in Chinatown. I realized it was probably the first time I had hung out with a tribal cousin off-island, without my parents or some other organizing adult around. We'd gotten closer throughout the pandemic, texting and having Zoom calls about tribal news and updates. I didn't know it, but things like online language classes and virtual membership meetings were exactly what I had been craving. For years, I had been feeling helpless to stop a slow, but inevitable drift away from the island and my tribal community. Learning about my family's choices to leave and then return to the island and discovering new ways to stay connected made me realize that I can't just wait for someone else to help me stay involved with the tribe; I have to work to create those opportunities for myself and for others in my community.

I became curious about what other tribes had done in the past for remote political participation and what they were doing during the pandemic. I started looking online for news about tribes conducting online meetings or elections. I also started connecting with Native people across the country working on creative solutions.

One Pueblo educator told me she wasn't exactly sure what her tribe was going to do in terms of elections, but her tribal governor had been posting update videos on Facebook, something she had never seen before. Meanwhile she was sending out iPads to Native students who didn't have internet at home. That summer, I talked to a range of Indigenous people across the country, including an artist in Brooklyn taking an Interior Salish language (ńsəl̓xčiń) course online, a Navajo woman helping to install internet infrastructure on the Navajo Nation, and the communications manager for the Prairie Island Indian Nation in Minnesota, who told me that their first online meeting had seen higher participation than any in-person meeting.

I had always felt that, until I understood my own tribe, I wasn't ready to begin to understand other tribes. It was around this time that I realized that while the Native experience was enormously varied, learning about other tribes and other Native people could help me understand what I was trying to work through.

The research and reporting I did that summer also made me realize that I had no idea how other tribes had been doing this stuff before the pandemic, or how they functioned in general. Through my reporting, I learned that some larger tribes had already had virtual meetings, or meetings with videos posted online, even before the pandemic.

In August 2020, the tribe put out an appeal for tribal members to help coordinate a virtual general membership meeting. My brother and I wrote to say that we would be willing to help, but they never got back to us. Shortly thereafter, the dates and details for the online membership meeting were announced. We heard the tribe had hired an outside company to run the meeting, which seemed like an unnecessary expense.

The day of the meeting, there were issues almost immediately. We were told to log in to the meeting with a special link and passcode for a Webex meeting and to call in on our phones. I wasn't sure why. A group text I was in with about two dozen tribal cousins began blowing up right away, with people asking questions about how to log in and complaining that their codes weren't working. Someone renamed the group "The People," as if to say that we represented the true community of Aquinnah, not our tribal government.

We spent almost the entire meeting discussing the logistics of the virtual meeting. It turned out that we needed the Webex so that the chair and council could share documents, including the agenda and report for the meeting. But we also needed the phone option because that's how the voting system worked. In person, people were called on to speak by raising their hands. The chair or another council member would make an informal list of who wanted to speak. With our new, virtual system, we could ask to speak by "raising our hand" on the phone, which was accomplished by pressing #2. There was a third-party moderator who was hired to handle those details and manage the list of speakers. Over four hours later, the meeting finally ended, with most of us feeling frustrated and exhausted.

That November, with many of the remote meeting details still being hashed out, we had an election. That led to another controversy—should the tribe, for the first time in our history, allow mail-in voting? In The People chat group, most of my cousins thought we should return to in-person voting and meetings. At the heart of the issue was an emergency declaration that our tribal council had passed, which was not unlike similar ones passed by cities, states, and the federal government that gave them more latitude and flexibility to respond to the ongoing crisis. The People wanted that to end. They no longer wanted Andrews-Maltais and her allies on the council to have the unrestricted power to change meeting and voting rules that had remained stable for over thirty years. Another factor was that most of The People lived in Aquinnah, or at least on the island, while many of Andrews-Maltais's supporters lived off-island. They worried that so many remote meeting and voting options were only increasing the power of the other side.

As the flurry of messages went back and forth, I felt like I had to say something. By then, my classes had transitioned back to partially in person and partially online. I can remember sitting on a bench outside of the university building where I had just taught and composing a long text in defense of keeping mail-in voting and virtual meetings. I made my case not just for myself and people like me, but on behalf of more transparency. The remote options had only increased participation, and wasn't that what we all wanted? I got a few thumbs-ups on my message, but I wasn't sure if I had really convinced anyone. Eventually, the election proceeded with mail-in voting and another virtual meeting.

Throughout those months, from wondering what the council was doing, to advocating for remote meetings, to figuring out how they could work best, to defending them from people who had supported them from the beginning but wanted to take them away, it felt like the first time in my life that I realized the tribal government was malleable, something that could and should be shaped, changed, and improved. It was also the first time that I felt like I could be a part of that change.

A few weeks after that first tribal membership meeting I attended in 2015, I went to see Tobias, the current chairperson. Growing up, I had always seen Tobias as a Wampanoag mentor, someone who understood our culture and community. His time in office had been challenging, and many people were disappointed with his leadership, but I still felt like he was someone I could have an honest conversation with. We talked about the challenges of tribal community. He told me that he wasn't planning on running for reelection, but he hadn't told many people yet.

Toward the end of that conversation, I asked if I could get a copy of the tribal constitution. I had realized throughout all my discussions that summer that we were talking about things in our constitution, but I had never actually read it. I wasn't sure if I was allowed to, which, looking back, shows just how untransparent I thought the tribe was. Growing up, tribal things always felt so secretive to me, things we either couldn't talk about or couldn't share, or both. But when I asked Tobias, he laughed and said that, of course, any tribal member could.

Later, as I pored over the constitution, I was surprised by how brief it was. Most of it seemed to outline the structure of the tribal council, and various election procedures. But I was also surprised by some of the things that were in there that I had never thought about, like freedom of information and freedom of press. Those were pretty standard First Amendment things that I understood in the US context, but I wasn't sure what they meant in a tribal context. I wondered what would happen if I requested documents that the tribal council wanted to remain secret or tried to start an independent newspaper reporting on council meetings. I wondered why those things were in there if we never used them, let alone talked about them. I later learned that these items were the battlegrounds for other tribes. The constitution helped open my eyes to what tribal government was and what possibilities it held, but it also helped me realize how limited tribal government really was in terms of constitutionally delineated powers.

It wasn't until years later, when I finally decided to do more research into tribal governments and tribal constitutions during the pandemic, that I learned one reason the constitution was structured that way was that it was based on a template created by the federal government nearly a hundred years earlier. As I researched, I wished I had paid more attention in the few moments I was taught about Native history in college. It always just felt so distant from the small, isolated tribe I grew up with. But we were always impacted by those national policies and movements.

In 1934, the US passed the Indian Reorganization Act, which represented an end to the allotment era, where Indigenous land was divided into private parcels. The IRA, as it came to be known, also provided a chance for tribes to gain federal funding and support if they agreed to the terms of the IRA, which included adopting new constitutions. Nearly two hundred tribes across the country voted in favor of the IRA, and many adopted constitutions at least partially based on the government's model.

While the IRA constitutions gave tribes structure and funding, they were far from perfect. A rough approximation and simplification of the US constitution, the IRA constitutions were, at best, a bit of an awkward fit for many tribes. "While the U.S. Constitution is a unique reflection of the country's traditions, culture and values, IRA and IRA-influenced constitutions are foreign, boilerplate documents that often conflict with pre-colonial tribal traditions of recognizing, organizing and allocating governance," wrote Eric Lemont, a research fellow at the Harvard Project on American Indian Economic Development, in 2002.

According to our constitution, the Aquinnah Wampanoag government is meant to be "dedicated to the conservation and careful development of our land and resources, to promote the economic well-being of all Tribal Members, to provide educational opportunities for ourselves and our posterity, and to preserve our heritage and culture for future generations." But like all constitutions, those lofty words can be interpreted in an unlimited number of ways.

By the time I was deep into trying to figure out the answers to all the questions I had about tribal government and sovereignty, Amira was on the tribal council and had experience working both inside and outside the system to try to change things. I decided to ask her about where she thought we were as a tribe.

As usual, she had a thoughtful, impassioned answer. "I think what we have now as a sovereign nation is very dysfunctional and does not work," she said. "And I think that we are very much stuck in the definition that America has created for sovereignty. We should never have to use a template offered by the BIA [Bureau of Indian Affairs] to govern us and fit that template of what our constitution should look like. I also don't believe that we have to do everything in the way that the BIA wants us to and we should be pushing back on that."

I hadn't always tied the dysfunction I saw in our tribal government to the BIA and US government policies, but it was becoming clear to me that positive change in our tribe would require a deeper understanding of our relationship with the US government. Even as I learned about the structure of tribal government, it occurred to me that I didn't just want to learn about that, I wanted to learn more about the underlying beliefs and why things were the way they were. The more I thought about it, the more I realized that sovereignty was this big term that I heard a lot, but I wasn't sure exactly what it was. So to understand more about how tribal government works, what it could be, and what its limitations are, I knew I needed to learn more about sovereignty.

7

RECOGNITION

In the same way I grew up hearing "we are still here" and began proudly repeating it without understanding exactly what that meant or how it had happened, I was proud to know that we were a sovereign nation before I really knew what that was. As a kid, I heard grown-ups talking about tribal leaders and elections, so I always knew we had our own tribal government, but it was hard for me to understand what they did and how it worked. I knew that federal recognition and the sovereignty that came with it was something that my parents' and grandparents' generations had fought for, so it never really occurred to me what sovereignty had looked like before, that it might be something we were regaining rather than being given for the first time.

After I turned eighteen in my senior year of high school, I got my tribal ID card. Like other forms of identification, the tribal ID has a photo of me, my date of birth, address, hair color, and so on. It also has my tribal enrollment number, which was assigned to me when my mom enrolled me as a child. Tribal members use their IDs for access to tribal events like meetings and to receive tribal services like health care. In theory, tribal IDs can also legally be used as IDs outside of tribal settings like bars and domestic flights, but the reality is that most TSA screeners and bartenders have no idea what a tribal ID is.

Unlike most teenagers, I was more excited to get the tribal ID than

I was to get a driver's license. For years, I had looked at my mom's card, impatiently waiting for the day I turned eighteen so that I could get my own. I craved something official I could point to that made me Wampanoag. The ID was the most legitimate thing I could think of, a physical card that I could actually show people. Looking back, I can see how I was simply craving external validation. No one in the tribe ever doubted that I was Wampanoag, but I wanted to be able to prove to outsiders—and to myself—that I was who and what I said I was.

After I got the ID, I showed it off to my high school friends. Flipping the card over to show the US government seal on the back, I proudly informed them that being a member of my tribe means being a citizen of a sovereign nation within the United States. That citizenship, like American citizenship, comes with the right to vote in tribal elections as well as to benefit from shared privileges like health benefits. I think I hid behind that ID card, telling myself that no matter what I did or where I lived, no one could take that away from me. And while that's true, it also stopped me from seeing the limits of relying on that kind of tribal identity, and just how narrow it was compared to the many other ways of expressing Wampanoag identity.

And now that I think about it more, it's strange that I would point to the US federal government as the validation of my tribal nation's sovereignty and my own Wampanoag identity. But I really was proud of that. I wanted everyone to know that the tribe wasn't just a cultural or racial identity, that being Wampanoag was a specific political identity. And that was all because of my tribe's sovereign status.

I remember my second-grade class talking about how the 2000 presidential election mattered to us because presidents had the power to determine educational policies and priorities. Even if that felt a bit abstract, I could at least understand the connection. But I didn't live on tribal land or go to a tribal school, so it was harder to make the same leap for tribal government. And I knew that in Aquinnah we had a separate town government that seemed to be in charge of most normal government responsibilities, like police and taxes.

As I began attending council meetings, I gradually began to learn more about how our tribal government is structured. The council, which meets twice a month, is made up of four officers—chairperson, vice chair, secretary, and treasurer—and seven at-large council members. The tribe's chief and medicine man also sit on the council in honorary, nonvoting roles. Council members are elected to three-year terms, and while the chairperson is a full-time job with a salary and benefits, the other council positions receive only small stipends for attending meetings or executing other duties.

Of course, like the federal, state, or municipal governments, tribal government is felt most often not through those elected positions, but by the administrative departments, like Education and Natural Resources. Education, for example, runs the tribal summer camp that I went to and distributes college scholarships to students. But as I learned more of these details and understood what our tribal government does, I had even more questions about sovereignty.

It felt hard to think of the tribe as sovereign, not just because we were so small, but because our influence felt small. It felt like it would be easy to live without the tribe impacting my life, while it felt inevitable for the federal or state government to have an impact on my day-to-day life. One of my cousins was married to a Ute guy who was on their business council, an elected position that was a full-time job with a salary and everything. I didn't know if there were degrees of sovereignty, but that seemed more sovereign than what we had. It was easy to compare our situation to larger tribes out west because their government structures more closely resembled things that I recognized as government.

Since most of the tribe's money comes from the federal government, it felt like the tribe just existed to manage and disburse that money. And so I began to wonder what the purpose of tribal government really is and what it means to be a sovereign nation within the United States, that phrase I had been so proud of.

Until that moment, I had been relying on a conception of tribal government and nationhood that depended on the US government's limited acknowledgment of that. But even once I realized that, I wasn't sure what else there was. Heritage and culture are part of tribal government, but figuring out exactly what that looks like is an ongoing question. Thinking about tribal sovereignty in comparison to the US government is useful when we are talking about authority and power, but I'm realizing it may be even more important to think about the ways that tribal governments are, or should be, different.

In attempting to work through these ideas, I knew I needed to learn more about the US understanding of what a tribal nation was and how that developed. For a long time, that kind of history and thinking felt inscrutable to me because I had never learned anything like it in school. But Indigenous scholars, activists, lawyers, and leaders have been studying and debating sovereignty for generations. By relying on the work of scholars like Vine Deloria Jr., I've been able to piece together a historical framework that helps me to understand my own tribe.

When the newly formed United States first began negotiating with Indigenous nations in the eighteenth century, the US made treaties with them that delineated trade agreements, borders, and so on. The treaties were approved by Congress and, according to the National Archives, "The form of these agreements was nearly identical to the Treaty of Paris ending the Revolutionary War between the U.S. and Great Britain."

This system, in which tribes were understood by the US as independent, sovereign nations, lasted until the 19th century, when the government began to consider tribes as domestic, dependent nations.

After the Civil War, Congress stopped making treaties with tribes. By the middle of the twentieth century, over one hundred tribes had been "terminated"—something I had always thought of in the context of land and rights, but not in terms of sovereignty and government. Termination meant that the US did not see tribes as having their own governments anymore.

But in the later part of the twentieth century, the federal government returned to a policy that acknowledged tribes as sovereign nations, and in 1978, the federal government created the Office of Federal Acknowledgment (OFA) and an official process for federal recognition. In the 1990s,

Congress passed the Federally Recognized Indian Tribes List Act, which outlined the three options tribes have to become federally recognized: congressional act, administrative procedures under the Federal Acknowledgment Process, or Supreme Court decision. Tribes that were terminated by the federal government can only receive recognition by Congress.

In sum, being federally recognized means all those things that I was so proud of on my ID—a domestic dependent nation with a government-to-government relationship with the US. Federally recognized tribes are also eligible for funding and other programs from the federal government. And that's where we are today. Tribes with federal recognition—there are nearly six hundred—are considered sovereign nations within the US. In other words, tribes with federal recognition have, in the eyes of the US federal government, sovereignty.

A few years ago, I downloaded our federal recognition application materials from the BIA website. The two main documents I spent hours reading and rereading are the initial proposed finding against federal recognition in 1985 and the revised proposed finding for federal recognition in 1987.

The first thing I had to understand was the BIA's specific criteria for federal recognition. There are seven criteria that a petitioning tribe must fulfill, including proving that the tribe has been a distinct group from historical times to the present and that it has historically identified and been identified by others as an Indian tribe. There is also a criterion that the tribe must have maintained political authority over the community throughout history.

The criteria sound relatively straightforward. But proving them in an official way takes countless hours and dollars to conduct the necessary research, advocacy, and organizing. Most tribes have to either already have or hire an anthropologist and a genealogist. And this massive, resource-intensive undertaking does not even mention the ways that colonialism and generations of oppression, harm, and erasure have made it more difficult to organize, gather history, and prove consistent community and political organization. And finally, there is what the OFA will accept, which often depends on relationships and advocacy more than simple fact.

My tribe's first application was found to meet only five of the seven criteria, and, since "failure to meet any one of the seven criteria requires a determination that the group does not exist as an Indian tribe within the meaning of Federal law," the petition was rejected. Even though these events took place only a few years before I was born, they still seem so distant to me, so far removed from the tribe that I grew up with. Partly because I can't imagine a tribe without federal recognition, and partly because the tribe described in these pages by the federal staff is not the tribe that I know.

I've read through the justification for the rejection countless times. It is strange being blamed for things that were done to you because you were Indian and then being told that because those things happened, you're not Indian anymore. It's also uncomfortable to see your community reduced to and analyzed as a summation of criteria for a government designation. Some of the complexities that I see in our tribe were things that made us not a tribe in the eyes of the US government. Our dispersed population and struggles to stay connected as a community, for example, were used as one reason to deny us federal recognition.

The two criteria that the Acknowledgment staff determined the tribe did not meet were the requirements to show a distinct community and political control over that community. The report says that the tribe did not maintain enough social contact with one another and that it did not have the structures to support community-wide contact. After several paragraphs describing the ways that our community ties had deteriorated over the past decades, the section wraps up by saying "We conclude, therefore, that the Gay Head Wampanoags do not meet the definition of community."

It's still somewhat shocking to read the matter-of-fact language. It's also revealing about what they thought is required for a tribe. It's one thing to see the specified criteria, but another to see what it looks like when an Indigenous community falls short. Each time I read through it, I find myself wanting to argue with each sentence. How much social contact outside of immediate families would be enough? What does social contact even mean?

There are also very clear historical reasons why we didn't have as many tribal institutions and events, not to mention the decline in "land-holding."

I was gratified to see that the proposed finding does accept that the Aquinnah Wampanoag have long "maintained a dispersed settlement pattern" and the fact that most of our people lived away from Gay Head at the time was not, on its own, reason for disqualification. But the same things that I've struggled with as an adult living away from the island, like staying in touch and staying up to date with tribal events, were being used as evidence for us not being a tribe. When I read these lines and think about people who want to limit voting in tribal elections to people who live in Aquinnah, or restrict access to meetings, I feel so frustrated. We should not have to adhere to colonial definitions of what makes us a people.

Intermarriage is clearly an important part of the federal government's definition of tribal community. In the report, there is an entire section on marriage patterns, including a percentage breakdown of marriages to "full blood Indians," "mixed blood Indians," "Non Indians," and "Foreigners." This kind of creepy race science is why I'm eternally thankful that my tribe does not use blood quantum as a requirement for membership, as many tribes across the country do.

Blood quantum policies determine eligibility for tribal membership based on the amount of Native "blood" you have. In some tribes, for example, a person needs their ancestry to be one-eighth from that tribe to be eligible for membership. Unlike the "one-drop" rule, where even a tiny amount of African ancestry was enough to make someone Black, American eugenics suggested that Indians needed a certain amount of Indian blood to really be Indian. If they weren't, it was that much easier to take their land. In other words, America had a vested interest in keeping Black people Black, whereas it could benefit from reducing the number of Natives. Seeing Indian marriages and so-called Indian blood percentages analyzed in an official document that would determine our tribe's access to funds and resources shows how dangerous blood quantum policies can be.

The explanation for why we didn't meet the requirement for political authority is longer and more complex, going on for a few pages about the distinctions between town and tribal governments, as well as the role that non-Indians played in Gay Head leadership over the years. But the result is no less devastatingly direct: "The Gay Head Wampanoags have not maintained tribal political influence or other authority over their members as an autonomous entity throughout history."

The OFA's Proposed Finding was published in June 1986. The tribe was given until December to submit rebuttal documents. An appeal, essentially, and an opportunity to submit more information that might support the case. On December 1, the tribe submitted a 147-page document, what the OFA called "an extensive rebuttal." The rebuttal worked and the tribe was recommended for federal recognition.

Although the revised proposed finding was a win for the tribe that affirmed its sovereignty and right to federal recognition, I couldn't help but find the tone distinctly scolding, pointing out the number of pages devoted to accusing the Acknowledgment staff of racism and discrimination or suggesting that the tribe did not understand the technical reports created by the OFA. At one point, the text says that although it may not have been easy to tell from the tone, the initial proposed finding was a very close decision, which is why the additional evidence presented was enough to push the case over the top. "However," it goes on to say, "the favorable determination in light of the new evidence was similarly difficult to decide, and this decision remains commensurably close."

I had to read this line a few times. It seems like a warning, as if to say, *You Indians got it, but only because we let you. And we can take it away whenever we want.* A reminder, even at this moment of triumph for the tribe, who is really in charge. Because what does it matter? Federal recognition is not a sliding scale. You have it or you do not.

There is also an unspoken thread throughout the whole document that there is no question that we were once a distinct tribe, but over time, thanks to a range of factors, we became less and less cohesive, distinct, and Indian. That's the same stereotype of Indians trapped in some unchanging, colonial ideal that I've had to overcome myself.

The revised finding is a much shorter document, merely addressing the new information submitted and how it changes the decision. It begins with the community cohesion requirement. One of the main issues in the initial petition was that the tribe did not have enough communication among dispersed tribal members. The rebuttal provided information about the island paper's local news column, which was written by a tribal member, as an example of one of the ways that tribal members stayed in touch despite living across a large geographic area. The 1986 Revised Finding wrote favorably of the columns, which "demonstrated the existence of the social boundaries between the Indians and non-Indians in Gay Head."

I've heard white people in Aquinnah scoff at the idea that a newspaper column could be evidence of community ties. And I get it—a newspaper column in a nontribal newspaper is a poor substitute for what I think everyone agrees would be a more robust form of tribal community. But we had no other choice: We were doing whatever we could to stay connected. And I can remember reading that column, written by one of my older cousins. Every year, I looked forward to seeing the news that my brother and I had arrived on the island for the summer. Seeing our names in the newspaper was a fun thrill, but it also made me feel like there was a genuine community that I was a part of.

As for the political control issue, the revised proposed finding had a discussion of what it actually meant for the Gay Head Indians. At one point, the document says that the tribe took parts of the town governmental structure that was imposed on them and made it their own. Like Wampanoags made Gay Head an identity to be proud of, there are countless examples of Indigenous people taking a bad situation and making it work for them. I was glad the OFA could acknowledge that doing so with town government didn't make us less Indian.

Finally, at the end of the section, I came to the words I had been waiting for, which is strange to say since this all happened decades ago: "We conclude that the Gay Head Wampanoag Indians have maintained tribal political influence or other authority over their members, independent of the control of any other Indian governing body, throughout history until the present." I knew that, once again, I was in danger of letting the US government dictate what it means to be Indian when I felt relief, but it was also oddly vindicating to read.

As much as I found the federal recognition documents interesting, I also felt myself instinctively dismissing them as I read. We have federal recognition now, so maybe there's no point in studying these documents. I think that's one of the features of the federal recognition system: Once tribes have it, they have no reason to look closely at the system. Tribes like mine are so relieved once they get it that they have no incentive or energy to think about the flaws in the system they just went through.

But maybe we should. The conversation about the importance and meaning of federal recognition is an ongoing issue that is much bigger than any one tribe. For example, at the National Congress of American Indians' annual meeting in 2023, the membership voted on controversial amendments that would limit voting membership to federally recognized tribes. The NCAI is a national nonprofit organization that represents hundreds of tribes across the country and advocates for Native and tribal rights. The proposed amendments would automatically exclude twenty-four member tribes that lacked federal recognition at the time and limit voting membership to only those with that status. Supporters of the amendments argued that it was required to combat fake tribes and protect tribal sovereignty. Opponents said that it would divide tribes and let the federal government decide who is Indian and who is not.

The more you look at federal recognition and how it works, the clearer it is to me that the system benefits the federal government, but not us. Federal recognition makes us part of a complex legal system that was never built to protect tribes. Of course, that doesn't mean that we can't find ways to make it work for us. I knew tribes were out there doing that, but reading all that history still didn't tell me what sovereignty actually looked like, or how tribes could exercise it. Reading legal theories and historical documents about sovereignty helped me understand how we got to where we are today, but not so much what was happening now and what different expressions of sovereignty look like.

Like Amira said, sovereignty should be more than just whatever the federal government declares. I realized that I had always thought of sovereignty in a reactive way, that it was a defense we could use when some outside force, whether that was the federal government or a private land owner, encroached on our land or violated our rights. And that's true—throughout our history, tribes have had to use their sovereignty as a shield, to defend our land, rights, and lives.

But in learning from other tribes, I discovered that sovereignty could be used actively, to accomplish big-picture goals rather than simply respond. That, I realized, was what I wanted to learn more about. As I started leaning more and more into reporting on Indigenous communities across the country, I also began to hear all the things that other tribes and Indigenous nations around the world were doing. All the things that my tribe had but felt like we never really used—freedom of information, freedom of press—other tribes were using and figuring out more creative ways to use them. And they were doing even more, negotiating major agreements and making waves on the national and international level.

8

WE CANNOT WAIT FOR OTHERS

In 2022 I got my first full-time job as a journalist, working for an environmental and climate news outlet on their new Indigenous Affairs desk, which consisted of me and an editor. I covered everything from pipeline lawsuits and tribal water rights to international human rights violations and Land Back efforts. As a small but ambitious desk, we tracked Indigenous stories from around the world, trying to focus on the kinds of stories that other outlets weren't covering.

One of the first stories that I worked on was about a legal theory called rights of nature, which some tribes and environmental groups were using to try to protect the environment. Rights of nature means legally codifying the rights of something like a river or a specific species to protect it. Countries like Ecuador had gone even further, recognizing the rights of Mother Nature, or Pachamama, in its constitution.

I was reporting on the Sauk-Suiattle Tribe in Washington State that had passed a law codifying the rights of salmon and sued the City of Seattle, saying that its hydroelectric dams were violating those rights. For decades, salmon populations had been declining in the Skagit River and tribes had been saying that the dams were to blame.

In its lawsuit, the tribe sought declaratory relief for the salmon's right to flourish, the tribe's right to protect the salmon, and that the city was purposefully violating both of those rights. To understand more about the legal concept behind rights of nature, Jack Fiander, the Sauk-Suiattle lawyer behind the case, recommended I call Frank Bibeau, who was using a rights of manoomin, or wild rice, law passed by the White Earth Ojibwe to fight the Line 5 pipeline in Minnesota. Fiander told me that he had based his lawsuit on Bibeau's rights of manoomin.

Bibeau explained that he believed rights of nature could be the legal key to protecting the environment, a secret weapon no one had thought of. He also said that he thought the rights of salmon had a better chance at changing the national narrative, since dying fish is a visceral thing that people can understand. Wild rice, on the other hand, might be a little more abstract to non-Native people.

Both lawsuits were based in part on treaty rights derived from decades-old agreements the tribes had signed with the US government, but Fiander and Bibeau took the issue way beyond simple treaty rights. They used tribal belief systems, tribal courts, and innovative legal theory to challenge the US colonial system. And the stakes were incredibly high.

The rights of salmon lawsuit came during a crucial period for the dams in Washington State—their relicensing process, which could renew the dams' license for another fifty years. When I talked to Fiander, he described it as an existential crisis. If they didn't do something, he said, the salmon could be gone in ten years. The city, for its part, disputed that the dams were harming the salmon and insisted that they were doing everything they could to protect the river, the fish, and the environment at large. From the city's perspective, holding up the dams meant depriving Seattle of green energy.

Fiander's legal argument relied on a combination of treaty rights and the tribe's relationship with and responsibility to salmon, which they call Tsuladx^{w}. I knew that tribes could sue for their rights, but I had never thought about how limited those rights were under the US system. Both Fiander and Bibeau argued that the rights of nature was a way to break out of those confines.

To help me understand some of the legal theories behind the movement and what it could mean for tribes, I called Matthew Fletcher, a law professor at the University of Michigan and member of the Grand Traverse Band of Ottawa and Chippewa Indians. Fletcher is one of the most prominent Indigenous legal scholars in the country and also runs *Turtle Talk*, a popular blog about Indian law and policy. He's the kind of guy reporters call when they want an Indigenous expert to weigh in on some complex legal situation.

Treaty law, he told me, is the law of the colonizer and it's not working for tribes. Rights of nature was an alternative that aligned with tribal beliefs and might have a better chance of protecting their rights and the environment. I still don't know how effective this alternative will ultimately be, but what I do know now is that it helps to show the kind of creativity that we need to use to find ways to work outside of the system and to change the system itself.

After the mini-lesson he had given me on treaty rights and sovereignty, I read some of Fletcher's papers on the complexities and nuances of sovereignty. Months later, when I was trying to think through some of the complicated questions I had about sovereignty, he was my first call.

"I think what you have to do is start with the notion that sovereignty is a European American legal facade that is totally fake," Fletcher explained. "The whole idea of sovereignty is that you can't have civilization without a sovereign government that controls enough of our lives, otherwise, we'll kill each other."

When I heard that, I sat up in my chair, my brain starting to whir. "And so if you start with that premise that sovereignty is a total lie, and is used to control people with less power, then that's a problem for tribal communities," he went on. Fletcher tied the idea of sovereignty to European ideas of kings and sovereign rulers. It seemed obvious when he said it, but I never really even thought about the origins of the concept.

How could sovereignty be fake? I wondered. It was the thing I felt I had been taught was the cornerstone of our rights and power. But sovereignty, Fletcher said, has to be earned. "You can put anything you want down on a piece of paper, but it doesn't mean jack shit," he said. "But if you go out and you govern better than those around you, and you constantly improve and develop the capacity of government and make human lives better, then you earn sovereignty."

Immediately I started to wonder whether my tribe had earned sovereignty the way he described it. When I showed my friends my tribal ID,

I was bragging about sovereignty as an idea, not something active, something we had accomplished. I was not only defining the tribe in relation to the United States, but I was thinking about what the tribe was in such a limited way. To get a different perspective on Wampanoag sovereignty, I called my cousin NaDaizja Aiguier-Bolling. NaDaizja grew up off-island but recently returned home, where she's gotten heavily involved in both politics and cultural events. We have both been frustrated with our tribal government, going back to those first virtual meetings during the pandemic. "We're not sovereign," she said. "We couldn't house all of our people if we wanted to right now. We couldn't feed all our people if we wanted to right now. And until we have the ability to do that, we're not sovereign, you know, we can't take care of ourselves."

NaDaizja and I talked about how we both grew up feeling like federal recognition and sovereignty were things to be proud of without knowing what they really were. It was only as adults that we both realized that those labels were dynamic, ever-evolving goals and maybe the tribe wasn't quite living up to them. As kids, we had to overcome the American-centric narrative of colonialism to say that we were still here. After that, questioning the tribe almost felt like a betrayal. It was later that I'd begin to feel that it was the reverse, that to let the tribe make mistakes unquestioned would be even worse. It's our responsibility to do what we can to make our community stronger.

NaDaizja talked about the need for our community to become more independent not just from the federal government, but also from the tribal council. "I think we have to focus on other ways to be a tribe and not depend on the tribal government for that," she said. Because of the pride I felt about federal recognition, it was hard for me to see past a form of sovereignty that was tied to the US government. But the more I thought about it, the more I realized that the kind of sovereignty that I was looking for was based on something else entirely.

As my reporting expanded to Indigenous nations outside the US, I wanted to see what sovereignty looked like in practice when removed from the unique legal system of federal recognition that the US had placed upon us. I knew the concept was just a concept, but it was still something that we talked about as if it was real. I wanted to know what that meant to different Indigenous nations.

In 2015, representatives from dozens of communities in the Peruvian Amazon established the Autonomous Territorial Government of the Wampis Nation, the first autonomous Indigenous territory in the country. Until that moment, Indigenous land in Peru was held only by individual communities or villages, rather than a regional government responsible for a contiguous territory. Unlike the US, Peru does not have a process for federal recognition of tribes. In fact, most countries around the world do not.

Instead of waiting for Peru to recognize their rights to sovereignty and self-determination, the Wampis simply did it themselves. Altogether, the Wampis Nation, as it has come to be called, consists of about fifteen thousand people spread across 1.3 million hectares, an area around the size of the entire state of Connecticut. The territory is located in northern Peru, by the border with Ecuador, and includes some of the world's most biodiverse primary forests. This is land that the Wampis have lived on and managed since time immemorial.

But the Peruvian government still does not recognize the Wampis Nation as a singular, united entity. According to Wampis leaders, this is at least in part because a legally recognized Wampis Nation is a threat to Peruvian state interests. The nation was formed primarily as a response to resource extraction and the ongoing colonization of their territory: oil pipelines and wells, in particular. Over the years, there have been hundreds of oil spills in the region, many of them major disasters that devastated the environment. And across the Amazon, extractive industries continue to lead to persecution, violence, and murders of Indigenous land defenders.

In 2021, Petroperu, Peru's national oil company, announced plans to explore oil extraction on a block of land that overlaps with the ancestral territories of both the Wampis and the Achuar, another large Indigenous federation in the Peruvian Amazon. The company has a long history of corruption, poor investment, and environmental hazards, so this was something that the Wampis and other Indigenous communities in the region would not accept.

Decades of spills and shoddy infrastructure had also limited Petroperu's profits, which meant the company relied heavily on foreign investment. Indigenous protest and resistance could derail the company even more. Major financial institutions in the US and abroad, like Vanguard and BlackRock, have invested millions of dollars in Petroperu. This money, the Wampis and Achuar argued, is powering a company that continues to violate their rights, threaten their lives, and hurt the environment. So after unsuccessful negotiations with the Peruvian government and Petroperu executives, the Wampis and the Achuar had a new strategy: Go after Petroperu's money in the US. By bringing their case to financial institutions that Petroperu was both a bad moral and financial investment, the Wampis and the Achuar hoped to cut off the company's lifeblood.

In November 2022, Nayap Santiago Velásquez, a delegate from the Wampis Nation responsible for justice and human rights, traveled with Nelton Yankur, the president of the Indigenous Achuar Federation, to the United States to pressure banks and investment companies to divest from Petroperu. They were accompanied by Carlos Chapilliquen, who represented an association of local fishermen from the coast who were also fighting back against Petroperu, and staff members from Amazon Watch, a nonprofit that advocates for Indigenous groups and the environment in the Amazon.

The night before one of their meetings with bank representatives, I met up with the group at their hotel in downtown Manhattan. When I arrived, they were eating a dinner of Peruvian chicken and rice in the hotel lobby. Gisela, one of the Amazon Watch staffers, told me that they had wanted to eat Peruvian food.

After they finished their dinner, our little group headed upstairs to the hotel restaurant, where we all sat around a large square table. Gisela and one of her colleagues from Amazon Watch translated between English and

Spanish. A few times, Nayap or Nelton taught us all a word in their Indigenous language.

I knew that the story of Indigenous representatives from Peru coming to the US to ask banks to cut their financial ties with an oil corporation was newsy. There was a version of a story that I could write about their call to action and what they were facing back in Peru, but what I really wanted to ask about was what it meant for them to be there as representatives of their respective nations. It seemed to me to be a pretty amazing moment—Indigenous leaders, representing tens of thousands of people from the Amazon rainforest, coming to negotiate with representatives from major international financial institutions in New York.

I asked them if they felt like this was a historic moment for them and their respective nations. Both Nelton and Nayap said yes and that they were proud to be representing their people, but that their main focus was simply stopping Petroperu. They were much more concerned about the health of their land and people. Once that was protected, they could get back to the business of living as Wampis and Achuar Nations. "The obstacle is extractive industries, which is the only thing that really makes it so that we couldn't fulfill this dream, this vision that we have of really living under our own customs and our own ways," Nayap told me. "Extractivism is the main obstacle, the influence that doesn't allow us to live how we want to live."

The formation of their autonomous governments, they both said, had changed very little about their internal processes. They saw it as a necessary step to defend their territory. "When we self-declared our autonomous government, we only formalized and wrote down for outsiders to understand, but it was just a formalization of an ancient process," Nayap said. That phrasing stuck with me, that what they had done was not for them, but for outsiders.

He went on to explain: "The Wampis Nation has always existed, and it has its own institutions inside. It has existed for more than seven thousand years, and we have been living there for seven thousand years. It doesn't have that occidental perspective of what the state is, or government is, it's our own vision of our institutions. And inside, we have education, health, and justice. All our institutions and arrangements are our own, and all of this forms our government. Ninety-eight percent of Wampis territory is untouched territory. And our ancestors have been taking care of this untouched territory for seven thousand years. So that's what we're preserving and continuing to preserve."

In other words, officially forming the Wampis Nation changed very little, if anything, in the day-to-day lives of its citizens. But what it gave them was a united front, an organized mechanism to advocate for their rights to the Peruvian government and the rest of the world. Historically their lack of that legal unity had allowed outside forces to exploit them and their land. In the past, corporations or government officials would approach one community and get their permission to do something, sometimes by tricking them.

"Right now under the Peruvian laws, the only thing that they recognize is the existence of particular Indigenous villages or communities. But we don't want that. We don't want to be recognized as this community and this community. We want to be recognized as a whole integral territory, as a nation," Nayap went on. "As the law concerns, we don't exist as a nation. So we are trying to change that."

To underline this point, Nelton explained that the Achuar Federation was hoping to change their name to just the Achuar Nation to make clear that it is a unified nation of Achuar people, rather than a group of individual communities coming together.

But while they advocate for the right to be recognized by the Peruvian government, the Wampis Nation and the Achuar Nation are already acting like autonomous nations, both domestically and internationally. Both Nelton and Nayap outlined the way their respective governments worked, the different structures, positions, and mechanisms that they had in place. They spoke with clear pride, wanting to demonstrate that they had an organized structure that could rival any Western government.

Their explanations of how their governments worked echoed something that Matthew Fletcher told me. He thought most of the real tribal leaders were people near the top of departments who were doing most of the work and making important day-to-day decisions, rather than those in official leadership positions. He distinguished between what he called statesmen, who signed treaties and gave speeches, and bureaucrats, who did things like run the health clinic. In other words, real governance was about the things that made a difference in the day-to-day lives of the people. But there are times when the statesmen are needed, when the existential issues like oil extraction or salmon extinction threaten the daily existence of the people. The Wampis and Achuar needed, and had, both.

So even beyond the day-to-day governance over its territory and people, it seemed to me that the Wampis and Achuar Nations were acting like independent, sovereign nations by traveling to New York to negotiate with and lobby these major financial institutions. That assertion of sovereignty on an international level made me think of something people from an Indigenous nation on the opposite side of the world had told me. While I was reporting at the United Nations Permanent Forum on Indigenous Issues at UN headquarters in New York, I met a group of Indigenous Ryukyuans from Okinawa who were there to deliver a statement condemning US military bases on their island. Okinawa is a prefecture of Japan, but it was once part of an independent nation known as the Ryukyu Kingdom.

Like millions of Indigenous people around the world, Ryukyuans faced persecution, abuse, and cultural eradication when colonizers—in this case from Japan—took control of their land. Today, US military bases, which cover about 25 percent of the island, are the focus of Ryukyuan activism. While Japan recognizes the Indigenous Ainu in the northern part of the country, it does not recognize the Ryukyuans as an Indigenous people. They say Japan refuses to recognize them because that official status might threaten Japan's relationship with the US military. According to the Ryukyuan delegation at the UN, the bases are violating their sovereignty, destroying sacred sites, and harming the environment. Just like the Wampis uniting represented a threat to Peruvian resource extraction and development, national interests take precedence over Indigenous rights.

One of the delegation members was Koutaro Yuuji, a former activist turned PhD student. When I talked to Koutaro about sovereignty and independence, he used the fact that the Ryukyu Kingdom made treaties with other countries like the US and France in the nineteenth century as proof that Ryukyu was in fact its own independent kingdom. That's the same time period in which the US was also making treaties with Indigenous nations in North America.

The Wampis and Achuar negotiating and lobbying financial institutions might not be quite the same as an international treaty between two kingdoms, but the scale felt similar to me. In 2023, BlackRock had over $9 trillion in assets, a sum that was many times greater than Peru's GDP. In fact, only China and the US have GDPs larger than $9 trillion. The Wampis Nation seemed to be exerting complete control over its land and people on local, national, and international levels. The only thing standing in the way was the Peruvian government.

Both Nelton and Nayap also said the idea of an Indigenous nation inside of Peru was another barrier because people didn't understand what that meant. "We understand that it's kind of hard to understand this concept of nation inside another nation," Nayap explained. "But the government has to understand we have been living here and we have been a nation since seven thousand years ago. But the Peruvian government is only two hundred years old. It's like a baby setting the rules for an adult man on how to live, so that's why we don't want it."

I told them that in the US we had something like what they were describing with our system of domestic dependent nations and federal recognition. They seemed happy that I understood what they were talking about, but nodded sadly when I said our system wasn't perfect, either, and we were still often disenfranchised, ignored, and abused. They knew that getting recognized by the Peruvian government wouldn't solve all their problems, but it would give them another tool to use to fight for their rights.

Later, when I was researching the Wampis, I came across a document written by Shapiom Noningo, who was at the time the technical secretary for the Wampis Nation. Noningo described how the Wampis Nation went about declaring themselves, including the creation of supporting documents.

There were four: an anthropological report detailing Wampis history on the land, a cartographic report that shows the territory's boundaries, a legal report on their right to the territory, and a statute with the collective rules for the Wampis. Since Noningo wrote that document other Indigenous nations have adopted this same process to claim and recover their territory.

Those four documents sounded very similar to the criteria required for federal recognition that tribes in the US have to go through, but the difference is that in this case, the criteria were not handed down from the federal government. The Wampis looked at their situation and collected information that they believed proved their right to the land and autonomy. It seemed to me like they had literally created a template for their own form of Indigenous-led federal recognition. This was another way that the Wampis were taking the colonial idea of sovereignty and turning it into a tool that worked for them.

The idea of sovereignty as a tool was also relevant to the Ryukyuans' situation. After talking to Koutaro, I spent a few days reading about Ryukyuan history and activism. I came across an article by Nozomi Nakaganeku Saito, an Okinawan American professor at Amherst College, about what she called "ossuopower"—the power over bones and ancestral remains—and how central it is to settler colonialism and militarism in Okinawa, where US bases are built on burial grounds, ancestor remains, and fragile ecosystems. While the idea of settlers and imperial powers trying to control ancestral remains or sacred sites and the environment being sacrificed for military expansion were not new to me, I found the ideas that Nakaganeku Saito was exploring to be incredibly haunting. Imperial powers, she seemed to be saying, wanted to have sovereignty over us forever, even in death. After reading the article online, I reached out to Nakaganeku Saito.

It's a complicated thing, she told me. In some ways, sovereignty is a completely colonial creation, and the need that Indigenous communities have for it is because of the colonial system that has been imposed on us. But political sovereignty, she said, was only one way of thinking about Indigenous rights and self-determination. The distinction between that type of sovereignty and more community-based ones reminded me of what Na-Daizja had said about the need for avenues outside of our tribal government to uplift the community.

Cultural and community-based forms of connection in Indigenous communities might be more important in the long term, but in the face of immediate and existential problems like oil extraction in the Amazon and unrelenting militarism in the Pacific, there was a clear role for political sovereignty to play. "In the short term, unless Okinawans achieve sovereignty, they're not going to get the bases off," Nakaganeku Saito argued. "So as the short-term goal it feels like it does have to continue to be a political project."

Political sovereignty, in other words, was something that could be used to defeat a specific problem. "We were a sovereign nation, but now we are just one of forty-seven small prefectures, a minority, powerless," Koutaro explained. "So the only way to counter that is to become a sovereign nation again, you know, get out of the Japanese nation."

The Wampis Nation, which has governed its people and land for thousands of years, only felt the need to organize in a way that might be recognized by the international community in response to an existential external threat. If Petroperu and other oil companies had never targeted their land, there might have been no need for the legal entity known as the Wampis Nation. The Wampis Nation could have simply continued governing as it has for over seven thousand years.

Thinking about sovereignty that way was really freeing for me. It had a specific utility within the system, but it wasn't the be-all and end-all that I had grown up thinking it was. And it wasn't some label that you got once and that was it; it was something you had to fight for, work on, and improve every day. Part of that work was also acknowledging the limits of the system and the danger of relying on a kind of Indigenous nationalism as the solution to everything.

And while that happens, we also have to focus on the rest of the work. That's what Koutaro is trying to do, working to revive Uchinaaguchi, the

Indigenous language of Okinawa. His dream is to have a generation of Okinawan kids growing up in Uchinaaguchi immersion schools. In addition to teaching and researching, he spends his days listening to Okinawan folk music and trying to rebuild his relationship with nature. The more he improves his language skills, the more meaningful the music and the natural world become for him. Political sovereignty is only one small part of that collective, generational process.

Tribal sovereignty is something that should be recognized and respected, but in colonial systems like Peru, the US, or Japan, true recognition may never come. But whether it is recognized or not should not determine every part of how Indigenous nations and people act. Or, as Koutaro put it, "We cannot expect Japanese people to change or respect us. We cannot wait for others." I know that many tribes have that attitude and are not waiting for the US to change. I wanted to see and learn from tribes taking matters into their own hands.

9

TIME IS ON OUR SIDE

The more I studied sovereignty, the more I realized that I could spend the rest of my life reading theory and asking people questions on the phone, but I might not get any closer to really understanding what I was trying to grasp. Every tribe's version of sovereignty was different. Theory didn't matter nearly as much as what tribes did with their sovereignty.

In September 2023, I went on a weeklong reporting trip to the Klamath Basin in Southern Oregon and Northern California. The trip was organized by the Institute of Journalism and Natural Resources, which is a nonprofit that organizes field trips for journalists to learn about environmental issues in remote places. There were about a dozen other reporters and photojournalists on the trip, including both Indigenous and non-Indigenous reporters. Some had covered the Klamath Basin extensively, while others, like me, had not.

The news hook of the trip was that four dams on the Klamath River, which snakes its way from the high desert in Southern Oregon, through the Cascade and Klamath Mountains, to the redwood trees on the Northern California coast, were scheduled to be removed after decades of advocacy from tribes in the area. It would be the largest dam removal in US history and open up around four hundred miles of fish habitat. Over seven days, we'd travel along the river, meeting with tribes, farmers, government officials, scientists, and water managers to hear about how they were going to be impacted by the dam removals. The idea of dams coming down because of tribal advocacy was almost impossible for me to fathom—that tribes could have such a huge impact on massive pieces of infrastructure. The tribes in the Klamath Basin might not have as much power as they deserved, but they definitely did have real power and real capacity.

Around the world, dams are often a symbol of colonization, built on stolen Indigenous land, flooding sacred sites and homelands, destroying water quality and habitats, and powering harmful industries. In some ways dams also reflect the difference in belief systems: Colonial powers want to change and shape the land to suit their needs and desires, while Indigenous people tend to value the land for what it is, and adapt their lives to its natural cycles, rather than the other way around. Because of this, from the Amazon to the Philippines, dams are frequently the focus of Indigenous resistance and activism.

Concepts like Land Back and decolonization are sometimes hard to understand in the abstract. But after years of advocacy in the Klamath Basin, they were finally going to become a reality. This was going to reshape a region where water had been an issue for years, and tribes were going to be a huge part of that conversation. I also wondered if it could be something like a fresh start—a new landscape where tribes could assert themselves.

Over the course of the week, we traveled by bus from the Klamath's headwaters to the mouth of the river, where it met the Pacific Ocean on Yurok territory. Along the way, we talked to tribes, farmers, ranchers, and other people who relied in some way on the river. Each new group or person that we talked to added another layer of complexity to the story we were all trying to wrap our heads around. So although the focus of the week was the dams, we quickly realized that the issues on the river and in the basin were so much deeper.

Our first stop was Iron Gate dam, an earthen dam built on the Klamath River in the 1960s near Hornbrook, California, which was scheduled for removal in a few months. Our guide for the morning was Mark Bransom, the CEO of the Klamath River Renewal Corporation (KRRC), a non-profit corporation formed specifically to manage the dam removals on the Klamath.

Standing on a hill above the dam, Bransom explained the plan for removing each of the dams and the status of the project. The KRRC, he explained, was a limited-term, fixed-funding entity created for the specific purpose of the dam removals. They owned the land and the dams, which had been transferred to them by the states and federal government. When the project was done, the dams were removed, and the land was restored, it would be returned to the state, federal government, and potentially tribes in the area.

After Iron Gate, Bransom took us to a few more sites, including another dam that was scheduled for removal, and Copco Lake, one of the large reservoirs that had been formed by the dams. He showed us spots where the water had turned a bright green color from the algae bloom that was caused, at least in part, by the dam's impact on the river. Our group got off the bus to take pictures of the fluorescent green water, but there was no way to capture the unmistakably toxic smell that permeated the area.

Small houses were scattered across the little hills along the lake edge. Bransom explained that many were vacation homes, and the owners were some of the most active opposition to the project because they would be losing their lakefront views when Copco Lake was drained. Some of these people, plus local Hmong communities, were still fishing in the lake, despite posted warnings about the water quality, Bransom told us.

Although the air in the morning was cool, as the sun moved higher and higher, the temperature continued to rise. By the time we stopped for lunch, the sun was scorching, and I savored every brief moment I could pause in the shade. Around midday we made our way to "Copco village," a kind of basecamp for the men working on the project. We arrived at a small seating area of picnic tables where two men were grilling burgers outside of a temporary building. Inside, there was, thankfully, air-conditioning and a bathroom. I splashed water on my face before heading back outside to eat.

While we ate sandwiches from a cooler, a few SUVs showed up with three members of the Shasta Indian Nation and an academic from the University of Pennsylvania Museum who had worked with the Shasta for many years. We would spend the rest of the afternoon with the Shasta, learning about their history and hopes for the dam removal project.

We were told that in 1851, one year after California became a state, gold was discovered in nearby Yreka, California. Later that week, we spent a night there. I woke up early in the morning to go for a run, jogging past Gold Rush–themed shops and restaurants on the town's small main street. But to Indigenous people in the area, the Gold Rush period is not remembered fondly. The Yreka discovery sparked a wave of violence and displacement for the Shasta, who had been living there since time immemorial. In Yreka, I thought about the intersecting history of the Gold Rush that helped bring my family over from China even as it simultaneously drove the Shasta, and other Indigenous people, from their lands. Many Shasta were killed or fled during the Gold Rush. Others, under the Shasta leader Bogus Tom, eventually settled along the Klamath River, where they gathered land and built a community.

But the six dams of the Klamath Hydroelectric Project soon threatened their new home. When constructed, the dams created Copco Lake, which flooded Shasta villages and sacred sites. Most of the good farmland, not to mention the fish, was gone. So once again, the Shasta had to leave their homes. When I met the Shasta, they had no reservation and were not recognized by the federal government. Many of the Shasta are spread across the state, and the tribal government is run largely on a volunteer basis.

Standing in a circle by the picnic tables at the basecamp, we smudged ourselves with sage that they had brought and then introduced ourselves. The Shasta delegation was made up of a council member, a natural resources officer, and a language expert. Unlike the morning session, where I had simply introduced myself as a freelance writer from New York, I made sure to say to the Shasta that I was an Aquinnah Wampanoag writer. I wasn't sure if they would know my tribe, but I wanted them to know I was Native too. Any time I needed to introduce myself to a group of Native people, I felt like I was back in tribal summer camp, practicing introducing myself in our language. That same awkwardness and insecurity about being Wampanoag enough came rushing back as it always does when I introduce myself to a large group of Native people.

After introductions, we piled into the SUVs and drove to a few sites with the Shasta. I followed the language expert, James Sarmento, to his car, sitting in the passenger seat next to him, as he blasted the AC to cool down the stifling car. He had come up from Sacramento to meet us. I wanted to ask him about his efforts and how long he had been working with the language. When I told him that my tribe has been going through something similar, he immediately said he was familiar with the Wampanoag language revival effort.

He wasn't the first person to tell me that he knew about our tribe through the language, but I always forgot that our project was internationally known. In some ways, it feels strange to be seen as a tribe that was further along on our journey than another. I was so used to thinking about how much we had lost and what we were trying to recover. It was a good reminder that colonialism is not linear.

As tribes in California know all too well, being on the West Coast was not some sort of shelter from the violence and destruction of colonialism. Even in the brutal and devastating history of the United States' colonization, California stands out. In 1851, the same year that settlers found gold in Yreka, Peter Burnett, the state's first governor, declared that "a war of extermination will continue to be waged between the two races until the Indian race becomes extinct." And he meant it. For decades, California supported militias that massacred Indigenous communities across the state, enslaved them, and did everything they could to exterminate their cultures, languages, and way of life. What happened to the Shasta was part of this history. Today, there are over one hundred federally recognized tribes and dozens of unrecognized ones across the state.

At one of the stops we made with the Shasta, in the middle of a dry, grassy path at the base of a small cliff, we heard a bit about this dark history. Standing in the hot sun in the field, Daniels, the academic from the University of Pennsylvania, read an account of a violent attack against the tribe. Shasta men, women, and children took shelter in the cave that stood above us on the hill. As he spoke, eagles began circling over the outcropping.

Afterward, we drove to the shore of Copco Lake. As we drove along the bumpy, winding road, I asked Sarmento about the lake houses that Bransom had pointed out earlier. He told me he understood that people were upset that their vacation homes were being devalued. I mentioned that on Martha's Vineyard, my tribe also dealt with tensions with vacation homeowners, not to mention how much land values have increased because of the summer homes. The land by Copco Lake was not as pricey as the multimillion-dollar estates on Martha's Vineyard, he told me, but most of it was still too expensive for the Shasta to buy back themselves.

For a long time, I had thought that being on such a desirable vacation destination made us unlike other tribes. The price might fluctuate from place to place, but the more I learn about other tribes and Indigenous nations, the more I realize that we're all dealing with the same issue. Everyone wants our land, no matter where it is or what condition it is in.

After driving along the lake for a few more minutes, we pulled off the road to a small shaded area next to a narrow offshoot of the lake. By the trees was some dry, tall grass that bordered a small, rocky beach area that led down to the water's edge. The water was still in a way that spoke not of calm, but stagnation. The toxic smell that filled the air matched the bright green color of the water. This was the same water that Bransom had pointed out before, the same water they were posting signs in multiple languages warning people not to fish in.

But it was also the home of the Shasta people. Standing by the edge of the lake, Sami Jo, the group's de facto leader, gestured behind her. Ancestral Shasta villages and sacred sites were out there under the water, she said. When the dams were removed and the lake drained away, they wanted the land back. When the dam removal process was complete, the state and federal government would work to restore the land and ensure that it was secure from landslides and invasive species. They would then return it to the states or a designated third party, which could be a tribe like the Shasta.

Sami Jo spoke about how her grandchildren and other members of the tribe deserved to have their culture and land. It was hard to imagine what kind of generational trauma was caused by the dams. I couldn't imagine visiting Aquinnah and finding it submerged under toxic green water. I also couldn't imagine what it would mean to get that land back. And even as I believed that my tribe needed to find a way to exist as a dispersed community, I felt humbled by the sheer willpower it must have taken to keep a community together without some kind of homeland that people could visit.

One of the other reporters asked Councilman Olson what getting the land back would mean and how he felt about it. He paused a long time before answering, seemingly overcome by emotion. It would mean a lot, he said. When he spoke, he spoke in short, slow sentences. It can be hard to be here, he told us.

When they got the land back, Sami Jo said she wanted to build affordable community housing modeled after traditional Shasta dwellings. That reminded me of tribal housing in Aquinnah. I thought back to what it was like growing up running around tribal housing with my cousins after camp. I felt a strange mix of sadness that the Shasta didn't have that and hoped that they might be on the verge of it. I knew what a long fight they had ahead of them, even once they got the land back. But the Shasta community was clearly excited about it. Like in Aquinnah, people were already reaching out to Sami Jo to put their names down for housing.

I asked Sami Jo what she thought about federal recognition and how their unrecognized status was impacting their Land Back efforts. She told me that they wanted federal recognition, of course, but it just wasn't a priority at the moment. They only had very limited resources, and federal recognition was a huge undertaking. Daniels, whose research would likely support such an effort, said the saying in academia is that you only can do one federal recognition in your entire career. That's how much time and energy it took. And for a small tribe run largely by volunteers, that was a lot to ask of the Shasta. We just want to be at the right table with the right people, Sami Jo told me. And for the most part, the State of California was allowing that, regardless of their federal recognition status. Maybe later they would try for federal recognition, but right now, Land Back was the main goal.

Although my feelings about and understanding of federal recognition have evolved since I first got my tribal ID, I was still somewhat surprised to hear that. Federal recognition, I ignorantly assumed, must be the main goal for tribes without it. But the more I thought about it, the more the Shasta's strategy made sense. There was no point spending so much time and money on something that might not work out when there were more achievable goals. This helped me reframe federal recognition as just another tool, just like the Wampis thought about it.

The Shasta hadn't talked about any of this with reporters before. Sami Jo said she knew that once they declared themselves and said they were interested in the land, people would come out of the woodwork to oppose them. They wanted to wait until they were ready. I felt honored to be one of the first to hear about their plans, but strangely nervous. Sami Jo made it all sound so straightforward, and I knew that we both knew that it would not be. Before we left the Shasta at the end of the day, I told Sami Jo that her housing idea reminded me of tribal housing in Aquinnah and I loved the idea. She gave me a tight hug and told me to stay in touch. Months later, I heard that the Shasta would receive nearly three thousand acres of land back, one of the largest land returns in state history.

Later that day, we began a long bus ride to Klamath Falls, Oregon, where we'd be spending the night. I spent the ride drinking cold water from a cooler on the bus and thinking about everything I'd seen that day. To the Shasta and the people living in the Klamath Basin, the big questions I wanted to ask about sovereignty were not theoretical, they were real. It was also a reminder about how lucky I was to have grown up with a tribal land base, tribal language classes, tribal community, and so much more.

The next morning, as we met with representatives of the Klamath Tribes, Oregon Department of Fisheries and Wildlife, and a nonprofit called Trout Unlimited by the Williamson River, I watched a couple of fishermen wade out into the river, casting their lines and periodically moving to a new spot. I chatted with Gary, our bus driver for the week, joking that we both wished we were out fishing with them. He had a vacation home not far from where we stood, and he clearly knew more about fishing than I did.

From the river, we drove to one of the Klamath Tribes' administrative buildings. We gathered for lunch in their meeting room, which reminded me of the big room in our tribal administration building. The room was circular, with benches lining the walls and beautiful designs all along the walls and floor. Don Gentry, a former chairman of the tribe and current natural resources specialist, explained that the room was designed to resemble a traditional Klamath structure. I could see that it was the kind of room that was used for many different things, just like ours. While we ate sandwiches and cookies, Gentry showed us slides of their land management practices, highlighting their fire management.

He showed us an aerial picture of the impact that their fire management had on the forest. The Klamath Tribes efforts, and others like them, were part of a wider effort by tribes to bring back prescribed fire and cultural burning as forest management practices, hoping to turn the tide on decades of harmful US policies that treated any fire as bad. By working to restrict all fire, rather than managing and using fire, the US had made forests into deadly fuel traps. A fire that should burn for an hour or a day in a confined area can now destroy thousands of acres, tearing through trees, homes, and people.

In 2021, the Bootleg fire burned 25 percent of the Klamath Tribes' treaty area, but in the picture, we could see the areas of forest that had received different treatment. It was shocking how stark it was. In the middle was an area that had received both thinning and prescribed fire. It looked completely untouched by the fire, with hundreds of bright green trees visible. To the left was an area that had been thinned but had not received any prescribed fire treatment. The trees were still visible, but almost all of them looked brown and dead, with very little green left. To the right was an area with no treatment. It was completely scorched, a black mark where a forest should have been. For months, I had been writing articles about how Indigenous land management was the most effective in the world, but it was still kind of amazing to see what that looked like firsthand.

Sometimes it's hard for me to see things other tribes are doing and not wonder why my tribe can't do the same. We're always harder on our own. It was so easy for me to visit other tribes and be impressed by everything they were doing, but only focus on the dysfunction in my own tribe. In fact, in many ways, the visit felt just like what I would imagine it would be to visit my tribe as an outsider. From the similarities of the room, to the small stand someone set up to sell T-shirts and stickers in the lobby, it felt a lot like my tribe.

We also met Clayton Dumont, the current chairman of the tribe, who talked about the tribe's desire to get land back. "Land Back is part of our constitution and we bring it up at every opportunity," Dumont explained. "Federal laws are not strong enough to protect the environment. The only way is if we own it."

The problem, of course, is that no one wants to just give tribes back land. If no one else was claiming the land, then maybe it could be that simple. But there were plenty of powerful interests competing with tribes for land, water, and power. And that afternoon and the next day, we spent time with some of those people: white farmers and ranchers in the Basin.

Talking to the farmers, the first thing I noticed was that they seemed to feel that tribes had the real power, that they were the little guys downtrodden by the powerful tribes. As we toured the area in our bus with Dumont and Gentry, a local rancher leader said that she felt so intimidated next to two chairmen. I don't know if she was just being polite, but I thought it was a kind of aw-shucks facade she was putting on, because to me, it seemed like white ranchers had all the power, or at least, way more than they should.

And I think that's the crux of the issue—it's not about how much power that is held, it's about how much is held compared to how much others think you should have. When tribes have more power than white people believe they should have, or than they were accustomed to them having, then suddenly it feels like tribes have all the power. In the Klamath Basin, tribes cannot be ignored. But that's not because they have inherently more power out there or because people are inherently more respectful, it's because they put themselves in that position. They have sovereignty in the way that Matthew Fletcher described: They earned it and continue to earn it year after year.

Talking to a group of farmers from the Tulelake Irrigation District, one of the common lines I heard was how long they had been in the Basin. They'd proudly introduce themselves as third- or fourth-generation farmers in the area. I wonder if they ever thought about how many generations the tribes have been there. And since the farmers had that history, they felt they had nowhere else to go. But all white settlers chose to go where they did, almost always for economic opportunity. It's one of the great American lies that the Pilgrims were on a mission of religious freedom. They were businesspeople on a for-profit expedition. The farmers in the Klamath Basin were no different.

Until the 1930s, Tulelake was a wetland area stretching over one hundred thousand acres. But then, the federal government drained the lake, creating around sixty thousand acres of farmland. Much of this farmland was raffled off to families of veterans, whose names were drawn out of a pickle jar for plots of land. Some moved to Tulelake from as far as New York, seeking a fresh opportunity. So, less than a hundred years after the US built dams and flooded Shasta land, they drained water in a nearby area so that white settlers could get free farmland. Tulelake was also home to Camp Tulelake, a Japanese internment camp during World War II, making it a kind of crossroads of displacement and oppression for multiple communities.

At the end of the day, the farmers took us to a rock in the middle of the grassy field. High up on the rock were petroglyphs, carved by Indigenous people hundreds of years before, when the lake waters were far above our heads. The rock was like a vertical record of the land. One of the farmers pointed out Japanese names carved in, just a few feet away from the names of local high school kids. As mosquitos buzzed around me, I felt numb in the face of the literal layers of historical oppression in front of me, which intersected with different aspects of my identity, even if my Japanese family didn't directly experience internment.

The day after we met with the farmers we began driving toward the coast, stopping in Karuk land around Happy Camp, California. As we drove along California's Highway 96, which runs next to the Klamath River as it twists its way toward the ocean, the air started getting smokier and smokier, the unmistakable smell of fire slowly seeping its way onto the bus until we were all wearing KN95 masks. Here and there, we spotted small tendrils of smoke spiraling up from the forest floor.

As the bus lurched along, I wondered if we were seeing good fires or bad fires. During a brief stop at one of the few convenience stores on the route, I picked up a dusty copy of something called "California Water Justice News" produced by a nonprofit called Save California Salmon. Finally, we pulled over on the side of the road to a large dirt turnoff, like the countless ones that our bus driver had used to let smaller, faster-moving cars pass us on the narrow, winding road. There, waiting for us were two trucks. There were three guys there: Bill Tripp, the director of natural resources and environmental policy for the Karuk Tribe; Clifton Whitehouse, the crew boss for the Mid Klamath Watershed Council Fire and Forestry Happy Camp Crew; and Silas Yamamoto, a cultural specialist and fuels technician for the Karuk Tribe and a Fire and Forestry field tech for the Mid Klamath Watershed Council.

After we all introduced ourselves, they pulled out a large map that they held against the tailgate of one of their trucks. The map showed a wide expanse of forest, filled in with different colored blobs. The three of them explained how each color signified different fire treatments and plans. They were working in the surrounding forest to manage the land through various fire treatments, including prescribed fires. They also spent a lot of time doing fuels reduction, which involves removing brush, litter, and other low-lying vegetation that can easily help a small fire accelerate and spread.

After they gave the overview of their work, we took a short walk up the ridge to see an area that had received prescribed fire treatment. As we walked up the hill toward the ridge, I asked Silas how long he's been doing this and how he got involved. He said that he was bicultural—Japanese and Karuk—and fire had always been a part of his life. Up on the ridge, they explained in more detail about the work they did and the various considerations. Silas explained the different impacts that prescribed fire and wildfire can have on the vegetation. Bill Tripp told us that words matter when it comes to sovereignty, that the Karuk did not want to define cultural burning in federal law, they simply wanted federal law to acknowledge it. I had to chew on the subtle but crucial difference between the two for a minute.

Federal law should not be the source of tribal sovereignty, but it must acknowledge and respect it. Cultural burning is something that the Karuk will continue to do, as they have for generations. The federal government just needs to get out of the way. Like the Klamath Tribes, the Karuk are trying to correct years of poor forest management by the US Forest Service.

"Why does the federal government need to own millions of acres of land if they're not going to treat it responsibly?" Silas asked. Year by year and fire by fire, the Karuk were proving what they always knew: that they could manage the land better than the US government. Silas's frustrated question reminded me of what Matthew Fletcher said, that you earn sovereignty by governing—managing the land, in this case—better than anyone else. To Silas, sovereignty was about the land, not necessarily tribal politics. "I think a huge step in the right direction in order to gain our sovereignty back is to do what we used to do: manage our lands, live off the land, you know, respect the land," he told me. "Sovereignty has a huge part in more than just government, like being able to just manage that Aboriginal territory the way that it used to be."

It was one thing to hear about sovereignty and protecting the land, but seeing Silas's passion for fire and the land was another. His favorite part of the job, he told me, was putting fire back on the ground. That phrasing stuck with me, that what he was doing was returning fire to where it belonged, rather than treating it as a problem. And in doing so, he was helping the land, his tribe, and himself. Since he had been working with fire, he told me, his relationship with the land felt stronger than ever before. "I definitely feel like a purpose of mine is to help heal the land," Silas said. "Because of the extensive amount of work that I've done with fire so far, and the way that I've seen it impact my friends and my family's life, like my life when my house burned down three years ago in the Slater fire. Yeah, it can be incredibly disruptive, but it can also bring some of the most beautiful life you've seen."

I had gone into the week thinking I was going to learn about sovereignty, and I definitely had, but I was also realizing all the different ways that Indigenous people had relationships with the land. Each relationship was unique and complex.

The next morning, we drove a few hours to Yurok land on the coast, where we met with Barry McCovey Jr., the director of the Yurok Fisheries Department, and Amy Bowers Cordalis, an attorney for the Yurok Tribe. We met at a brush dance site and sat on wooden benches as the wind from the coast whipped around us. We talked to McCovey and Cordalis about how everything we had seen on the river came to a head on their land and could be seen through the health of the fish populations.

In 2002, tens of thousands of adult salmon died on the Klamath after farmers and ranchers diverted water during a drought. It was the largest salmon kill in the history of the US. The cultural, environmental, and economic impacts of the 2002 fish kill are still felt today. Like the Wampanoag, the Yurok are fishing people, but as the health of the river has declined, their fishing activities have been increasingly limited. The dam removal is just one step toward finally restoring the river they have called home since time immemorial. But the Yurok and other tribes we met that week know that taking out the dams will not fix the river overnight.

"We're fine with it taking generations," McCovey said of the restoration process. "Time is on our side." I knew exactly what he meant. The way Indigenous people think about the problem is much longer term than the way white people do. We understand long cycles. It reminded me a little bit about how Sami Jo focused so much on what getting the land back would mean for her grandchildren. She had also said the same thing about federal recognition, that they were thinking in terms of generations and as long as they were moving in the right direction, that was enough for now. But it was still a little surprising to hear McCovey say that. So much of the reporting I've done focuses on urgent, existential issues, like how Jack Fiander said that unless something changed in the next few years, the salmon could all be gone. I had never really heard an Indigenous person say that time was on our side.

But the more I thought about it, the more I understood that the idea comes from the core understanding of everything that we have survived. After disease, stolen land, persecution, violence, racism, and near extermination, Indigenous people across the country are still here. And we aren't going anywhere. Our sovereignty is based on our status as nations, but it is built on the people who make up those nations and the work those people are doing to protect our land.

After we wrapped up our conversation with Cordalis and McCovey, we walked on a short trail over to a wide expanse of beach. It was the last stop on our trip, and stepping out from the trail onto the sand, the Pacific Ocean stretched out in front of us. Driftwood was scattered across the beach while the tide lapped at huge rocks. We took photos, climbed on the rocks, and skipped stones. Standing high up on one of the rocks, I tilted my head back and let the ocean air ripple across my face. Closing my eyes, I could have been standing on the beach in Aquinnah, not just because of the ocean air, but because of the ideas swirling around my head.

10

THE WILL OF THE PEOPLE

As immersive as the Klamath trip was, it was missing one component that made up a big part of my personal understanding of tribal sovereignty and government. Most of my experiences with tribal politics were not about taking down dams and challenging white farmers, but unpopular council decisions. Because of that, when I thought about tribal government and sovereignty, I thought more about internal tensions, rather than external threats. I realized that to move toward what I saw other tribes doing, I would first have to look more closely at the conflicts we had been dealing with as a tribe. The biggest one during my life has been over a casino.

Today, casinos are one of the first things Americans think about when they think about Indians. There's a strange stereotype that Indians are either dirt poor or filthy rich from casino earnings. Growing up, the possibility of a tribal casino was something always floating around, but I never really knew that much about why tribal casinos were a thing. Figuring that out was one of my first steps after learning about the settlement.

In the late 1970s, the Seminole Tribe of Florida opened a high-stakes bingo facility, the first official Indian gaming operation in the country. According to a recent Supreme Court decision, because federally recognized tribes were sovereign nations, state laws prohibiting gaming did not apply on tribal reservations. News of the success of the Seminole operation quickly spread across the country.

In 1988, the federal government passed the Indian Gaming Regulatory Act (IGRA), a law that created three classifications of gaming allowed on Indian land. Class I is traditional Indian gaming and is not regulated by IGRA. Class II, which includes high stakes and electronic bingo, became legal on Indian land regardless of state laws against it. Class III gaming includes all other types of traditional casino gambling, like blackjack, poker, and slot machines. Class II does require approval from local governments.

In 1992, the Mashantucket Pequot tribe in Connecticut built the first Native-owned Vegas-style resort casino, the Foxwoods Resort Casino. Foxwoods would soon generate billions of dollars in profits. Suddenly, almost every tribe wanted a casino. In 1996, tribal casinos generated over $5 billion in gross gaming revenue. Today, there are many examples of successful tribal casinos around the country. These casinos can bring jobs, money, and opportunity to tribal communities. Tribes often use casino profits to invest in education, culture, public safety, health, and infrastructure projects. Some also send out direct payments to tribal members. But there are also many smaller tribal casinos that do not bring in millions of dollars. And there are plenty of tribes with no gambling operations at all.

In the 1990s, as a newly federally recognized tribe with virtually no source of income beyond federal grants, casino gambling represented an enormous opportunity for the Aquinnah Wampanoag. For decades, different tribal leaders and councils tried to build a casino, both off-island and in Aquinnah. All those attempts resulted in lawsuits, internal tensions, and virtually no progress on an actual casino. In 2011, Massachusetts Governor Deval Patrick announced that the state would issue three gaming licenses, one of which would be reserved for a Native American tribe. The Mashpee Wampanoag tribe on Cape Cod got the license, shutting out the Aquinnah Wampanoag. This set the stage for the casino fight to come back to Aquinnah. If we couldn't build a casino off-island, there might be a way for us to build one on the Vineyard.

Andrews-Maltais, who was chairperson at the time, decided to pursue a Class II gaming facility, an electronic bingo hall, in Aquinnah. She chose to do so because IGRA had created a pathway for tribes to operate that kind of facility regardless of what state law said. The problem was the 1987 settlement agreement the tribe had signed with the town. In that agreement, there was a provision that said the tribe will follow all town laws, and gambling of any kind was not allowed. That question of whether the settlement agreement or federal law and sovereignty would take precedence would go all the way to the Supreme Court. The other open issue was whether tribal members actually wanted a casino in Aquinnah. A casino in New Bedford or somewhere else off-island, where it could generate profit away from our homeland, was one thing. A casino in Aquinnah, a town that didn't even have a school or grocery store, was another.

At the May 2011 general membership meeting, the membership voted narrowly to use our unfinished community center building as a temporary gaming facility. Opponents of the casino were outraged, saying that the vote was not publicized, and that they would have organized more people to come to the meeting if they had known the vote would happen. I didn't go to that meeting, but it is one of the first times I can remember being aware of a tribal meeting.

Tribal government was always something for grown-ups to care about. I knew that people argued about tribal government, that there were fierce disagreements and debates. I just never really knew what they were about or how they might impact me. The more I paid attention to tribal politics over the years, the more acrimonious it all seemed. Having grown up without really feeling the presence of tribal government, when I finally became aware of it, the context was this massive internal conflict.

Of course, as the tribe argued over whether it should build a casino or not, there was also plenty of external opposition. The Taxpayers' Association, which changed its name to the Gay Head Community Association, joined the town in a lawsuit against the tribe's right to build a gaming facility in Aquinnah, based on the language in the settlement agreement. To help pay for their lawyers, the Community Association, which normally donated substantial sums to the library, lighthouse, cultural center, and other causes in town, suspended all charitable contributions in town, except for a small scholarship given to high school graduates.

* * *

Over the next few years, the tribe was enmeshed in a messy, complicated legal battle with the town over the right to build a casino. Meanwhile, internal tribal politics focused almost entirely on that singular issue. Andrews-Maltais was eventually voted out of office, losing a 2013 election to Tobias Vanderhoop. My mom and many other Aquinnah residents helped run a phone bank for Tobias, calling every tribal member they could and encouraging them to come out and vote. Tobias made a Facebook page and a Twitter account for his campaign. Amira and another cousin were his campaign managers. It was the first time I had seen a tribal campaign that resembled the American political campaigns I followed.

With Tobias in office, many of us thought that the casino issue was done. Even though the membership's last vote on the subject was the controversial 2011 vote in favor of using the community center building as a casino, we never expected it to go anywhere with Tobias in office and the legal battle still dragging on. But within the tribe, the pro-casino lobby kept working. Andrews-Maltais, even though she was no longer in office, was the head of the tribe's Gaming Corporation, an independent entity within the tribe dedicated to pursuing all gaming options for the tribe.

When the council voted in 2015 to turn over control of the community center to the Gaming Corporation, I was pretty surprised, along with many other people in Aquinnah. And when Tobias ended up backing the council and the Gaming Corporation in their efforts to convert the community center into a gaming facility, I think a lot of people felt betrayed. Tobias always said that he did what he did because it was the "will of the people" and it was his job to execute whatever the membership decided.

In response to the vote, a small group of tribal members decided to organize a referendum petition for a vote to overturn the council's decision. A referendum vote required fifty signatures of tribal members. Someone brought the petition up to the store, where I was working with my mom, and I signed, happy to play a small role in the casino resistance. Once the petition was accepted by the tribal secretary, the vote was scheduled for that August. For a referendum vote to succeed, a two-thirds majority was needed.

Three weeks before the vote, all tribal members received a postcard in the mail from the Gaming Corporation. The postcard firmly rejected the claims made in the referendum petition about the casino's lack of feasibility, its harm to the community, and various other points. To help rally support and votes, someone came up with the idea of circulating a letter to counter the postcard and outline the key reasons to oppose the casino decision. Eager to help, I drafted a letter and emailed it around to a few cousins who my mom and I had been talking to about the issue. The letter focused on the logistical and economic challenges a casino in Aquinnah would face, rather than coming out completely against gaming.

There were six bullet points highlighting specific facts about the proposed casino, like the $1 million in federal grants used to build the community center the tribe would have to pay back if we converted the building into a casino. After some debate over how to sign the letter, we eventually agreed on the label "Aquinnah Wampanoags for a Better Community." I created a Gmail account for the group and added the email at the bottom of the letter along with an invitation to reach out with any questions. Looking back, I regret not signing the letter with our names. I don't think it would have made a difference to the vote, but there's such a culture of secrecy, paranoia, and lack of transparency in the tribe that I should have known better than to have contributed to that ongoing problem.

Once we agreed on the final text of the letter, we sent it off to a local shop to print out hundreds of copies. One cousin ordered envelopes on Amazon, while another bought stamps. My mom gave her $50 to help pay for the stamps. I called a couple people to make sure they'd be there to help with the dull work of envelope stuffing. Our loosely organized opposition group got together one night after work to fold the letters, put them in envelopes, and slap address labels on them for each and every tribal member. We ended up sending out around seven hundred letters.

Two days before the election, the Gaming Corporation mailed out a six-page packet laying out all their arguments for the casino. The packet included a schedule for a chartered bus that would pick up off-island voters and shuttle them to the ferry and then to the tribal building. Rumors were going around town that the Gaming Corporation was bringing in "hundreds" of voters from off-island. My dad joked that the boat would be so full of off-island voters it might sink. We all agreed we'd be lucky to get a simple majority, hoping for at least a moral victory.

After the meeting that day, I hung around the tribal building to wait for the results of the vote. While we were waiting around, Amira, who was on the Elections Committee, came up to say that there had been a problem with the counting and they needed volunteers to recount the votes. I volunteered and headed downstairs to the library where the chief and medicine man were leading the vote counting. I wasn't sure if it was somehow a conflict of interest for me to count the votes, but I figured that everyone had a conflict of interest. Plus, I wanted to see how it all worked.

As we counted the votes, I tried to keep track and see if we were looking good for the two-thirds majority. It became quickly apparent that we did not have enough votes. But when we finally got to the end and finalized the tally, it made us all pause: the vote was a dead tie at 110–110. Two hundred and twenty votes was also one of the highest turnouts ever for a tribal vote, especially one without an election for chair. Just like years without presidential elections see lower turnout, tribal elections without a chair election typically get much lower numbers.

No one thought turnout would be this high or the vote so close. The vote was supposed to be a measure of what the community wanted to do, but the answer was we couldn't decide. While the big-picture meaning of the vote may not have been clear, the immediate result was. Since a referendum vote required a two-thirds majority to pass, the results of the vote meant that the Gaming Corporation retained control of the community center, but the actual casino was still tied up in legal battles with the town and the Community Association.

In November of that year, the tribe lost the court case. Fourth Circuit US District Judge Dennis Saylor ruled that the tribe did not exercise "sufficient governmental authority" on its lands for IGRA to apply. Even to those of us who opposed the casino, that sounded like a challenge to the tribe's sovereignty. Or, in other words, Saylor said that we had not earned our sovereignty. Reading the decision, I felt like he was saying we weren't a tribe at all. The tribe appealed the decision. Facing a grant deadline from HUD on the building that the council voted to turn into a bingo hall, Tobias decided to finish the project as originally intended—a community center.

On April 10, 2017—the thirtieth anniversary of federal recognition—the First Circuit appellate panel ruled in favor of the tribe, overturning Judge Saylor's ruling and affirming the tribe's right to operate a Class II gaming facility under IGRA. By then, Andrews-Maltais was back in office and she welcomed the ruling as an affirmation of the tribe's sovereignty. Even though the ruling was a narrow one, the town and the Community Association elected to pursue an appeal. Eventually, the Supreme Court declined to hear the appeal. Despite that legal victory, the community center was eventually completed as originally intended. The tribe's after-school program, meetings, and other community events now take place there. There's another property where the tribe's casino push has stalled out again.

That experience became foundational to the way I think about my tribe. When I began writing, I focused on the issues that had come up during the casino fight, exploring issues like the tension between on-island and off-island tribal members. I wanted to write about my tribe, family, and experiences because I thought they deserved to be shared with the world, but also because I wanted to tell a different kind of Native story than the ones I was used to seeing. I was afraid of being accused of airing dirty laundry or focusing on internal problems when there were so many external problems to care about, but I was probably even more afraid of being yet another voice that simplified Native communities and issues.

It seemed like so many stories I read about tribes were simple, like modern versions of Cowboys vs. Indians. Indians vs. Pipeline and Indians vs.

Language Loss were probably the most common. And that's not to say that those aren't important stories, but the truth is that they felt so foreign to the experiences I had. It rarely felt like we were locked in existential fights over land and water. Instead, we were fighting with one another over power, battling our way through and around bureaucracy, or just unsure about what the best step forward was.

And that's what always felt so different to me about stories about other tribes. When I read books and articles or watched movies and TV shows that touched on the Native experience, I rarely saw representations that reflected my own experience. I think part of that was because East Coast tribes were so rarely depicted, but also because those stories were more complicated and therefore more difficult to tell.

The idea of tribal government as flawed was not new to me, but in the content I consumed about tribes, it was never really talked about. If my experience was anything to go by, there were things that were impacting the lives of Indigenous people across the country, but that, by and large, we were not talking about.

11

BIG SLOW-MOVING THING

In early 2022, I heard about tribes in western Alaska who were trying to stop what would be the world's largest open-pit gold mine, known as the Donlin Gold project. The mine, if built, could threaten the health of the Kuskokwim River and dozens of tribes that rely on it for food, transportation, water, and culture. Loosely translated, Kuskokwim means big slow-moving thing.

At first I was hesitant to look more into the story. I felt like there is already so much coverage about the environmental, health, and cultural impacts on Indigenous communities from mines and pipelines that I wasn't sure what else I could add. But when I did a little reading about the mine project, something immediately caught my attention. The mine was being backed by Calista Corporation, an Alaska Native Corporation (ANC) that represents around thirty thousand Alaska Natives, most of whom live in the Yukon-Kuskokwim region.

Located in southwestern Alaska, the Yukon-Kuskokwim Delta (YK Delta) is one of the largest river deltas in the world, covering an area around the size of the state of New York. The area is made up primarily of tundra, with wetlands rich in wildlife, including millions of birds and other species. The vast majority of the roughly twenty-five thousand people who live in the YK Delta are Yup'ik people who have called the area home for thousands of years. Many of these people still live at least partially subsistence lifestyles, relying on the abundant landscape for food. Bethel, a city of about six thousand, is by far the largest population center in the area and is home to a regional hospital. The city is also a transit and shopping hub for about fifty villages that surround it. None of the villages are connected by roads, which means that bush planes, boats, and snow machines are the only ways to get around.

I knew that Alaska had hundreds of small federally recognized tribes, by far the most in any state, in addition to the larger Alaska Native Corporations, but I didn't quite understand what the relationship between the two was. Some of the tribes, it turned out, were suing Calista, their own Native Corporation.

I decided that complexity was worth looking into more. To begin reporting the story, I spoke with a number of tribal members who were anti-mine activists and also Calista shareholders.

While each person had a slightly different perspective about the impact the mine would have, they all spoke in deeply serious tones about the threat that it represented to their way of life. "Right now there's so many other things that are coming on the horizon that are very, very scary, but this one has more potential to destroy us, our river, our land, our Earth, than any other thing that is out there," one elder told me. "So we are fighting to survive."

In particular, they spoke about the importance of the river as a source of subsistence lifestyle, in particular fish. Many families, they told me, got almost all their food from the river. Because of its remote location, food in the region is extremely expensive to buy from stores, not to mention the centuries of subsistence living that have conditioned their gut biomes to thrive on foods from the tundra rather than processed foods from the supermarket. The youngest person I talked to, a woman named Sophie Swope, said she had always dreamed of having children and sharing traditional Yup'ik foods with them. The possibility of the mine destroying the river, however, made her wonder if she even wanted a family anymore.

Several activists spoke about their frustration with Calista, which most of them were shareholders in. One man told me that he felt Calista was trying to keep them blindfolded from the true dangers of the mine and described their actions as a slap in the face. Threats from an outside corporation were one thing, but coming from an institution that was supposed to benefit the community, they were even harder to swallow. When I talked to Indigenous representatives from Calista, they told me that Donlin was an almost unimaginable opportunity for their communities. They said it could bring hope and change to the next generations.

Calista is one of thirteen Alaska Native Corporations that were all created in 1971 by the Alaska Native Claims Settlement Act (ANCSA), which gave the ANCs forty-four million acres and $900 million. In return, the tribes and ANCs had to give up all land claims in Alaska. Because of this system, those forty-four million acres are owned by these private, for-profit corporations, rather than by federally recognized tribes. ANCs, which are run by Indigenous boards of directors, provide dividends to shareholders, along with scholarships, cultural programs, and other community benefits. It's a complicated arrangement. Individual tribes have local governing authority, but don't own the land. To make matters even more confusing, there are also regional and local corporations.

During our conversations, several elders mentioned that they felt like they were playing catch-up with tribes in the lower forty-eight states in terms of asserting sovereignty. The ANCs had all the money, land, and power. Tribes were small and extremely resource-limited. I remember feeling surprised that they would say that. In some ways, I always thought that the later a tribe was colonized, the more sovereign they would probably be, since they had more years to live under their own systems and rule without colonial interference. But like I had seen in the Klamath Basin, there was no linear way to measure the impact of colonialism.

In Alaska, the new system disrupted a way of life that had existed for countless generations by putting most of the land and resources into the for-profit system. And so tribes had little power and little recourse. Seeing the complexity of the ANC system made me question some of my own ideas about sovereignty. In Aquinnah, people have always talked about ways of making the tribe more economically self-sufficient. While I can understand the need for financial independence, the ANC system reminded me that economic power can be a useful tool, but it can also be detrimental when money becomes the end goal.

Sophie Swope told me how she went to a shareholder meeting in Tuluksak, a nearby village, to speak out against Calista's support of the mine. It was her first time and the experience she described reminded me of my first tribal meeting, on the day of the casino referendum vote. She was interested to see how shareholder meetings worked, but she was also frustrated and felt like the community was not being heard.

The article I eventually wrote focused on the environmental danger of the mine as well as the complexity of the fight Sophie and others were waging against their own corporation. Over the next year, I stayed in touch with Sophie. We talked about everything from her old job working in a dental clinic and the differences between our tribes' language efforts to the dynamics of tribal councils and fish camps.

Sophie grew up in Bethel with a Yup'ik mom and white dad, surrounded by Indigenous culture and tradition. Some of her earliest memories are seeing her grandmother giggle and smile at how much Sophie enjoyed traditional foods like dried fish and fish skin. Sophie also learned bits and pieces of the Yup'ik language, but never became fluent. It wasn't until she went away to college in Colorado that Sophie really began to understand what she calls the "huge disruption" to Indigenous life that was colonialism. She had never really thought about her community's history and how it might have been shaped by colonial forces until college. And so it was around that time, she told me, that she decided she wanted to, maybe even needed to, learn more about the systems that had been imposed on her people. She also began to realize that some of the complexity that made her and others shy away from trying to analyze those systems was intentional. "I need to understand this super complicated structure because I feel that they've created it to make it complicated and not want people to go near it," she told me about her feelings around that time.

And so even though she had always looked forward to leaving home and going away to live in a city when she was younger, the older she got and the more she learned about her community's history, the more Sophie wanted to return home and work to make things better. She started working for the Yukon Kuskokwim Health Corporation, first as a dental assistant, and then eventually in HR. Although she enjoyed working with the community and sometimes getting to travel to villages to take services to community members, her frustrations with having to work with old systems, people unwilling to change, and messy internal politics began to build.

And so, a few years after college, Sophie took a new job with her tribe as the self-governance director. "I just became overwhelmingly fascinated in how much power there is to be a quote, unquote, domestic dependent nation of the United States," she said of her time working as the self-governance director. "There's just so much that we could do and it really takes this visioning and step-by-step plan to create the things that we desire for our community."

Hearing Sophie talk about her frustrations with working in tribal bureaucracy sounded familiar. I never actually worked in the tribal administration building, but my experiences told a similar story, not to mention the stories of countless cousins who cycled through working for the tribe over the years, quitting when they couldn't take it anymore.

As we talked, we found other parallels between our family stories. I couldn't help but compare Yup'ik subsistence ways to how my family had lived in Gay Head just a few generations ago. Both our grandfathers started commercial fishing businesses when there were few other opportunities to make a living. Sophie's grandmother can remember seeing a Japanese warplane during World War II as it flew over Mekoryuk, her small village on the remote island of Nunivak. It was the first plane she had ever seen. My grandmother, who was born in Japan, had almost the reverse experience when she came from Tokyo's urban sprawl to remote Gay Head.

When Sophie described her experiences growing up, it was clear to me that Yup'ik community, culture, and tradition were core parts of who she was, but tribal government and politics weren't really a major factor until later. She grew up feeling the real effect of Yup'ik foods, but not necessarily tribal government. And I know that's normal. American kids grow up immersed in American culture, but not thinking about American government and history. I never really felt a shortage of tribal culture or community when I was in Aquinnah, but all that always felt so separate from tribal government, almost in spite of it, rather than because of it. It was almost like the tribal government was weaker than the culture and community that it was in theory trying to protect.

For both Sophie and me, it was only as we grew up that we began to learn about why that was and that things could actually change. "I had to start to educate myself on what our actual rights to self-governance were," she said. "We're able to make tribal laws and all of these guidelines for our people and our nation, but I was also very confused by the fact that we have no land and there's no real way to kind of govern anything when there's already a city council that makes the laws and imposes taxes and everything."

And, like me, sometimes it took visiting other tribes to see that other options did in fact exist. Sophie told me about a recent trip to Kwigillingok, a nearby village that is unincorporated. In other words, the tribal council is the only local authority. As she listened to elders and community leaders talk about their community, she began to realize that they never mentioned a town government or municipal council. "I wish that we had that in Bethel. We should have one governing body," she said. "We shouldn't have that separation between people that are coming into the community and a completely separate governing body for the Indigenous people that have been there for forever."

During one of our first conversations, when I was explaining the complicated relationship between my tribe and the town of Aquinnah, she paused me to ask if we had a municipality. I hesitated for a second. We did, but I had never thought about it that way. Or, to be more precise, I had never thought about the possibility of a system in which there was no town government that shared authority with the tribe.

In Bethel, Sophie's tribal government, the Orutsararmiut Native Council, is buried under multiple layers of external authority, from the city of Bethel and the regional corporation to the State of Alaska and Calista, the huge corporation with over thirty thousand shareholders across the region, not to mention the other thousands of nonshareholders who are in the area. With all these entities, tribes often get pushed out of the picture and have little resources to force their way in. "How are the tribes supposed to govern themselves when they have no land and there's another governing body that makes all the rules?" Sophie wondered.

At age twenty-six Sophie was serving on both the Bethel city council and her tribal council. She told me she wanted there to be more collaboration between the two. "It's been really interesting, the dynamic of holding both seats," she explained. "The municipality is more steered toward, you know, this economic foundation. It's very different from the traditional values that are held on the tribal council level."

She was also the director of the Mother Kuskokwim Coalition, a group of activists and organizers working to protect the river, support tribal sovereignty, and build community. Nearly two years after I wrote my initial article on the mine, I flew out to visit Bethel in the middle of winter. I didn't know quite what to expect. I had never been to Alaska, and certainly not to somewhere like Bethel, a city that was large by western Alaskan standards, but one without any roads in or out. To get there, I flew from New York to Seattle, Seattle to Anchorage, and finally Anchorage to Bethel.

There was a light snow as we left Anchorage, and as the plane climbed upward, it hurtled through the increasingly thick and fast flakes streaming past my smudged window, the wing's flashing signals illuminating the snow like streams of light in the ocean depths. Unlike my previous two flights, which had been completely full, bags and coats crammed under seats and into overhead bins, the flight to Bethel was, at most, half full. The two seats next to me were empty. Most people on the flight looked to be Native. As we neared Bethel, a flight attendant made an announcement to please clean up after ourselves because "as most of you know," there was no postflight cleaning service in Bethel before the next flight boarded the plane. What struck me wasn't so much that there wouldn't be anyone to clean the plane when we landed, but that most people flying this route already knew that. I wondered if I was the only person going to Bethel for the first time.

As the plane began its descent toward Bethel, I saw a few small clusters of lights on the ground. They were villages, I realized. Soon, a larger cluster emerged from the darkness and I knew that must be Bethel. As I stepped off the plane, cool air hit my face, but it was not the bitingly cold weather I had hoped for. That evening, the temperature was around 30 degrees, and during the five days I was in Bethel, temperatures were generally in the 20s, with one day dipping into the teens. The weather app on my phone told me that these temperatures were 10 to 20 degrees above the average January temperatures. Although the warm weather meant more pleasant walks, it also meant we couldn't do some classic Bethel winter activities.

A few weeks before I arrived in Bethel, Sophie had said we could probably go ice fishing, but by the time I was there, the weather had warmed up enough that the river was no longer fully safe to travel on. A 150-mile dogsled race that I had been hoping to watch was postponed because the trail conditions were too slushy. Like with so many Indigenous issues, climate change was the looming context.

The next morning, Sophie picked me up, along with a friend who was a reporter for the local radio station and joined us for the day. Sophie had planned a day trip to Tuluksak, a small village about thirty miles upriver. She was bringing a box of groceries, including fruit, milk, and eggs, along with sweatshirts branded with Mother Kuskokwim and No Donlin logos. Part of her work was doing outreach in the dozens of villages around Bethel. She wanted to help the communities develop alternative solutions to Donlin that could also generate income, jobs, and opportunity without destroying the land and their way of life. It struck me as a fine line, going into villages to spread her message about the mine, while also trying to learn from them about what they need and want.

She understood that it was hard for many people in villages to say no to Donlin when it promised jobs, money, and other economic development. She told me she didn't just want to be saying no, she wanted to find alternatives, which is why she spent time in villages listening to what people need and want. It could be lonely work, she explained, since many people in the community were supportive of the mine. But every once in a while, another young person from the area would randomly tell her that they were so grateful that someone their age was out there fighting to protect the land, and those moments made it all worth it.

The three of us, bulky in our winter coats, piled into the six-seat plane. Since it was my first time in a small plane, they let me take the front seat. Before I knew it, we were tilting upward, the low roar of the engine and propeller filling the small cabin as we set off into the early morning sky. The sun had just risen, casting faint orange light across the pale blue sky. Low bunches of clouds hung over the horizon. Rather than obstructing the view or spoiling the sunrise, they seemed to add extra canvas for the beautiful scene. The growing morning light dipped and poked its way through the clouds, while the yellow glow above the cloud line grew brighter and brighter as the sun rose.

Below us, even frozen and immobile, the Kuskokwim River was a mighty sight. I could immediately see how this one river sustained an entire region, providing food, transportation, and so much more. Winding its way through the tundra in a broad curve, the river was covered in ice and snow that looked rippled, almost soft from the air. Here and there, I could see snow machine tracks cutting through the river, but I didn't see any people. On either side of the river, there were countless tributaries and lakes, some of them circled by dark trees, others blending in with the snowy tundra ground around them. The entire landscape seemed to be snow, scattered trees, and frozen water all the way to the horizon. About halfway through the flight, the pilot nudged me and pointed past my shoulder to a few moose standing in a small clearing. After that, I began noticing small clusters of moose every few moments. The giant animals looked tiny from the sky. I wondered what smaller wildlife I wasn't able to see from the plane.

Before long, I saw our destination, a single, icy runway in the middle of a large clearing. Stepping off the plane and into the cold air, I breathed deeply. All the different legs of my trip to Tuluksak reminded me of taking three or four different buses and a ferry to Aquinnah. By the time I got there, all I wanted to do was breathe in the island air. Aquinnah is far less remote than Tuluksak, but I had a similar sensation of having earned that first breath of fresh air.

We waited there on the ice for a few minutes before our ride showed up. By posting on the Tuluksak Facebook group, Sophie arranged for a ride to take us from the airport to the middle of town. Some of the fruit she brought would help compensate them for the ride. A young man picked us up in his car. As we rolled slowly along the snowy road into town, Sophie asked him if he knew some of the people she had connected with. He apologized, explaining that he only really knew people's Yup'ik names, not their English names.

The village was made up of small, one-story wooden houses. Snow-covered dirt roads crisscrossed their way through the houses. Dogs paced over the packed snow, looking curiously in our direction as we walked. A few came up to us, prodding their noses at the food in our bags. We made one quick stop to drop off a few groceries and sweatshirts for one woman that Sophie knew. Then our driver dropped us off at his grandparents' house. As we stomped up the steps to the entryway, snow shaking off our boots, Sophie knocked on the door, asking if we could come in, calling out that we brought fruit. From inside, I heard a muffled shout to please come in, especially if we had fruit.

Inside, we met two village elders, Dora and Peter. Dora eagerly accepted milk and fruit from Sophie, announcing that she was going to make coffee for everyone. While she chatted, Peter was busy running in and out of the house, desperately trying to fix frozen pipes before he left for church. As happy as Dora was to receive the food delivery, Peter might have been even more excited. He told us that he had just been saying that he hoped someone would show up and help him and suddenly there we were.

The gas pipes, it turned out, had frozen because he forgot to close the tank lid when it rained. When the temperatures dropped, the water froze, clogging the pipes with ice. Peter handed me a blowtorch and had me stand outside passing the flame over the pipe to melt as much ice as possible when he blew into the pipe from inside the house, forcing the ice out. It felt good to help even if I didn't feel like I was doing that much. Eventually, the torch and Peter's blowing cleared the pipes and I headed back inside to help clean up.

Peter changed into warmer clothes for the snow machine ride to church and the rest of us stood around, sipping coffee while they told us a bit about their lives. They had met in boarding school in Wrangell, over a thousand miles from where we stood. Before Peter left for church, he showed us a bucket filled with small blackfish that he had caught. They told us that he could catch trash bags full of fish and they'd post online for others to come and pick some up. I thought of how some of my cousins would drop fish off in our refrigerator when we weren't home. One of the grandkids told us that elders would eat them raw, but he preferred them cooked. It reminded me of my grandfather, who would happily slurp down raw clams at the beach before we could bring them home.

After we left their house, we wandered around the village. The air was cold, but still unseasonably warm. A few people passing by asked if we were teachers. I gathered that the vast majority of outsiders, if not all of them, in the village were teachers. The village had two stores. We stopped by both of them, browsing the jarringly high prices for chips, soda, and jam. These prices were why food from the river and tundra were so crucial to people in the region. In the second store, above a doorway leading to a back room, there were about a dozen framed photos, with a handmade sign that read "Tuluksak Elders." Based on the dates below the photos, many of them had passed away years ago. In the tribal building in Aquinnah, we have a gallery that is almost exactly the same. Every time I go to the tribe, I find myself browsing the black-and-white portraits. I didn't know who any of the Tuluksak elders were, but I felt strangely emotional looking at their pictures. I loved that the residents wanted to honor and remember local elders that way in a local store. I think it spoke to the strength of community as well as the different roles that stores play in small communities.

Before heading back to the airport, we sat on some snowy steps and ate peanut butter sandwiches. Some of the dogs trotted up, keeping their distance but clearly eager for any food we might be willing to share. At the airport, while we waited for our plane to come pick us up for the ride back to Bethel, another plane landed. This plane was so loaded up that the tail was weighed down until it was almost resting on the ice. We helped the pilot unload what seemed like an endless series of packages from the plane, stacking them on the ice. A moment later, a man on a four-wheeler with a long sled showed up. It turned out that he was the village package guy. We helped him load the heavy packages, which included a couple of packed suitcases, Amazon packages, cases of soda, and other unmarked boxes, onto his sled. The pilot asked if he was okay for food, since apparently some deliveries had been canceled because of the weather. He said yes, but I wondered what the solution would have been if he had said no.

A few minutes after we loaded up the sled, our plane arrived to fly us back to Bethel. On the ride home, I tried to take in more of the beautiful tundra. This time, I noticed a few people on snow machines and one dog sled zipping across the snowy ground. I wondered if they were going to church too.

Over the next few days, I spent my time exploring Bethel. In the mornings, I walked through the darkness to the Yukon-Kuskokwim Fitness Center. Bethel has about fifteen miles of roads, and they were all covered with snow and ice. There are no roads out of town. Because there is no way to drive a car to Bethel, they need to be shipped, which is expensive. The roads—bumpy, gravelly, and icy—are also pretty tough on vehicles. Many people walk, even throughout the freezing winter. I came to enjoy the slow pace of walking in the packed snow on the wide shoulder of the roads, saying a quiet good morning to the people I passed. The sun didn't come up until nearly eleven in the morning, and I enjoyed how long the quiet mornings lasted, even though I could see how the short days would quickly grow old.

One afternoon, Sophie brought Yup'ik foods from her grandmother's freezer over to my bed-and-breakfast, where we had a small feast of muktuk, dried salmon, dried whitefish, tundra greens, and seal oil. These were the foods she had been telling me about since the first time we spoke, the foods she was trying to protect. She considered them to be her soul foods, things she had loved eating for as long as she could remember. I loved it all, savoring the unique texture of the muktuk, the flavor of the seal oil, and the smokiness of the dried salmon. But even more than the differently delicious flavors, I just felt privileged to be in Bethel and eating foods that had sustained people in the region for countless generations. Knowing that these foods were in danger made it all the more special.

Throughout my visit, as she showed me around her hometown, Sophie also asked me about my tribe, Martha's Vineyard, and New York City. One afternoon, as we shuffled along the frozen river, my coat zipped up against the wind, we talked about challenges both of our communities faced, like housing and low wages. We also shared traditional stories and legends from our tribes. It seemed like by taking up the fight against the mine, a fight that was unpopular with many who wanted the promised economic benefits, Sophie was shouldering a huge burden. I think that burden made her seek connection with people outside the community.

Sharing some of our stories with Sophie made me realize how much I do know. I brought her a small jar of multicolored clay from the cliffs that one of my cousins had made and explained the story of how Moshup had stained the cliffs red with whale blood. Whales had long since been fished to near-extinction in the waters around Martha's Vineyard, so it felt especially meaningful to eat muktuk in a Native community thousands of miles away from my own.

This trip helped me see how lucky I was to have what I do, to have grown up with tribal community, culture and language, not to mention access to our traditional foods like clams, fish, and cranberries. Part of that was also because I never really thought of those things as traditional foods. We didn't have many traditional recipes and even when I went out for clams, I never really felt like I was getting them in any kind of traditional way. I always resented the stereotype or assumption that if Natives didn't do things the way we did them hundreds of years ago, we weren't really Native. But my time in Alaska helped me realize that I was holding myself to that flawed standard.

One afternoon, Sophie and I went to Lucy's Cache, a small gift store in the airport. Lucy, the owner, had been there for decades. She was busy making a kuspuk (a hooded overshirt) for a family member and was overjoyed to see Sophie, greeting her with a huge hug. Around the shop, above the earrings, bags, scarves, and soap for sale, Lucy had hung old photos, newspaper clippings, and Yup'ik clothing and footwear. Sophie and Lucy went through all the photos, with Lucy asking Sophie if she remembered various elders and community members. Like the store in Tuluksak with elder portraits, I appreciated how unexpected places like a store could be places of community memory and history just as much as, if not more than, a museum or cultural center. For most of my life, my family's store on the cliffs had played a similar role.

While I was in Bethel, there was a ribbon-cutting ceremony at the new Yukon Kuskokwim Health Corporation Customer Lodging building. The building was essentially a hotel for patients and their families who came from villages to go to the regional hospital in Bethel. Before the new building was open, there were very few options for them to stay in Bethel. According to some of the speeches at the ceremony, elders often had to sleep on cots on the hospital floor. Before the ceremony, I went on a tour of the facility, checking out the rooms, which seemed almost identical to some of the nicer hotels I had stayed in. While community members on my tour marveled at how nice everything was, my attention was caught by the signs written in both Yup'ik and English.

The Yukon-Kuskokwim Health Corporation (YKHC) is a nonprofit organization that has been authorized by dozens of tribes in the region to work with the Indian Health Services to provide services. Because of this unique arrangement, YKHC receives federal funding designated for Indigenous people in Alaska and the tribes it acts on behalf of. Today, YKHC is the largest employer in Bethel. This is where Sophie worked as a dental assistant before she became her tribe's self-governance director. Although YKHC does tangible good in the community and the mood at the ribbon cutting was festive, Sophie told me that she wished YKHC was more transparent with how it spends money. She also said that she believed tribes should have more control over their own money and health care. Individual tribes, she believes, need to reclaim some of their power and sovereignty. It seemed that everywhere I looked I found another layer of complexity.

At the ceremony, I also met Beverly Hoffman, another anti-mine activist I had interviewed in my original article. She had to run to another appointment, but she invited Sophie and me over for coffee the next day. At her house, Beverly served us sourdough toast made from a 122-year-old starter and some dried salmon. We talked briefly about the mine, but mostly we swapped stories.

She asked me about my tribe and our homelands, looking Aquinnah up on Google Maps on her laptop. As we zoomed in and out on the satellite view of my house, I explained how my grandparents' house was moved by oxen when the state built the road and that we were the last town in the state to receive electricity. I showed them the distance between Aquinnah and the more populous, well-known parts of the island. Like Sophie, it seemed that Beverly was as interested in learning about where I was from as I was interested in Bethel.

On my last morning, I walked down to the river, where I sat on the seawall and watched the sunrise. It was the coldest morning yet and the sky was perfectly clear. The sun wouldn't come up for over an hour, but I could see a dim red glow behind the horizon. The river was quiet, but after about ten minutes, I saw a single snow machine headlight in the distance. It took longer than I expected for it to pass me, the morning light growing with the snow machine's accompanying drone. Because of the distance, it almost seemed like it wasn't moving, just a gentle light in the distance. But it steadily moved toward me and as it passed me, I saw how fast it was moving, and how far the light in front of it extended, illuminating fifty feet of frozen river as it zipped past.

Later that day, at the Bethel library, Sophie pulled a giant binder from a shelf, just one of several enormous tomes marked with Donlin Gold logos. These were some of the environmental impact statements that Donlin had prepared. Sophie flipped through the binder, showing me a page that had a key for different statuses for land that the proposed pipeline would travel over. There were dozens of different border and land designations, including four types of federal land and three types of state land, not to mention Native allotment land, ANCSA land, and private land. This was all the stuff she had to learn, she told me, just to try to protect the river. It was easy to see why she felt that these systems were designed to confuse them.

After that, we went to the tribe, where Sophie had a council meeting. In the hallway there was an enormous Mother Kuskokwim banner, painted with the original design that was now on the shirts and bags that Sophie brought on village trips. During the meeting, I waited out in the lobby, chatting with the receptionist about what it was like to live in Bethel.

Before I headed to the airport, Sophie and I stopped for dinner. While we waited for our food, I asked Sophie if she'd ever think about leaving. She told me she would only do it if she left to do something that would ultimately help the community. Sovereignty, money, political power—it was all just a means to an end of protecting the land and our communities. For all the tension and strife that I had thought about before visiting Bethel, the trip turned out to be much more about community. Instead of providing answers about tribal sovereignty, the trip helped give me some perspective and refocus the questions I was asking. Helping Peter defrost his pipes and delivering fruit to Tuluksak isn't less important than protecting the Kuskokwim; they're all part of the same bigger picture. Sovereignty is a crucial part of that, but it's not the complete answer. Like the Wampis and Ryukyuans had told me, it was a tool. We need to speak out and work to make our tribal governments better, but real change comes at the community level.

12

SOVEREIGNTY ISN'T JUST "I'M GOING TO DO WHAT I WANT"

The more I tried to tackle big questions about tribal sovereignty, the more distinct they felt from the other questions I was working through about Indigenous identity.

After grad school, I had started to read more about other Indigenous communities, to see how they thought about and shared their stories of identity and sovereignty. I had also realized by then that to understand some of the big questions of community and belonging that I had about my own experiences, I needed to go outside my tribe.

Around that time, I was seeing a lot of news about two complicated conflicts around tribal sovereignty and identity. One was about Cherokee Freedmen. Before the Civil War, the Cherokee Nation had enslaved about four thousand people. After the war, in 1866, the tribe signed a treaty with the US that said, in part, that all their former enslaved people, "and their descendants, shall have all the rights of native Cherokees." Since then Cherokee Freedmen, as they came to be called, have faced fluctuating levels of inclusion and discrimination from the Cherokee Nation. This issue had flared up again because one woman had mounted a legal challenge against the tribe's policy of exclusion.

Marilyn Vann grew up knowing that she was part of the Cherokee Nation, but never enrolled. Becoming a tribal citizen means submitting enrollment paperwork. After that, you get a tribal ID card. So there is a difference between being eligible for enrollment and actually enrolled. After she retired and her daughter was off to college, Vann tried to enroll in the tribe. But when she applied for membership in 2001, she was denied. The reason, she came to find out, was because the tribe was excluding Freedmen. Different people give different reasons for the exclusion, but Vann believes it came down to simple racism. She eventually sued the tribe, and after a long, drawn-out legal battle, a US federal judge ruled in 2017 that Cherokee Freedmen should be eligible for Cherokee enrollment, reversing an earlier decision by the Cherokee Nation Supreme Court that upheld a constitutional amendment barring Freedmen from citizenship unless they could prove their "blood" status.

In 2021, the Cherokee Nation removed the phrase "Cherokee by blood" from its constitution. That decision effectively ended the system of exclusion that Freedmen had faced and Freedmen began to enroll in the tribe. Today there are over ten thousand Cherokee Freedmen citizens.

In 2017, I called Vann, who is a retired engineer at the US Department of the Treasury and the current president of the Descendants of Freedmen of the Five Civilized Tribes. As one of the most prominent advocates for Cherokee Freedmen rights, Vann had been speaking out, sometimes alone, for years about the injustice her community was facing.

When I first spoke to Vann, she compared the 2017 ruling to *Brown v. Board of Education* in terms of its civil rights impact. I had gone into those conversations not quite sure what to make of the Freedmen—I didn't think having "Indian blood" made you Native, but I also wasn't entirely sure what did. Before that, I had only ever heard of people falsely claiming tribal membership, not being legally barred from it. Turns out that Freedmen weren't the only ones facing challenges over the right to tribal citizenship.

Tribal disenrollment is when a tribal government terminates a person's citizenship or membership in that tribe. At first, I thought disenrollment was an isolated phenomenon, but I soon learned how widespread it is. Over ten thousand people have been disenrolled from over one hundred tribes across the country. And the true totals are likely higher, given how hard it is to track tribal enrollment data, especially across tribes.

But a few prominent examples stand out. Since the Picayune Rancheria of the Chukchansi Indians built a successful casino in 2003, it has disenrolled many of its own citizens, who claim remaining members are simply trying to get a larger share of casino profits, which have totaled hundreds of millions of dollars. Reported numbers for the monthly payments members receive have ranged from a few hundred to over ten thousand, depending on casino revenues at the time. As for disenrollment estimates, some estimate that over one thousand tribal members have been disenrolled, a shocking total for a tribe of less than two thousand people. For individual members, this kind of culling would mean additional thousands of dollars in profit per year. In 2011, an eighty-seven-year-old woman, one of the last living speakers of the tribe's language, was disenrolled.

As insecure as I have felt about my Wampanoag identity, it never occurred to me that it was something I could lose, something that someone could take away. Although I was learning about the epidemic of tribal disenrollments for the first time, activists had been fighting for years to stop what many have called a new form of genocide. One of those people is Gabe Galanda, a member of the Round Valley Indian Tribes of California and lawyer who has represented many families facing disenrollment.

I called Galanda and he told me that disenrollment is an existential threat to Indian Country. He said that Native people across the country should do everything in their power to make tribes realize that this is not our way. If tribal identity is nothing more than a political identity, he argued, then it can be taken away by a political process. Galanda said that we needed to find a way to understand and build tribal community around kinship, beyond politics. Disenrollment, he went on, wasn't just harming disenrolled families, but the entire community. "The absence of human rights protection means to me that we're dulling our brains, we're draining our brains. We're not coming up with the best ideas," he said. "Maybe our best criticisms resulting in some reform of tribal government are never expressed, because we're afraid of it."

Through Galanda, I spoke with some people facing disenrollment from their tribes. Some of his clients were from the Confederated Tribes of the Grand Ronde Community of Oregon, which was trying to disenroll them thanks to a tragic, colonial quirk of fate. The Confederated Tribes were formed in 1854 and 1855 when the individual tribes signed treaties with the US government to create a sixty-thousand-acre reservation. After a brutal forced march in 1857 from a temporary reservation to their new home, an executive order was signed confirming the Grand Ronde treaties. Chief Tumulth, one of the signees, was hanged by the US Army after a tribal attack on settler camps, and never made it to the new reservation, where the basis of today's membership roll was created. Over 150 years later, the disenrollment committee used this history to challenge Chief Tumulth's descendants' status in the tribe. Like with the Chukchansi, the Grand Ronde disenrollments followed the opening of a tribal casino. In 2013, the Grand Ronde enrollment committee notified sixty-six citizens that they failed to meet enrollment criteria and would be disenrolled unless they were able to provide acceptable documentation. Although the disenrollment action would be reversed a few years later after a long legal battle, the scars lingered. Some family members remained bitter, preferring to withdraw from tribal activities rather than try to reengage with a tribe that wanted to kick them out.

Disenrollment helped me understand what I always sort of knew but had never nailed down—that tribal government was not this inarguably good thing, that sovereignty was not simply something to be proud of, that it meant tribal governments were infallible. It was something I had seen in my own tribe and in other tribes like in Alaska. I learned a feature of disenrollments was that the tribe almost always said it was their sovereign right to decide who belongs and who does not. It was the same argument that anti-Freedmen politicians made. Galanda told me that it was hard to fight disenrollment because there was often no remedy or place to seek recourse within the tribe.

Later, I asked Matthew Fletcher at the University of Michigan about tribes using sovereignty as a kind of cover. "When things start to go to shit is when you're asserting sovereignty, and you're doing things like disenrolling people or denying financial accountability for your slips and falls at the casino," he said. "When you go down that road, and when a government actor is saying 'we're doing this because we're sovereign,' nine times out of ten in the twenty-first century, it's because we're doing something really shitty to someone and they're trying to cloak it in something that's invisible. I mean, sovereignty is not even a real thing. It's just your ability to persuade somebody."

These conversations completely changed the way that I thought about tribal governments and sovereignty. It also helped me think about tribal governments as fully fledged governments and that tribal sovereignty could be used as a cover for abuses and discrimination against Indigenous people. This perspective shift allowed me to see things I never would have been able to otherwise.

In 2020, when the pandemic ripped through the world, I thought of the Freedmen. Tribes across the country were receiving federal aid money and shipments of vaccine doses, and in many cases, tribes were being hailed as more successful in their vaccine rollouts than the federal government. I received several checks from my tribe, direct COVID-19 payments like the ones sent out by the federal government to all American citizens. My family and I called them Wamp Bucks.

But, I wondered, given all the historical discrimination the Freedmen had faced, if they were receiving the same services and benefits that non-Freedmen Cherokee citizens were getting. I emailed Vann and she wrote back, saying that Cherokee Freedmen were indeed getting vaccines, but Seminole Freedmen were being turned away at tribal clinics. She recommended I reach out to her friend LeEtta Osborne-Sampson, a Seminole Freedman who sat on the Seminole Nation tribal council, to learn more.

Over the phone, LeEtta told me about how she had gone to the Indian Health Services clinic in Wewoka, the Seminole Nation capital, where she was told that she was not eligible for a vaccine. Meanwhile, members of LeEtta's extended family were dying from the virus. At first I was nervous; this was real life and death news, and I didn't know if I was up for it. But I asked LeEtta to stay in touch.

Over the next month, I spent hours on the phone with LeEtta and other Freedmen in Oklahoma. Another Seminole Freedman council member sent me an audio recording of when he called the clinic to ask if he could get a COVID-19 shot. The clinic, he was told, did not "honor the Freedmen" and he could get a vaccine only if he lived with a full tribal member. One young woman told me that she did not want to take her grandmother to try to get a vaccine because she didn't want to subject her grandmother to being turned away by her own people. She told me she hoped that her grandmother would not have to die as a second-class citizen in the tribe.

I also looked into the stories of Freedmen from the Chickasaw, Choctaw, and Muscogee Nations. While Cherokee Freedmen had the most rights thanks to the 2017 ruling that gave them full citizenship and benefits, the Seminole Freedmen were a step below, considered citizens with the right to vote and hold seats on council, but without access to other benefits. LeEtta and others sent me pictures of their tribal ID cards, which read "0/0 Indian Blood" on the front and "voting benefits only" on the back.

Freedmen from the other three tribes were in even worse situations, not considered tribal citizens at all. Once again tribal leaders from these tribes often said it was an issue of sovereignty, that the tribe had the sovereign right to decide who was a citizen and who was not. While I was interviewing Freedmen and learning more about the situation, the Seminole Nation ignored my repeated requests for an interview or any kind of comment. When I asked IHS about the Freedmen being excluded, their response was that the agency was "not involved in determining tribal enrollment of individual citizens."

In mid-March 2021, I published an article about this, and it got thousands of retweets, shares, and hundreds of thousands of views online. It was also picked up by other outlets, including local TV stations in Oklahoma. In the aftermath, the Seminole Nation put out two statements, finally responding in the face of public attention.

They said, "The United States Indian Health Service is the entity in charge of administering COVID-19 vaccinations to the Seminole Nation, and it is the Nation's understanding that such vaccine dissemination is being administered entirely consistent with federal law and policy in providing such vaccinations." The statement added, "Any allegation that the Seminole Nation is denying access of the COVID-19 vaccine to a group of people is entirely false." It seemed to me like the Seminole Nation was blaming the IHS, saying that they did not run the clinic, while the IHS put the responsibility on the Seminole Nation, saying that the IHS had no involvement with determining or judging tribal membership.

Later that year, in October, the IHS sent out a press release saying that they had been reviewing the situation and determined that the Seminole Freedmen were eligible to receive health services. According to the press release, the IHS would begin instructing the clinic in Wewoka and other clinics and hospitals in Oklahoma to provide services to Seminole Freedmen. After I got the press release, I called LeEtta. She was thrilled. Now, she said, she was focused on getting even more of their rights back.

About two years after the IHS finally gave the Seminole their health care rights, I went to Oklahoma to visit the Seminole Freedmen. I was hoping to learn about not just the exclusion and discrimination the Freedmen were facing, but the inclusion that they had felt in the past, their deep connections to the land and the tribe. It was one thing for me to hear and read how Freedmen were always part of the tribe, but it was another to see their land, and see how their histories were interwoven with the history of the Seminole Nation.

On a cool Saturday morning, I drove from my hotel in downtown Oklahoma City to LeEtta's house in a suburban neighborhood. From there, we got in her car to drive down to the Seminole Nation. Along the way, I noticed how many different reservations we were passing through. As we drove, I asked LeEtta more about her family history and her hopes for the Seminole Freedmen. She told me that she first began doing more research into Freedmen history when her father, who was suffering from dementia, started talking about how his people had left him behind, forgot about him. She didn't understand what he was talking about at first, but realized that he was devastated that no one came to visit him when he was sick, the way he had done for other community members as a child. Growing up, LeEtta said, she never heard the word *Freedmen*. It wasn't until she was an adult that she even knew what it meant. As a kid, she felt like she was just part of the tribal community. This is what made the exclusion she faced later in life so painful.

She told me about the stomp dances she grew up doing, staying at the church for three days, playing in the mud, eating pig that had been cooking in the ground for hours. "Those are the days that I sometimes yearn for," she said. "Because it was the best days, playing with people, it didn't even matter what you look like. Nobody talked about people's color."

She told me that later in the day we could stop at the old church her family used to go to that was right next to their allotment land. "It is sad that we're being treated as outsiders in our own land, in our own community, and in our church," LeEtta told me. "You know, when I get old, and if I get feebleminded, I'll probably be living my memories down here in this red dirt. So that's something that can never be taken from me."

After driving for a little over an hour, our first stop was a small cluster of buildings on an otherwise empty road cutting through the flat countryside. We parked and as we walked around, LeEtta pointed out the various buildings: the gym, Head Start building, old council building. There was a large community center building where I saw signs for an Indian market.

It all seemed rather impressive. Even though I knew the Seminole Nation was many times larger than my tribe, it was still something to see so much tribal infrastructure. But LeEtta lamented that none of their people lived there. Most of them, she said, lived in the city like her or in other surrounding towns. She felt the tribe should be working to build more housing and create more jobs there.

Across the street from the market was a circle of what looked like headstones. The Nation is made up of fourteen bands, distinct familial and community units led by a band chief, and named after the band's original leader. We walked over and stood in the middle, where I could see that each stone was engraved with the name and brief history of each band. LeEtta pointed out the Caesar Bruner stone, for her band. I strolled around, pausing to read the histories. "All these bands are mighty people that worked in our nation, that stood in our nation to make it what it is today," she said. "They had to have been working with each other, all of them, back to back. What are we doing today? We don't have to do this anymore. We need to work together for everybody's benefit."

We stood there in silence for a few moments before walking across the road to the community center, where the Native market was taking place. Walking in, there was an entrance hallway where one vendor was set up. LeEtta introduced herself as a councilwoman and me as her friend from New York. The room was huge, with dozens of folding tables set up along the walls and in rows in the center. Glancing around, I could see that people were selling a range of jewelry, bags, blankets, T-shirts, stickers, and other items.

LeEtta and I started slowly walking around, browsing the tables. At one table, a mother and daughter were beading at their table, which was filled with earrings and bracelets. LeEtta introduced herself as a councilwoman and said that she had been trying to organize beading classes for the community and would love to have them come and teach. They seemed bashful at first, saying their stuff wasn't good enough to teach, but LeEtta kept pressing them and saying it was okay as long as the whole community was learning together. She exchanged numbers with the mother before we moved on to the next table. A few minutes later, I saw LeEtta give the same spiel at another table.

While we browsed the market, LeEtta's cousin, who was also a Seminole Freedmen council member, met up with us. He was the one who had sent me the recording of the call with the clinic that said he wasn't eligible for a vaccine. LeEtta chatted with him while I continued to browse the tables, stopping to buy a couple pairs of earrings. There was a small stand in the corner of the room where some people were selling chili and cornbread from what looked like a small kitchen. Other people were milling around, chatting with one another.

It was nice, if unexpected, to experience the Seminole Nation this way. For a long time, I had been thinking of the Seminole Nation only in terms of its government and policies, and how those things were impacting the Freedmen. But walking around the market, it reminded me so much of my own tribe and other Native gatherings I had been to.

Even though I had been reporting on the life and death consequences of Seminole Freedmen exclusion, it was at the market that I really felt what that meant. LeEtta and her cousin were the only Freedmen at the market. There was nothing stopping the Freedmen from going to the market—like there had been from them getting a COVID-19 vaccine after the IHS policy change—but they had been made to feel that they weren't welcome and so they wanted no part in it. It seemed to me that as much as LeEtta was fighting to get Freedmen rights restored, she was also fighting with her own community to get them to trust the tribe and make efforts to engage with it. Offering beading classes or computer classes (another idea she mentioned in the car) was just one way to entice people to participate, to show them that being part of the tribe could be a good thing, not just a source of pain and racism.

It also occurred to me that this was a reminder that tribal identity is best rooted in community and events like the Native market, not tribal government and council policies. Those structures should support, fund, and uplift community events, but too often they get in the way of community, not to mention actively destroy it, like by disenfranchising the Freedmen. Since I had been so focused on learning about and exposing the discrimination the Freedmen were facing, I found it hard to think of the tribe as a community rather than a hostile political entity, even though I knew that it could be both and that not every member of the community wanted the situation with the Freedmen to continue.

But that's the position that years of anti-Freedmen policies had put the Freedmen in. They did not have the luxury of seeing past tribal government. I said this to LeEtta in the car, that I could understand why some Freedmen might feel bitter. But she immediately replied that she does blame them for feeling that way, that if they want to be part of the community, they need to rise above and work to make the community better. Bitterness had gotten them here and it would take something different to get them out.

From the market, we went to lunch with LeEtta's cousin and his girlfriend at a Chinese buffet that LeEtta said they often ate at after council meetings. As we ate plates of noodles, chicken, and vegetables, we talked about some of the challenges that stood in the way of making change. They told me that many people worked for the tribe and were afraid of retaliation and losing their jobs or their family members' jobs if they spoke up for the Freedmen. I said the same thing happened in my tribe, where people were afraid to criticize tribal leadership because they worked at the tribe. It's the same problem Gabe Galanda had told me prevented many people from resisting disenrollments in their tribes.

We also talked about how some people simply could not be bothered to participate, whether that was because of apathy, busy schedules, or some other reason. I told them how my tribe regularly struggles to get a quorum at our general membership meetings and about tribes I've heard about where they hand out per capita payments at the door to motivate people to come to the meetings. I think it helped them to see that other tribes were going through the same problems.

After lunch, while we waited for LeEtta's cousin and his girlfriend to run an errand, she and I went to Wewoka, the capital of the Seminole Nation. As we drove slowly along a dirt road off the main, paved road, LeEtta pointed out houses that looked like they were falling apart, what she called "sick houses." We drove past the health clinic that had been the subject of my article. Even though Freedmen now had full access to the clinic's services, LeEtta said that many were still hesitant to take advantage of it—the relationship completely broken under years of mistrust and acrimony.

In Wewoka, we stopped at the Seminole Nation Museum, located in a one-story building in a quiet, suburban-looking part of town. Inside, the museum had different artifacts, paintings, and historical documents tracing the tribe's history from the Seminole wars in Florida in the nineteenth century to their removal to Oklahoma. There were also exhibits on Seminole culture and life, including band structure and cultural events like the Green Corn Dance.

LeEtta was pleasantly surprised at how much Freedmen material and history was there. This wasn't like this before, she said, it was like we didn't exist. Even in just a few years, the narrative had changed, she told me. As we walked around, I also noticed that Freedmen history was just as LeEtta had described it to me—central and integral to Seminole history. They had fought the same battles and lived the same struggles and triumphs as the rest of the tribe. That history was reflected in the content and tone of the museum. Several times, as she passed by a piece of Freedmen history, LeEtta would exclaim "This was not here before!" her delight growing as we went through the museum.

She said she had been trying to get Freedmen to donate more of their artifacts and documents to the museum and would now definitely redouble those efforts after seeing how included they were. In the gift shop, she asked a staff member about the increase in Freedmen history. It turned out that the woman behind the counter was the curator responsible for the change. She told us that it was one of her main goals to keep increasing the Freedmen material. She and LeEtta agreed that the more people could understand about their shared history, the less strife there would be. Like with the women at the market, LeEtta exchanged contact information with the curator, promising to stay in touch.

After the museum, we drove to Sasakwa, to LeEtta's grandfather's land allotment, where LeEtta had spent childhood summers with a gaggle of cousins. Today, the property is collectively owned by all those cousins—around forty in total. The landscape around us became more and more rural as we drove toward Sasakwa. As we drove, the sun began to set, golden light streaming through the windshield into our eyes. Somewhere, we made a sharp right-hand turn onto a red dirt road. The road gently rolled through the grassy countryside that was interrupted only by the rare wooden house. After a few minutes, we came to another right-hand turn, this time down into a bumpy, muddy driveway separated from the road by a cattle guard.

As the road flattened out, I saw that we were in a large clearing, covered with scrubby grass and dirt patches. In the middle was a dilapidated, one-story wooden house. Scattered around the house was an assortment of cars, lawn mowers, and other equipment, all in varying stages of rust and disrepair. Something about the land, clearly used, loved, abandoned, and loved again by multiple generations, reminded me of pieces of land in Aquinnah. Looking across the field, I saw two chestnut horses nibbling on the grass, the setting sun beginning to dip below the barren trees behind them.

As we got closer to the house, I saw a large white truck parked in front. It was clearly newer than the other vehicles decomposing in the grass. LeEtta seemed surprised to see anyone there. It turned out to be one of her cousins, a man she had not seen for years. Although the family collectively owned the land, LeEtta didn't think anyone else spent time down there. He bred horses and as we talked, I realized that in addition to the two I first saw, there were another half dozen or so trotting around. While LeEtta caught up with her cousin, I walked around the house, taking pictures of the soft red dirt under my boots, the horses, and the rusting equipment. When I circled back to them, LeEtta was saying how they should apply for state funding to fix up the house and the land. Her cousin seemed interested and told her to check it out and let him know.

The sun slipped below the horizon and as the sky darkened, the air grew cooler. We said our goodbyes and began the drive back to the city. In the car, LeEtta told me that she had been trying to get her cousin on board with the state program for years, but he had always been resistant. Because it was a program for tribal members, he never trusted it. She was thrilled that he had given his blessing for her to look into it, saying she had more hope for the land now. On the ride back, we talked about that hope, and how much of it rested on the next generation. LeEtta seemed to accept that she might not see all the changes she is working for, but she wants to create a foundation for those to follow and build on.

The next day, I met Marilyn Vann at a Panera Bread near her house in Oklahoma City. It was our first time meeting in person, and since I had first spoken with her, she and the Cherokee Freedmen were in a very different position. In 2021, Vann was appointed to the tribe's Environmental Protection Commission, making her the first Freedman to work in the Cherokee government. At the time, Cherokee Nation Chief Chuck Hoskin Jr., who appointed Vann, called her a "highly qualified trailblazer." She had also run for tribal council, finishing third, which she told me she thought was very good for a first-time candidate. But she said that the progress she had seen from Cherokee Freedmen was beautiful and more important. It also meant they were in a very different place than the Seminole Freedmen.

Cherokee Freedmen were voting, getting medical services, and participating in community events and groups. This was not just benefiting the Freedmen, Vann explained, it was benefiting the entire tribe. "The tribe was the one that was losing," she said. "The focus could have been on let's make our tribe bigger, let's make it better, let's make our tribe the most powerful tribe in the country, instead of us having to fight for things that are legally ours." Her words reminded me of what Galanda had said about disenrollment dulling our brains.

And now that the tribe was including the Freedmen, she believed they could focus on building the whole community. Vann talked about how by honoring treaty agreements to Freedmen the tribe was able to do things like demand a Cherokee delegate in the US Congress. In other words, when the tribe lived up to its own obligations, they had a much stronger position to tell the US to do the same and respect tribal sovereignty. "Of course, as an Indian, I believe in tribal sovereignty, but I believe there's responsibility that goes there," she said. "Sovereignty isn't just 'I'm going to do what I want.' "

I also asked Vann about her advocacy for Freedmen from all five tribes. She said she hoped that the other tribes would follow in the Cherokee Nation's footsteps. She had sympathy for LeEtta's situation and said it was preventing the whole Seminole Nation from making progress the way the Cherokee Nation is. "The tribe will never move forward the way it could be while this energy is going to be used to hold back the Freedmen," she said.

The kind of tension, bitterness, and drama that LeEtta dealt with were no longer part of Vann's daily struggle. She could simply focus on the work and the community. She no longer had to worry about treaty rights and court cases; she could simply focus on real, action-based sovereignty.

After talking to Vann, I headed to Tulsa, where I was spending the night. As I drove, the sun set behind me, casting faint red light across the horizon. I didn't know exactly what I had gone to Oklahoma looking for, but I was more convinced than ever that the answers to the big questions I was asking wouldn't be found in tribal government.

13

WE KNOW WE ARE NOT ALONE

Every year, the United Nations Permanent Forum on Indigenous Issues, a two-week international gathering, is held at the United Nations headquarters in New York City. The Permanent Forum is the world's largest gathering of Indigenous leaders, bringing together thousands of Indigenous leaders, activists, and representatives from all corners of the globe. Over two weeks of all-day sessions, Indigenous delegates make statements in the hopes of using the UN system and international platform to bring global attention to key issues and put pressure on their home governments.

Beyond the official sessions, Indigenous leaders also host dozens of side events, designed to delve deeper into specific topics. And before and after the main sessions and side events, delegates gather during breaks in the café and build relationships over dinner. There's nowhere else in the world where so many Indigenous people from around the world can come together to share stories, ideas, and community with one another.

For a few years, I covered the Permanent Forum as a reporter. In daily stories from the Forum, I wrote about everything from cyclone relief in New Zealand and antimilitary protests in Okinawa to land grabs in Tanzania and the unique challenges facing Indigenous migrants to the US. I learned more than I ever thought I would about different Indigenous nations and communities. I also learned about the complex and long-standing international advocacy groups and networks fighting for Indigenous rights.

Those weeks I spent at the Forum were the first time I had been with so many Indigenous people from around the world. I met people from Indigenous communities from Ecuador, Indonesia, Tanzania, Mexico, Sweden, and so many more places I could only dream of visiting. Every year, I was one of only a small handful of reporters covering the event, which did not draw the crowds of journalists that larger UN events like COP (Conference of the Parties) climate conferences or General Assembly sessions. To help elevate the event and the messages of Indigenous delegates, I did my best to report on as many issues and communities as possible. It was a reminder how diverse the range of Indigenous nations, identities, and experiences really is around the world. Unfortunately, it was also a reminder of the ongoing impact of colonialism around the world.

The kinds of stories I was reporting on at the Forum were urgent, often about human rights violations like violence, evictions, and land grabs. Focusing on those important stories meant that I had less time to explore the deeper questions about Indigenous identity and community that I was also interested in. I was curious what Indigenous identity looked like in other parts of the world and what I could learn from it. Each year, after the Forum ended, I stayed in touch with many of the people I met, continuing our conversations. I found that often they were just as curious about my experiences as I was about theirs. I saw the same thing from Sophie Swope and LeEtta Osborne-Sampson—they were both so focused on their own situations they had little time to learn from other communities, but they knew there were answers to be found out there.

One of the first Indigenous delegates I met was Majo Andrade Cerda, a young Kichwa woman from the Ecuadorian Amazon. Indigenous communities in the Amazon face a series of violent threats, including government persecution, invasive mining projects, agribusiness, and environmental degradation. From a couple of illegal gold miners encroaching on Indigenous territory to massive government land grabs, these issues form a multipronged threat to Indigenous life, culture, and community. Majo is one of the leaders fighting not just to protect her people, but also to build a stronger, more resilient community. Some of that work comes in the form of international advocacy, while other projects are more community-based efforts.

Majo grew up in Serena, a small Kichwa village located between two rivers: the Hatun Yaku and the Ilokulin. The community is named after the peaceful feeling that the village's first inhabitants felt when they arrived there. Majo grew up swimming in those rivers with her community after spending the morning and early afternoons harvesting local fruits and vegetables like cassava, cacao, and plantains. Today about 150 people live in the community. Looking up pictures online, I was amazed at the natural beauty of the lush rainforest, rocky riverbanks, and rippling river.

That upbringing gave Majo a powerful sense of place, identity, and community. Although Majo left Serena to go to school in the nearby town and then to Ecuador's capital city, Quito, for university, she always returned whenever she could. These days, her work takes her to international conferences and gatherings in places like New York City and Cairo, where she advocates for her community and the broader rights of Indigenous people around the world. "Everything I do is for our community because I personally think that all that I am and all that I do, it's because of my community," she told me. "Maybe in a physical way I sometimes go out from the community, but in my mind, in my thinking, the community's always in me."

The way Majo distinguished between physically and spiritually leaving the community resonated with me and gave me hope for my relationship with the tribe. At the same time, I also wondered whether I was embodying that deep connection enough.

Majo is a focal point for the Latin American and Caribbean region at the Global Indigenous Youth Caucus and a cofounder of the International Indigenous Youth Forum on Climate Change. She also works on economic and community development for the Confederation of Indigenous Nationalities of the Ecuadorian Amazon (CONFENIAE). In these roles, Majo regularly advocates at major international summits like the Permanent Forum and the UN's annual COP climate change conference. Majo also works with Yuturi Warmi, the first Indigenous guard in the region that is led by women, and Runa Yachay, a local school focused on Indigenous values, tradition, and language. Majo is also part of a network of Indigenous leaders developing their own legal protocols that outside governments and corporations must follow when negotiating with Indigenous communities. Together, all these roles and organizations form a web of advocacy, education, and community building.

I asked Majo about her international work and how it connected to her work back home in Serena. What I had seen at the Forum showed me how difficult it is to make any meaningful change through the UN's nearly endless layers of bureaucracy. To make matters even worse, everything I had learned in school and read in the news told me that even the highest levels of the UN struggled to make a difference in world affairs. Powerful countries were unlikely to listen to a UN statement of condemnation. The General Assembly and the Security Council are the most powerful arms of the UN. The Forum's entire purpose is to get Indigenous concerns through the UN system and in front of the General Assembly. And the Forum was perhaps the lowest rung of the hierarchy, laboring behind the scenes to get its message heard by the more powerful UN bodies and agencies, the same agencies that struggled to influence global politics.

But I figured that someone like Majo would not spend time and money traveling to the Forum and other international summits if they were not useful to her mission. "At the beginning, when I started to do a lot of things in my community, I thought being in the community was the only correct way of working because I studied international relations, and all my experiences with diplomacy and the UN were like they are just talking and they're not doing anything," she told me. "But in nature and in our territories, everything is interconnected. So that is the same way for the work that we're doing, you know, connecting from the local to the international level."

In other words, there cannot be just one approach to addressing the issues Indigenous communities are facing—there are just too many and they are too deeply entrenched in our societies. Although it is daunting, I find Majo's perspective rather moving, that from the smallest local levels to the biggest international stages, the work is all connected by the same commitment and devotion to land and community. One type of work is not better than the other. They are all connected and necessary.

I think it also means an understanding that each avenue cannot solve the whole problem, maybe just a piece. Put enough of those pieces together and we might get somewhere. Until then, I had never really thought about it that way. I think I was putting too much pressure and responsibility on a space like the Permanent Forum. If we expect something like the Forum to solve all our problems, we'll always fall short. The kind of progress made at the UN is different from the kind that comes from language classes or cultural revitalization, but they are all important.

The Forum itself, which has been around for over twenty years, came after decades of international advocacy for Indigenous people to have a more prominent role on the international stage. Even the term Indigenous was something that had been fought over for years. It can be easy to dismiss changes in terminology or UN policy, but when I see what international Indigenous solidarity looks like and can achieve, I understand that those fights are part of a bigger picture.

While I was first covering the Forum, it occurred to me that I had never really thought about what Indigenous means. The word was relatively new to me, but I couldn't pinpoint when it had entered my regular vocabulary. I grew up saying Native American or Indian, but by the time I had graduated from college, it seemed like Indigenous was becoming more and more popular. I knew that it was a more global term, something that united Native Americans in the US, First Nations in Canada, and Indigenous people around the world. Starting with my experiences at the UN, I've come to learn that just as American Indian and Native American were terms supported by Indigenous activists during the Red Power movement, Indigenous is not just a neutral term, but a collective identity that has been promoted through years of hard work and organizing across the world.

In 1981, before the Permanent Forum or other Indigenous mechanisms at the UN were created, José R. Martínez Cobo, the special rapporteur of the Sub-Commission on Prevention of Discrimination and Protection of Minorities, conducted one of the first major international studies of Indigenous peoples. In the study, Martínez Cobo developed a broad working definition of Indigenous peoples and nations. In part, the definition reads, "Indigenous communities, peoples and nations are those which, having a historical continuity with pre-invasion and pre-colonial societies that developed on their territories, consider themselves distinct from other sectors of the societies now prevailing on those territories, or parts of them."

Martínez Cobo expanded to say that Indigenous historical continuity might consist of factors like occupation of ancestral lands, language, shared ancestry, and other factors. This definition first struck me as incredibly broad and flexible, allowing for a range of Indigenous peoples, communities, and nations to be accepted under the umbrella term. Since Martínez Cobo's seminal report, Indigenous peoples have created more and more space for themselves at the United Nations, but the UN has resisted adopting any kind of standardized definition of Indigenous peoples, generally preferring to identify rather than define, leaving self-identification in the hands of the Indigenous peoples themselves. In that way, self-identifying as Indigenous can be seen as a kind of choice, a decision to opt into a global consciousness and collective.

Sometimes, I wondered what connected us all, and what it meant to fall under the Indigenous umbrella. I always thought that it was a definition based on colonialism, that to be Indigenous meant to be a people that had faced colonialism in some form. And while that is a part of it, I've come to think of it as more of an identification that is based on solidarity and collective identity. Part of that shared experience is definitely the ongoing struggle against colonialism, but it is so much more than that.

The kind of international collaboration that I saw at the UN reminded me of something that Gabe Galanda had said to me. "The best strategies for success in the face of an existential threat are when tribal peoples come together," he explained. "The winning strategies come on an intertribal basis, because people are willing to get together to think, talk, strategize, and act." He believes that because so many tribes in the US are squabbling over disenrollment and per capita casino payments, those conversations aren't even happening.

At the UN, I felt like I was constantly learning about parallels that I never thought of. For example, Indigenous Sámi from Norway spoke repeatedly about the massive wind farm that was violating their land rights and threatening generations of reindeer herding communities. It reminded me of the large wind farm project off the Aquinnah coast that had been in the works for years. At first, I had wondered why the tribe couldn't support the project, since green energy was something we would normally support. But over time, and especially as I listened to Sámi delegates talk about how they refused to sacrifice their land, lives, and rights in the name of the supposed green transition, I realized it was all the same fight.

A few days after I wrote an article about Indigenous Ryukyuans and their call for the US military to remove its bases on their land, I ran into Koutaro, one of the Ryukyuans I had interviewed, on the floor of the UN. He was dressed more casually, wearing jeans and a hoodie rather than the traditional Ryukyuan outfit I had previously seen him in. He mentioned that he was studying with many other diverse Indigenous people in his PhD program in Hawaii and was hoping to connect with more young Indigenous people at the UN.

I noticed a woman I knew across the floor with a few other young Indigenous delegates and I introduced them to Koutaro, who said he wished he was still wearing his traditional outfit. He asked if I would take a picture of them. That afternoon, I saw that he posted the picture on Twitter with a caption in Japanese, which Twitter translated for me as "Ryukyu people, Kanaka Maoli (Native Hawaiian people), Alaska Native peoples, Samoan/Fiji Indigenous peoples, Sámi people at the United Nations Indigenous Peoples Forum."

Later, I connected with Koutaro on Zoom. He said he really valued sharing stories about colonialism and trauma even when it was difficult. "It sucks we experienced this, but sharing these kinds of stories really empowers me because we know we are not alone," he told me.

For Koutaro, those connections are especially important because he thinks most Okinawans are not actively engaged with the anticolonial struggle. Ryukyuans are not considered Indigenous by the Japanese government and their language is seen as a dialect of Japanese, rather than a distinct language. Japan's national culture promotes the idea of a united Japanese people, which erases the history and experiences of Indigenous people like the Ryukyuans and Ainu. Because of this, many Ryukyuans do not see themselves as Indigenous. "I think we need to be more angry about the current situation because we are too comfortable," he told me. "Today nobody wants to fight for social justice. Everyone is so focused on individualism. Many people don't want to fight for a collective good."

Koutaro's dream is that Ryukyu will eventually have language and cultural immersion schools. He hopes that this will help new generations of Okinawans learn not just their language, but to embrace their Ryukyuan identity. Focusing on language, he believes, is also the key to help shifting focus back to collective, community-based goals from the more capitalistic individualism that mainstream Japanese culture promotes. He knows this will take a long time, but Koutaro's own journey to awareness reflects the kind of journey he thinks many other Okinawans should make.

He grew up in Nishibaru, the traditional name for Nishihara, a town in the southern part of Okinawa island, just a few kilometers from the US Marine Corps Air Station Futenma, a massive base home to thousands of American marines. Growing up, Koutaro was into basketball and American music. Because the stores near the US military bases sold American clothes, he grew up thinking that the bases were generally good for the community. He was aware of the protests that many Okinawans led against the bases, but never had any desire to join in. He learned some traditional Okinawan dance and culture, but didn't pay much attention. He preferred to play basketball and listen to hip-hop. It wasn't until he went to Hawaii that he began to understand more about Indigenous resistance.

It was practically an accident that he went to Hawaii at all. When his grades were not good enough for local universities, his mother suggested the University of Hawaii at Hilo because they had some family there who were part of the large Okinawan diaspora in Hawaii. Once in Hawaii, he connected with the local Okinawan community and began going to cultural and community gatherings, where he says that for the first time in his life, he felt really proud of who he was. But when people at those events would ask him for updates about things happening back at home, he realized he did not know that much.

Koutaro began going to Ryukyuan culture and history workshops organized by local activists and academics. It was in these workshops that he finally learned about the history of Ryukyu, Japan's colonization, and how the US military got there. He wondered why he never knew any of that before. "The fact that I didn't know anything made me really angry," he told me.

After learning about the history and problems with the US military bases on Okinawa, Koutaro's new, radical stance led to conflict with friends and family, including a near fistfight with an uncle in front of his grandmother. Back then, he says, he thought that activism was all about political ideology, but he couldn't see how to get past the division that it caused in the community. But thinking about how he was so pro-US before, Koutaro realized that resistance is about identity more than political ideology. Okinawans needed to awaken their sense of collective Indigenous identity, but he wasn't sure how to do that. After observing Native Hawaiian activism and organization, Koutaro thought he figured it out. "I realized language is the center of Indigenous culture," he told me. "And culture unites Indigenous people. So revitalizing the Indigenous language means almost the same thing as protecting the Indigenous land from any desecration. I originally didn't have much love for my language, but when I saw the relationship between the language and political activism, I felt that this was the missing piece."

Koutaro firmly believes that learning the language is not just about learning vocabulary and grammar. It is a way to change the way you think. He says that learning Uchinaaguchi has already changed how he sees the world, and he can't wait for even bigger perspective shifts as he becomes more fluent. He doesn't know what he is going to discover, but he knows it will be powerful. When I asked, Koutaro shared one example: In Uchinaaguchi, you don't say "my mother," you say "our mother," since a mother is not just a mother for her child, but for the whole village. These are the kinds of little lessons that he is taking from the language to influence his worldview. He wants to help more Okinawans follow that same path. One time when we spoke over Zoom, his roommate Manato was on the call too. Koutaro said that Manato was involved in a lot of Ryukyuan cultural activities but wasn't so outspoken about political issues. He hoped by bringing him along to conversations like this, Manato would get more comfortable speaking out.

Koutaro said that in some ways it is easier to do his language revitalization work in Hawaii because people there understand its importance more than back home in Okinawa. In fact, he never thought that the language could be revitalized until he went to Hawaii and saw what they had managed to achieve. He said that in Okinawa many people were stuck in the Japanese mindset and may be proud to be Okinawan, but felt that it was something from the past. "Most of our people love our culture and tradition," he said. "They just don't know it's possible to keep it for the future."

Talking to Koutaro made me realize that physical distance has helped me work through some of these issues too. In the same way that it is hard for Indigenous activists to work on the big picture, in Aquinnah it can be hard to keep that perspective in mind. Of course, there is a limit to that. If I want to engage with the community, I can't stay away forever.

The way Koutaro described language also reminded me of how Majo described some of her work. Yuturi Warmi believes that territorial defense does not just mean physically protecting the land from miners and other extractive industries. It means building and strengthening community practices, including education and traditional crafts. This kind of holistic approach was echoed by almost every Indigenous person I talked to at the UN. Language is not just about language, it is about identity, community, and so much more.

And in the same way, Indigenous identity is complex and multifaceted. I was surprised by how much I identified with many of the stories I heard about people's experiences of understanding their own Indigenous identities. Because I had always struggled to claim my own, I never thought I could have so much in common with Indigenous people representing their communities at the highest international level. But I realized that working to figure out and understand identity does not make that identity any less real. I think I understood that for other people but never really believed it for myself.

In fact, Majo told me that she didn't fully realize that she was Indigenous until she left home. "In my community I was just part of the community, not even realizing we were Indigenous," she said. In many of my conversations with people from the UN, I asked about how they thought about their Indigenous identity. I was curious about the different journeys and experiences people have had.

In 2023, my second year attending the Permanent Forum, I met Amba-Rose Atkinson, a Gumbaynggirr PhD candidate from Australia. Over the next few days, I ran into Amba a few more times at the Forum and we talked about how intense the Forum was and that we wished there was more space for conversation and connection. After the Forum, we stayed in touch, finding time across a fourteen-hour time difference for Zoom meetings. We were both in the midst of finishing huge writing projects—for me, this book, and for Amba, her PhD dissertation—and used those meetings to write, sharing ideas and stories during our self-imposed breaks.

Amba grew up in Lismore, Australia, where she was raised in a spiritual way, going to Indigenous ceremonies and dances with her family, along with protests for Indigenous rights. From a young age, her family also taught her about some of the horrors of colonialism, helping to prepare her for a society that did not want Indigenous people speaking up. That combination of celebration and resistance helped form her early understanding of Indigenous identity.

Amba can remember being in kindergarten and her teacher saying that her language skills were quite good for an Aboriginal person and understanding that the comment was not really a compliment. In school Amba was also learning the national narrative about Australia's founding, a country that is only about 3 percent Indigenous today. Until university, she was often the only Indigenous person in the class.

She told me how throughout these years, her own understanding and perception of Indigenous identity shifted. At times she felt very close to her localized community, while at others, she might identify more with the national Indigenous population in Australia, or even the international Indigenous community. In high school, for example, Amba tended to identify with the collective Australian Indigenous as she was learning more about contemporary Indigenous issues, while in university, surrounded by more Indigenous students, she reverted back to a more specific, place-based Indigenous identity. I had never broken it down to anyone the way Amba did for me, but her experiences echoed a lot of what I had experienced.

After university, Amba completed a master's in public health and then got a job in the corporate world. She hated it, quickly feeling like it was sucking out her soul, that she was not having the kind of impact on Indigenous peoples and communities that she had always hoped she would. And so, after a particularly devastating bushfire season in 2020, she felt guided by the ancestors to begin a PhD program in 2021 that focused on the relationship between Country, health, and community. Amba's PhD thesis is based on interviews conducted with Indigenous elders, rangers, and knowledge holders about their relationship with Country. She described the project as a healing journey, being able to go back to her communities and spend time with Country and the people there. "I think that that identity and connection to culture is also being reflected in my relationship to Country," she told me. "But you know, I've also spent a lot of my time in the city. And so it's, like, well, how do you feel that spiritual connection when you're literally surrounded by skyscrapers? And sometimes it will manifest in the most bizarre ways and sometimes you go through weeks without being, like, oh yeah, I'm Indigenous."

That reminded me of a line from Tommy Orange's novel *There There*: "We are Indians and Native Americans, American Indians and Native American Indians, North American Indians, Natives, NDNs and Indians, Status Indians and Non-Status Indians, First Nations Indians and Indians so Indian we either think about the fact of it every single day or we never think about it at all." I always thought I had to be a certain kind of Indian and wondered if that meant the kind that thinks about it all the time or never.

These days, Amba said she has fewer of those days where she doesn't think about being Indigenous because of how much her life is now dedicated to thinking through and working on Indigenous issues. That's been my experience too. When I've had other jobs, like working in publishing or teaching, it was easy to settle into a rhythm where that part of my life wasn't as relevant. But now that I write about Indigenous people every day, it's impossible not to also be constantly thinking about my own Indigenous experience and identity. It makes me wonder how much of identity comes down to choice, the choice to be involved and engage.

Of course, not everyone has the freedom to make that kind of choice, to make a career out of thinking about Indigenous identity and community. "I think that's one of the challenges that a lot of young Indigenous people face," Amba explained. "How do you work on that relationship when you're also working and you've got all these other pressures of what it means to live in this society?"

That question, about how to balance those pressures with whatever it means to be Indigenous, also came up in a conversation I had with another person I met at the UN. While working on an article about the Māori call for more disaster relief and land rights, I met Renee Raroa, who is Ngati Porou Māori from Rangitukia on New Zealand's East Coast. Rangitukia is a rural community located about one hundred kilometers up the coast from Gisborne, a small city that is the main city in the region that is known as the East Coast. On New Zealand's North Island, the area is marked by dense forests and steep cliffs and stunning ocean views. Growing up in Rangitukia, Renee was immersed in Māori culture and community. "You're walking through the forest constantly, or you're working with the land," she said. "The relationship you have to the environment is so intertwined with your life that you take for granted that that's even a thing, until I moved to the cities and saw that, hey, this isn't the way that everyone's experiencing their daily lives. And some people have never had that opportunity to really experience that close relationship with nature."

The Gisborne area is about 50 percent Māori, while the country as a whole is only about 17 percent, with many areas being less than 10 percent. It wasn't until she moved to Gisborne as a teenager and then to a larger city for university that she realized how rare that experience was, even for other Māori. Renee became a high school science teacher and eventually transitioned into working on finding ways to incorporate technology into education. That led to working on the connections among technology, environment, and community. Today Renee works with nonprofits that are trying to create infrastructure to have data that proves the value of Indigenous environmental work and land stewardship. One of their projects is to find ways to fund Indigenous land stewardship work.

I asked Renee about how she felt using these kinds of digital and economic tools to uplift Indigenous communities, rather than working outside of the system. She connected it to language. Her grandfather grew up speaking only the Māori language and was convinced that it was better for his children to speak only English. So Renee's parents' generation grew up with that kind of instruction, while she grew up in a time with much more focus on language revitalization. She described it as a process of one generation, because of the situation they were forced into, picking one choice as the best, and then the next generation seeing that they could actually have both. So for Renee, it's not about giving in to a colonial system of capitalism, but finding ways that the system can help Indigenous people, with an understanding that it also won't solve all their issues. If they can see and understand those limits, they can use those tools to help.

"The ultimate might actually be that every place has sovereign independence and is able to live fulfilled, strong, happy, healthy lives based on their own regional resources," she told me. "The challenge is that that's not currently what most communities are dealing with. So how can we use the bits that can work for us and leave other parts behind?"

I think that was true about the UN, that there were things we could take away from it and use, but the entire system was not there to serve us. In our first conversation, Renee and I quickly connected over our shared experience coming from an East Coast Indigenous community. She is from Te Tairāwhiti, which means "the coast upon which the sun shines" in Te reo Māori. She loved it when I told her that Wampanoag means "people of the first light." Many local businesses and organizations in her area, she told me, use "Firstlight" in their names. Those connections might feel small or obvious. I'm sure there are many Indigenous and non-Indigenous East Coast communities that use similar language. Japan, after all, is known as the land of the rising sun. But in a world and a system that seems designed to destroy opportunities for connection and solidarity, it felt both remarkable and beautiful to connect over those simple shared things.

After Renee and I spoke over Zoom one afternoon, I sent her a picture of the Gay Head cliffs on WhatsApp so we could compare what our coastal homes looked like. I didn't mention the lighthouse, but she noticed and sent back a picture of herself in front of the lighthouse in Rangitukia. "Is that a lighthouse? Here's ours!" she said. I sent an old, black-and-white photo of my great-grandfather in front of the lighthouse when he was keeper and mentioned our family history with the lighthouse. There's something strangely powerful about making those kinds of connections that makes me not only feel connected to the person I am talking to, but more connected to my own family and history. There is a kind of warmth that I feel when I share my grandfather's story with people who I know will understand.

These conversations helped me develop a more nuanced way of looking at Indigenous identity as something dynamic, ever-changing and adapting. Indigenous work can look like academic research, language revitalization, activism, and so much more. But the goals are the same. There are so many different ways to do and to be. I just needed to find ways to let myself embrace and embody that complexity. Indigenous identity is rooted in the past, in our ancestors, our land, and our communities. But that doesn't mean that is all that it is. It is also about how we choose to engage with it going forward.

14

WHOLLY AND ALWAYS AND FOREVER—INDIAN

While exploring the different parts of my family history has led me to embrace my multifaceted identity, I still get uncomfortable when people assume I speak Chinese at restaurants or on the street. But I no longer carry any resentment about it. I'm no longer running away from who I am or trying to divide myself. I thought I had to pick Wampanoag or Chinese or Japanese, but now I am choosing to pick them all.

I think for a long time I didn't really understand what that meant. Equal doesn't mean the same. I used to think that there was no way to accept all the parts of who I am without somehow diluting them all. But just like Freedmen's tribal citizenship seemed like a powerful expression of tribal sovereignty—the tribe would determine who belonged, regardless of what American perception or racialized notions of Indian identity might say—accepting the discrete parts of my identity as part of, not separate from, one another seemed like the very embodiment of a more progressive, inclusive understanding of what it means to be Indigenous.

One of the reasons those questions are so fraught is that Indian identity has always been heavily persecuted, regulated, and policed. In my research of Aquinnah history, I discovered just how long we've been fighting for the basic right to be recognized as Indigenous.

In the historical materials in our federal recognition documents, I found an 1869 quote from William Claflin, then the governor of Massachusetts, about the Gay Headers. "These persons are not indian in any sense of the word," Claflin said. "It is doubtful there is a full blooded indian in the state . . . a majority have more or less the marked characteristics of the Aboriginal race, but there are many without a drop of indian blood in their veins. The marriage of a foreigner with a member of the tribe transforms the foreigner into an indian. The result of this singular system has been a heterogenous population, in which the characteristics of the white and negro races have already near obliterated all traces of the indian."

Claflin's words came at a time when the state was trying to incorporate Gay Head into a town and eliminate what he called the "political anomaly" that the Indian district represented. It was more convenient for the state if the Gay Head Indians were not Indian at all. This was a tactic repeated across the world. When I was reporting on the Indigenous Maasai in Tanzania getting evicted from their land, I heard representatives from the Tanzanian government repeatedly insist that there were no Indigenous people in their country. All Africans were Indigenous, they said, and beyond that there should be no distinctions. If the Maasai are not Indigenous, then it is much easier to say that they have no greater claim to the land than anyone else.

And in the US, multiple policies worked in conjunction to achieve the same goal. Indian boarding schools operated under the infamous "Kill the Indian, save the man" philosophy, land allotment policies eliminated collective land ownership, and blood quantum policies reduced Indian identity to a simple mathematical formula based in race science. Not only were blood quantum policies based on false racial absolutism, but they were also designed to gradually eliminate Indigenous people and, more importantly, their power and land ownership. If Indians were legally dissolved, it would be that much easier to take their land.

But for at least as long as Indian identity and Wampanoag identity have been questioned, we have been standing up for a less reductive understanding. Edwin DeVries Vanderhoop was the son of my great-great-great-grandparents, Beulah Salisbury and William Vanderhoop, the original Vanderhoop from Suriname. After the Civil War, Edwin was teaching in

Pine Bluff, Arkansas, where he met Mary Cleggett, the daughter of a free Black man. The two married and eventually returned to Gay Head, where Edwin became a prominent political figure, the first Wampanoag elected to the state legislature. His homestead is now the Aquinnah Cultural Center.

Mary wrote a number of articles documenting the tribe's history and traditions. In one of them, written for the New Bedford *Evening Standard* in 1904, she wrote that "in the offspring of the intermarriages the strongest blood may show externally and the predominant features are those of either the white or the negro, but the inner self, the ego, the soul, the mind, the living principle, is wholly and always and forever—Indian."

Having met her Wampanoag husband in Arkansas, Mary was well aware that being Wampanoag did not mean living in Gay Head for your whole life. She also knew that it had nothing to do with physical appearance, but something innate, something deeper. As much as I found her words moving, I wondered if I had that innate something, that indescribable part of my soul that is Wampanoag.

To help me understand it all, I asked some of my cousins how they thought about their identity and relationship to our community. Amira grew up in the Boston area and remembered hearing her mom talk about Aquinnah and taking a boat over there. Amira imagined a small rowboat. When she first moved to the island, she felt in awe of the community and culture. She wanted to learn and be a part of as much as she could. Over the years, Amira became a youth leader, participating in national Native youth gatherings, and worked for the tribe in a variety of roles. She would go on to work for the City of Boston, Harvard University, and serve on our tribal council.

"Being Native is not about my blood quantum or my DNA," she told me. "It's more than just that. It's about how I see the world and how I see community, how I hold my people's history and how I share that and how I look at the world. That's what for me is the most important."

I think I wasted so much time worrying about what Wampanoag identity wasn't or didn't have to be that I didn't spend enough time building up the things that it is and can be. I've also come to learn that there are different ways of being Wampanoag, and what works or is meaningful for someone might be different from the way I approach things.

My other cousin NaDaizja recently moved back to the island and has been working in both political and cultural spaces to try to make a difference in our community. She's part of my extended Vanderhoop family and, like me, it took the new virtual and remote options during the pandemic for NaDaizja to get more involved in the tribe. Today, NaDaizja works as the director of the Aquinnah Cultural Center, the museum located in the old Edwin DeVries Vanderhoop homestead at the cliffs. "Coming back home has been a chance to explore Aquinnah culture and also try to create opportunities for other people in our community who might not have had the experiences that they might have desired," she told me.

We also talked about what traditions and culture really look like. Clamming, fishing, spending time on the water, picking cranberries and beach plums were all things that we agreed were less overt examples of Wampanoag culture. "I think that people have this picturesque view of what tradition looks like that doesn't always make room for some of those old Gay Head traditions," she said. "And those are totally a part of our story and should be valued in the same way as the things that we're trying to reclaim from precontact."

That really resonated with me because I think that I was always looking for a perfect version of Wampanoag identity and a perfect form of Wampanoag culture. Part of the challenge for me is that identity and the way I've thought about it has shifted. I think I not only had this ideal of what it should be, but a misconception that someday I would arrive at it and stay there, not that it would evolve throughout my whole life. Wampanoag identity is not just political, but there were times when my engagement with the tribe was focused on tribal politics. It's not just about community, but there have been times in my life when the way that I thought about being Wampanoag was based around the people and community in Aquinnah. And there have been other times, especially as I grew older, where my sense of Wampanoag identity was more rooted in a broader Native or Indigenous identity, connecting with other people from across the country and around the world.

The more I talked to other people, the more I also realized that people had similar experiences, figuring out different ways to engage with that identity and with their community. It struck me how many similar stories I heard.

About a month after I went on the Klamath trip, I called up Silas Yamamoto, the Karuk-Japanese firefighter I had met in Happy Camp. Silas told me that he grew up going to Karuk Head Start programs and felt like the tribe was part of his identity ever since he was a kid. But it wasn't until he started participating in ceremonial dances when he was around eleven or twelve that being Karuk became a conscious part of his identity.

But around that time, he also started to get bullied. Silas is not an enrolled member of the tribe because he does not have a high enough blood quantum. He could still participate in Head Start, but he wasn't able to participate in certain programs and ceremonies. Although some kids accepted him, the bullying from those who felt he was not Karuk enough stung. "I think that was probably a pretty big development point in my life because I started getting less and less interested in my Native culture as I got older because I got bullied," Silas said.

These are the kinds of issues I never had to think about, but unfortunately stories like Silas's are far too common in Indian Country. As he drew away from tribal events and culture, Silas devoted his time to other pursuits, like Boy Scouts, sports, and school. He eventually left home for college in San Francisco. It wasn't until he came back and began working with fire that his interest in Karuk culture was reignited.

Silas never intended to work with fire and initially took the job just to pay off college loans, but now, he feels that he's found his purpose and his place in the tribe. He loves working with fire and has found a small network of tribal fire experts and elders he can ask questions about Karuk fire traditions. He wants to keep learning about fire, from Karuk elders and from other communities across the country. In the past couple years, he's traveled to other places, including three months in South Carolina and a few weeks in Idaho, to learn from their fire practices. "There's been many instances where, because of my use of fire, I feel more connected to the land," Silas said. "I've seen the effects that I can have with fire. I can either bring back a lot of life or I can take it all away, just depending on how I use it. It's definitely allowed me to build a deeper respect and connection to the land."

Silas has worked to build his relationship with his land and his community through literal work with his fire jobs, but he's also had to gain cultural knowledge on his own. Silas's grandmother is enrolled, but his mother also doesn't have a high enough blood quantum to enroll. And even though his grandmother is enrolled, Silas said that she is not that involved with the tribe, which is one reason that not a lot of Karuk culture and traditions were passed down in his family. "The whole integration into our Native culture is a journey that we've had to take on our own, because we've had to track down elders to tell us the stories or teach us basket weaving," he said.

I was so interested in that journey of discovery because it reminded me of my own. There was stuff I had as a kid, but then as I grew older, I realized it was up to me to figure out what I wanted and where I could get it from. I think, if anything, that has been the hardest thing to adapt to about Wampanoag identity, the idea that a lot of it is up to me. It is still community based, but I have to make decisions about how and when I engage with the community.

Neilson Powless is a professional cyclist who races in major international races like the Tour de France. He is also a member of the Oneida Nation of Wisconsin. In 2020, Powless became the first member of a federally recognized tribe to ride in the Tour de France. I grew up riding bikes, raced for my college's road racing team, and loved watching professional racing. Seeing one of the best riders in the world, who is also Native, felt like an almost unbelievable crossover, especially since bike racing is historically a very white sport. I read interviews where Neilson talked about his Oneida heritage and what it meant to be a trailblazing figure. I wanted to ask him what that was all like, especially since I knew that he had not grown up on the reservation. We spoke on Zoom during his offseason break.

Neilson grew up in California, but every summer he went back to the

Oneida reservation in Wisconsin, where his grandfather lived. "I had a lot of fun on the reservation," he recalled. "I think when I was younger, I didn't really fully understand everything that was going on with tribal dynamics and politics. I think my parents tried to keep me a little bit protected from that and just try to keep the trips always positive and with a focus on reconnecting with family, and gaining appreciation for the background that I had and the people that I came from."

That's how I felt too. My parents felt it was important for us to spend time on the island to get to know the place and the people, but generally shielded us from some of the nasty politics and internal tensions in Gay Head, not to mention the brutal history of colonialism.

I asked Neilson about the attention he's received for his tribal heritage. "Sometimes it feels strange, because it doesn't really feel like that's my whole identity," he said. "But people definitely try to make it that because it's something that's different." On the other hand, he explained that if his position can help to inspire Native kids to ride their bikes or chase any kind of dream, then he's all for it. He said he definitely hoped to become more involved with the tribe in the future, but right now it was hard while he focused on a racing career in Europe. "I feel like at this point, I've just been focusing so much on my career and becoming someone that people would hopefully see some relation to and use as a motivation tool," he said. "But at some point, I've got to go the other way too: not just talk about who I am, but try to be involved with who I am." That made me wonder how much time I should spend out in the world asking questions before, like Neilson, I need to just go back home and do the work in Aquinnah. What I've come to accept is that in a lifelong relationship, it is okay, perhaps even good, for there to be different phases in that relationship.

Neilson said that his grandfather passed away around the time that he felt their relationship was starting to get to the point where they would talk about deeper stuff. But now he mostly relies on his father to share information and pass down traditions. The struggles that Neilson, Silas, and I have experienced to learn more about our tribal history shows just how fragile it can be, and how hard we have to work to preserve it. It was also a reminder that we can't just wait around and rely on adults forever. By the time I became really interested in learning about my grandparents' lives, they had passed away.

Less than a year before we spoke, Neilson and his Korean American wife had a baby girl. Because we had just talked about the importance of passing along Native culture, I asked Neilson how he was planning to navigate identity with his daughter. "She is going to be Korean, Native, and white," he told me. "It's going to be difficult to understand which part of her is the most dominant and which part of her is really where she came from. And, you know, I think it's going to be up to us as parents to teach her that all parts equally are who she is." What he said was a reminder that the world is always going to try to pigeonhole identity. We have to work to share and embrace all aspects of our identity.

We also talked about tribal enrollment policies. Neilson's tribe has a blood quantum requirement, but he wasn't quite sure how much was required for membership. While we talked, he looked up the details. Neilson's blood quantum is a quarter, the minimum required for tribal membership, which means his daughter will not be eligible unless the policy changes. He told me that his dad had recently been on the reservation talking about the issue and hopes a change might be made soon. "It almost makes me feel like I'm less Oneida if my kids cannot be considered Oneida," Neilson explained. "It's like I wasn't enough. I wasn't Oneida enough to give it to my kids."

Because my tribe does not have blood quantum and I've never believed in any biological race science component of Indigenous identity, I've kind of ignored it. But it is a reality for Silas, Neilson, and thousands of other Indigenous people, so I called up Krystal Tsosie. Tsosie, Diné, is a geneticist-bioethicist at Arizona State University, where she leads the Tsosie Lab for Indigenous Genomic Data Equity and Justice. Tsosie is also a cofounder of the Native BioData Consortium, the first Indigenous-led biobank in the US. Through her work, Tsosie is committed to uplifting Indigenous scientists, tribal and Indigenous data sovereignty, and the nuances of Indigenous identity. In the popular media, Tsosie has spoken out prominently about DNA testing, cautioning people about the flaws in both the tests and reducing Indigeneity to a biological category.

While working as a freelance journalist, I had written a profile of Tsosie for a science news magazine. The article was pretty straightforward, mostly talking about her career journey and current work, but I wanted to ask her more about some of the complexities of Indigenous identity, including the dangers of reducing Indigeneity to a biological category. "These racial biological constructions have also been used to inform medicine, so sometimes it's useful, but a lot of times it can be really harmful," she told me. "Using a colonial genealogy here was really meant to dilute our rights to our lands."

For Tsosie, these issues are both personal and professional. "As a Navajo woman in our matrilineal culture, I had this sort of unspoken, but heavy pressure that I must marry a Navajo man and bear children with this Navajo individual," she went on. "And that caused a lot of guilt for me. It's a pressure I felt maybe not from my parents, but from other elements of family and certainly from my culture and other people who are Indigenous."

I asked Krystal where she thought this was all going and what tribal identity might look like in a few generations. She seemed surprised by the question. "I've honestly been so focused on trying to get recognition that Indigeneity is not just rooted fully in genetics—that there are other factors at play, especially as it relates to health inequities. That has been my challenge right there," she said. "I haven't been permitted an opportunity to think about, well, what is this going to look like several years or even several generations down the line? All I know is that for my nuclear family, I'm a little scared." That's just another example of how the problems in front of us take away from our time to think big picture.

We talked about the ways that Indigenous identity was so often reduced to biological or political categories and how neither was sufficient. In her lab, Tsosie is conducting a study involving social, structural, cultural, and traditional identity factors to help create a more thorough picture of Indigenous health outcomes. "It comes down to these questions: What is the next generation going to claim as tribal enrollment, and what will they claim as their identity? What are the impacts if those are not the same?" she wondered.

It's clear to me after talking to all these people how complicated and personal Indigenous identity is, but it's also even more clear that we need a collective way to move past these outdated and often dangerous ways of thinking about it. I think the understanding that blood quantum is not the answer is growing, but not quickly enough. And beyond that, I've come to understand that Indigenous identity is about how you engage with the community more than anything else.

Gabe Galanda, the lawyer representing disenrolled people, wrote an article about tribal kinship relationships as a response to phenomena like disenrollments. Galanda, more than many people, has seen how blood quantum, disenrollment, and financially driven policies have divided and destroyed tribal communities. "My biggest concern about the state of Indigenous Americans today is we are overly consumed with economies and monies and individualism rather than relationships based in reciprocity and duty to one another, to land, to water, to air, to animals," he told me over the phone. Galanda cited the debate at the National Congress of American Indians over tribes without federal recognition as an example of how lost tribes are. Tribes care more about casino money than sovereignty and community bonds, he believes. He explained that at least the NCAI debate about state recognized tribes put that reality out in the open, rather than behind closed council doors.

Kinship, he believes, is a way of returning to positive relationships. "It's getting back to decision-making that first and foremost venerates Indigenous humanity and the relationship between Indigenous peoples and their lands, their waters, and their air," Galanda told me. He is asking tribal citizens to step back and ask who they are as individuals and collectively. He thinks the way we think and talk about belonging and tribal citizenship needs to change. "My biggest concern is, five hundred years in, that a great many of us have forgotten who we originally were. We've forgotten our original instructions, and individualism has supplanted reciprocity."

I think there is some truth in that, that hundreds of years of American colonialism has changed the way we think. Sometimes I think I am so deep in the American system that it's hard to see another way even as I reject it. It is one thing to resist what has been imposed on you and entirely another to find a new way forward. From elementary-school lessons about Pilgrims to blood quantum and federal recognition, the way that I understood Indigenous identity was so dominated by American structures and myths that I realized looking outside the US might help. Like the Wampis Nation helped me understand the limits and realities of sovereignty rooted in federal recognition, I thought that Indigenous people around the world might help me understand more. I wasn't so much looking for answers to specific questions, but crumbs to follow, hints at a future and a mindset out of the only one I knew. For a long time I never believed that I could have much in common with Indigenous peoples from other countries. But I realized that just like Indigenous sovereignty should not be decided by colonial rules, Indigenous identity should not be divided by colonial borders. The more we can push past those, the more ways we'll find to connect.

CONCLUSION: OUR OWN MAP

In all the conversations I've had with Indigenous people over the past few years, one of the most common themes was looking to the future. There are so many urgent threats today—floods, fires, violence, racism, persecution—that it can be hard to think about the bigger picture. But in talking to lawyers, activists, scholars, and other Indigenous people fighting for their communities, their biggest goal was almost always making the world a better place for the next generations, even if the specific work they do looks different.

The stereotype about Indigenous people is that we live in the past, but I've found that Indigenous people are some of the most forward-looking people in the world. I think that's part of what collective identity means. It's not all about what we are feeling or experiencing in this moment; it's about how we can use the time and resources we've been given to benefit our community now and in the future.

Renee Raroa, who has two children, told me that she hopes her kids will grow up with an understanding of and appreciation for the land. But she also knows that not every relationship with the land looks the same, so she is doing what she can to help preserve the land for them but also to give them options. "When I think about what I want for my kids, and what I am hopeful to have for the next generations of young ones coming through, is the ability for them to connect all the way back to place, whether that means going home and helping to grow the forests and looking after our food sovereignty, or just knowing where they come from, and knowing the responsibility that they have to place, even if you're away from it," she told me.

Renee and I talked about how relationships to land have shifted across generations, but the importance of having that relationship has not. And as the demands of our lives change, we have to remember that. So doing the work means protecting and preserving the land, but it also means building a world where the next generation has the option to leave the land and come back to it again and again, like my family and I have.

Amba-Rose Atkinson doesn't have any kids yet, but she is still thinking about making a better world for them. When we were talking about the sheer scope of the work ahead of us, and reflecting on how much culture, tradition, and community has been taken from us, she told me that she tries to think about progress in the long term. "I know that there's ceremonies that we can probably never get back and that's so devastating and heartbreaking on so many different levels," Amba explained. "But I think it's important to keep going because we have to. Maybe I didn't have that growing up, but my children will have that more so, and then etc., etc."

That sentiment echoed what I heard from so many other people. I thought about how Sami Jo from the Shasta Indian Nation spoke so passionately about providing culture and home for her grandchildren and future generations. I thought of Barry McCovey Jr. from the Yurok Tribe saying that he was okay with the restoration of the river taking generations. I thought about LeEtta Osborne-Sampson's acceptance that the change she is fighting for will not happen within her lifetime, but her hope that it would continue to improve for future generations.

The way we think about Indigenous identity may shift from generation to generation, but what really matters is that we do what we can to ensure future generations have as many options as possible and a strong relationship with land and community. Sometimes, I wonder what Aquinnah will look like in fifty years, or a hundred. I don't think my great-grandparents could have imagined what it would look like today, but they still did what they could to hold on to land, create opportunities for our family, and build a stronger tribal community. I don't think it's about trying to guarantee or preserve a certain version of Aquinnah beyond one where Aquinnah Wampanoag people can still live and build community together.

When I think about how much Aquinnah has changed in the past few decades, I find myself wishing it would stay the way it is. The things that loom on the horizon terrify me. I don't know what is going to happen to my family's land in a couple generations. Climate change will continue to erode the cliffs, property values in Aquinnah will keep rising, and more Wampanoags will probably live off-island.

But even though I can't control the land or predict what new challenges will emerge, I can keep working toward a community that is prepared to handle them. That is our responsibility. My parents' and grandparents' generations fought for the right to be proud to be Wampanoag, for sovereignty, for language. My generation is using the tools and experiences they gave us to fight for different goals. Whether it was Moshup preparing his family for invaders, King Philip's resistance, or my grandfather's generation fighting for our land, we have always risen to the challenge.

"We stand on the shoulders of all of those who came before us and who had to fight the fight in order for me to be here," Amba told me. "The fight through each generation has looked different, but we're still fighting the same thing: the machine of colonization. I can acknowledge that I have a lot more space in my life to contribute to that fight and in a different way. Before it was literally just trying to keep your family together, trying to keep your children safe."

As the fight evolves from one generation to the next, part of the work is accepting what the previous generations were able to survive and accomplish, while also understanding that the work is not finished. That doesn't mean blaming them, it simply means picking up the torch. When I talk to Indigenous people there is not just hope for the next generation, there is hope in it. Hope that they will be better, that they will move past some of the trauma and conflict that burdened previous generations. In Oklahoma, Freedmen tell me that they think there is less animosity and racism toward them among younger tribal members. Young Indigenous people across the country seem to care less about blood quantum than their parents and grandparents.

"My hope actually does not lie in our generation or our parents' and grandparents' generations," Gabe Galanda said when I asked him if he felt hopeful tribes would stop disenrolling their people and embrace kinship models. "In fact, that's where my cynicism lies. My hope lies in the youth that are coming up behind us who have had a different experience, who maybe have not been jaded by a sovereignty fight, who are open to democratic ideals, open to human rights norms, to more traditional ideas of who belongs and how we belong."

I've talked to some of my tribal cousins about how we grew up thinking that federal recognition was the best thing ever and being a bit confused the more we learned about the system and saw the flaws in the tribe. But we can understand why our parents' and grandparents' generations, unintentionally or not, instilled that message in us. It was the fight of their generation to achieve federal recognition, to gain back things that I'd grown up taking for granted, like language programs, tribal housing, and sovereignty. And with each accomplishment, new challenges and debates emerged.

In Gay Head, after fights over the settlement and federal recognition, a younger generation began to pick up the mantle. In 1991, younger tribal members led by Carl Widdiss, the son of Gladys proposed changing the name of the town from Gay Head to Aquinnah. "An Indian place should have an Indian name," Carl said. Older tribal members, including my grandfather, were proud to be Gay Headers and opposed the name change. The vote failed by a large margin.

In 1997, Carl and others brought the name change to a vote again, and this time, it passed. Later, I found out that the change only passed by three votes. Many Gay Headers were upset at the name change and plenty of people still call the town Gay Head. It's a strange mix of older white people who have been visiting for decades and refuse to accept change and the older generation of tribal members who grew up being proud to be from Gay Head. Even though Gay Head was the name given by white settlers, those elders made Gay Head identity their own. That always struck me as a perfect example of the complexity of Indian identity. We are not simply trying to reclaim things from the past, but create new ones.

We get to decide what our own traditions are. Sometimes people in Aquinnah say there aren't very many Gay Headers left. When I reflect on childhood summers in Gay Head, I think about tribal elders who were around. I remember Gladys teaching us how to make pinch pots from the clay. I remember my grandfather's cousin Phiddie coming over to our house for dinner with her famous rum cake. I think of my grandfather Charlie, sitting in his armchair, eating seafood, or telling another one of his stories. They are all gone now.

Changing the name to Aquinnah was the beginning of the end of one chapter, and the beginning of a new one. Gay Head was an identity people created and used to empower a community. Now, Aquinnah is that core. There is not a new generation of Gay Headers, but the next generation has taken up the same fight, just with different tools. It reminds me of a line from Muscogee poet Joy Harjo's "A Map to the Next World." The line, which comes near the end of the poem, reads like this: "Crucial to finding the way is this: there is no beginning or end."

I first read that poem in Oklahoma City. The day after LeEtta showed me around the Seminole Nation, I went to the Oklahoma Contemporary Art Center in downtown OKC, where there was an exhibition featuring thirteen artists exploring the history and future of Oklahoma. The exhibition, which was called *The Soul Is a Wanderer*, was inspired by Harjo's poem. On the wall, there were lines from the poem printed here and there. I knew Harjo's work but hadn't read that particular poem before. Above one painting, a sweeping and swirling multicolor landscape, there was a line that made me suddenly pause: "You will see red cliffs. They are the heart, contain the ladder."

I don't know if it was just the way I was feeling in Oklahoma, thinking deeply about Indigenous land and what it means to us, but that line transported me back to Aquinnah and the cliffs. I'm not sure what red cliffs Harjo might have been imagining when she wrote that line, but I felt as though it was speaking to me directly. In so many ways, the cliffs are the heart of how I understand what it means to be Wampanoag. The cliffs are where Moshup killed whales to feed our community, where my family has made a living for decades, and where I grew up getting to know Aquinnah.

But it is the last part of that line that struck me the most. Land is the heart, but it also contains the ladder, a way up. I think I'm finally understanding that there doesn't have to be a choice between the land and moving forward. We can take that ladder toward a better way and a stronger community. The land holds all that, if only we can protect it enough. And protecting the land doesn't mean never leaving it. I never thought that caring about Aquinnah could take me to Oklahoma or Alaska or allow me to meet Indigenous people from around the world, but it has. And the more I learn about other Indigenous communities, the more I want to learn about my own. The more I travel to other Indigenous lands, the more time I want to spend on mine. The more stories I hear, the more I want to share.

Later, in my hotel, I looked up the rest of the poem, and as I traveled around Indigenous lands, met Indigenous people from around the world, and wrote this book, the last line kept coming back to me: "You must make your own map." At first, that line made me think of big journeys across the world, meeting Indigenous people from faraway places, or deep spiritual journeys. But lately, it's making me think about clams.

When I go home to Aquinnah every summer, the thing I look forward to the most is heading down to the beach to go clamming. Walking carefully over the rocks and out into the cold water, I toss my bucket out ahead of me, where it bobs gently, filling up partially with water and sinking halfway under the surface. I take a deep breath and plunge forward, pushing my bucket out into deeper water. When I get deep enough, I force my bucket to the bottom, weighing it down with a rock or small clam I found on my way out. I leave the bucket in a central location before circling out to look for clams.

A foot or two above the gently rippled sand, I flatten my body and begin to pull my way through the water, scanning the sand as I navigate around the seaweed patches. From close up, I can see how the sand is speckled with different colored fragments of rock, shell, and seaweed. I use the geography of the seaweed—seemingly randomly placed clumps of dark green strands—to guide my search. I think of the areas between patches as forest clearings. I've dug up hundreds of clams, but there is still something amazing that makes me pause in the water every time I spot the unmistakably alive breathing holes of a clam. I work my way from clearing to clearing, retracing my path every time I need to return to my bucket to deposit the heavy clams weighing down my bathing suit. In my hand, a sea clam feels nearly indestructible. The dark shell, streaked with white and gold, seems to hide another world inside. When I find a too-small clam, I clutch it in my hand, enjoying the feel of the smooth shell in my hand before tossing it toward deeper water.

These are the same waters that Moshup once caught whales in and where countless ancestors and cousins have swum and fished over the years. They are the waters that gave my grandfather a career and a life away from the island, and the same ones that brought him back. Every summer, those waters draw the tourists that supported my family and continued to threaten the tribe.

No matter how many times I go clamming in those waters, I never feel entirely comfortable. A striped bass might dart in front of me, startling me, or my foot might kick an unexpected clump of seaweed. Mysterious sounds break the silence. Sometimes the sun passes behind a cloud while I'm underwater and suddenly the ocean floor turns from sun-dappled to dark and ominous. I never know if it's in my head or not, but it always seems like the water instantly gets colder in those moments. On some days, the water looks flat, clear, and calm from the beach, but is murky and swirling below the surface.

Then there are the days when I could stay in the water forever. I navigate smoothly around and over seagrass. The water feels somehow cool and warm at the same time, refreshing and nourishing. Sometimes in a deep sandy clearing, I'll plunge to the bottom, blowing bubbles out as I descend, trying to gently settle on the sand and stay as still as possible, letting the moment linger before my body pulls me back up to the surface.

I can't explain why some days I feel like I belong in the water and others I almost feel like I am trespassing. But I've come to accept that it's okay to not feel the same thing every time. I don't have to understand every aspect of the land. I used to think that someday I could memorize where all the seaweed patches are and remember exactly where I tossed smaller clams so I could get them later when they had grown.

I thought that was the kind of map I needed to make, a kind of detailed catalog of the land. But, of course, the ocean is always changing, shifting, and evolving. Clamming is not about mastery or memorization. It's about the time I spend in the water and on the beach, hanging out with my family. It's about sharing clams with my cousins and showing them how to get clams themselves. And that's all part of the map that I'm making, the map that I'll continue making for the rest of my life. It's not a map to or away from somewhere, I've realized; it's a map that shows us how to live, how to be, and how to care. And that's enough.

ACKNOWLEDGMENTS

First, thank you to the entire Aquinnah Wampanoag community for supporting, inspiring, and teaching me. Thank you especially to those of you who patiently answered my many questions for this book.

I spoke to so many amazing Indigenous people while writing this book, which could not exist without their insights and ideas. Huge thank you to Majo Andrade Cerda, Matthew Fletcher, Amba-Rose Atkinson, Gabe Galanda, Nayap Santiago Velásquez, Nelton Yankur, Sami Jo Difuntorum, James Sarmento, Michael Olsen, Amy Bowers Cordalis, Barry McCovey Jr., Don Gentry, Clayton Dumont, Bill Tripp, Koutaro Yuuji, Nozomi Nakaganeku Saito, Silas Yamamoto, Krystal Tsosie, Marilyn Vann, Neilson Powless, and Renee Raroa. I only wish I had more time to spend with you and more space to share your words. There are countless other people who contributed their time and wisdom with me across many years. Thank you all.

I owe a special thank you to Sophie Swope and LeEtta Osborne-Sampson, who welcomed me into their homes and went above and beyond to show me their beautiful land and communities. My cousins Amira Madison and NaDaizja Aiguier-Bolling were also especially helpful and generous with their time.

My editor Alessandra Bastagli was the perfect partner for this book. From our very first conversations, she helped draw out ideas that had been swirling in my head for years and helped me find a way to put them together. Thank you to the entire team at One Signal and Atria: Rola Harb, Abby Mohr, Joanna Pinkser, Libby McGuire, Erin Kibby, Annie Probert, Paige Lytle, Kelli McAdams, and Laurie McGee.

My agent Alia Hanna Habib has been a steady hand and friend throughout this process, and believed in me for years before this became anything resembling a book. Thank you also to Sophie Pugh-Sellers and everyone at the Gernert Company.

I have had many excellent teachers, but there are a few who went above and beyond to encourage and challenge me. David Weintraub, Courtney Bender, Colm Tóibín, Margo Jefferson, and Leslie Jamison all showed me that I might have something to say and helped me find ways to say it. I've been fortunate to work with many exceptional editors, especially Tristan Ahtone, who taught me how to be a better writer and journalist. Thank you to my incredible friends and colleagues at the Indigenous Journalists Association, who are out there doing the work every day of making journalism, and the world, a better place.

Plympton & The Writer's Block bookstore, Millay Arts, and the Cuttyhunk Island Writers Residency gave me support and space to work. The Institute for Journalism and Natural Resources supported my trip to the Klamath Basin. The Robert B. Silvers Foundation provided valuable support in the final phase of writing. When I needed it the most, the Asian American Writers Workshop gave me time, resources, and belief to become a writer. A special thanks to Jyothi Natarajan, Lily Philpott, and Yasmin Adele Majeed for all the help and encouragement along the way. AAWW also introduced me to Mitchell S. Jackson, who was an invaluable mentor in the early stages of this book.

I'm extremely lucky to have wonderful, supportive friends who have been there for me at every step of this long process. Emmanuel Felton is one of the best friends anyone could ask for and the world is lucky to have his work. I have no idea where I'd be if we never met in that basement. Cara Blue Adams is a gift to everyone who cares about books and helped me get this book off my computer and into the world.

Thank you to Alex, Victoria, Marylen, José Luis, Alexis, Isabella, Catalina, and the rest of the Martinez and Montañes family for welcoming me into your family, for your support, and for all the delicious food.

This book would have never existed without the self-belief and support my family have always given me. My brother, Sam, who read to me when we shared a childhood bedroom and bought my first literary magazine subscription, has always been my first teacher and role model. My parents taught me how to ask questions, how to think for myself, and how to work for what I wanted. Their lifelong support and encouragement have made everything possible. Thank you.

Finally, thank you to my wife, Chanel, who first heard about the idea for this book when we were both clueless college kids. You've made my life better in every way and I could have never done any of this without you.

NOTES

INTRODUCTION: LAND AT THE END

5 *Mittark's Will:* Early Texts in Massachusetts, Jaime Battiste, Juana Perley, Donald Soctomah, Carol Dana, Lisa Brooks, Cheryl Stedtler, et al. "Petition from Gay Head Sachem Mittark, 1681," in *Dawnland Voices: An Anthology of Indigenous Writing from New England*, ed. Siobhan Senier (University of Nebraska Press, 2014), 435–36, https://doi.org/10.2307/j.ctt1d9njj2.206.

A STILL PLACE AMONG THE CURRENTS

9 *English colonizer Bartholomew Gosnold:* Louise T. Haskell, *The Story of Cuttyhunk* (Waterford Printing, 1953), 8–14, https://massrods.com/dukes/wp-content/uploads/sites/19/2017/10/The-History-of-Cuttyhunk.pdf.

10 *a devastating plague hit Indigenous populations in the Northeast:* Linda Coombs, *Colonization and the Wampanoag Story* (Crown Books for Young Readers, 2023), 103–14.

10 *four separate Wampanoag villages:* Ibid., 163–64.

10 *dozens of other tribes were forced off their homelands onto foreign lands:* "Removal of Tribal Nations to Oklahoma," Oklahoma Historical Society, accessed August 20, 2024, https://www.okhistory.org/research/airemoval.

11 *In 1827, the lighthouse keeper in Aquinnah*: "Evidence for Proposed Finding Against Federal Acknowledgment of the Wampanoag Tribal Council of Gay Head, Inc." (United States Department of the Interior, Office of Federal Acknowledgment, 1985), 23.

11 *When gold was discovered in the Black Hills:* "Black Hills Expedition of 1874," PBS American Experience, accessed August 20, 2024, https://www.pbs.org/wgbh/americanexperience/features/custer-timeline/.

11 *When the Ojibwe refused to leave their timber-rich land:* David Treuer, *The Heartbeat of Wounded Knee* (Riverhead Books, 2019), 147–48.

11 *American whaling continued to grow:* "The History of Whaling in America," PBS, accessed August 19, 2024, https://www.pbs.org/wgbh/americanexperience/features/whaling-history-whaling-america/.

12 *a bell sounding whenever a slave catcher came into town*: Skip Finley, "A Bell of Freedom," *Martha's Vineyard Magazine*, July 9, 2021, https://mvmagazine.com/news/2021/07/08/bell-freedom.

13 *In 1862, Aquinnah was designated an official Indian district and renamed Gay Head:* "Evidence for Proposed Finding against Federal Acknowledgment of the Wampanoag Tribal Council of Gay Head, Inc." (United States Department of the Interior, Office of Federal Acknowledgment, 1985), 4.

13 *Aquinnah Wampanoag Indians were under state guardianship and not granted American citizenship:* "Evidence for Proposed Finding against Federal Acknowledgment of the Wampanoag Tribal Council of Gay Head, Inc." (United States Department of the Interior, Office of Federal Acknowledgment, 1985), 4, 11, 21.

15 *In 1871, the state commissioned an assessment of land titles*: Ibid., 30.

15 *newly instated property taxes proved impossible for many Wampanoags to pay:* "When Gay Head Was Just Still a District," *Vineyard Gazette*, February 26, 1937, https://vineyardgazette.com/news/1937/02/26/when-gay-head-was-still-just-district.

15 *the 1887 General Allotment Act:* Treuer, *Heartbeat of Wounded Knee*, 145–51.

16 *Indians had lost about one hundred million acres:* Ibid., 150.

17 *traditional lifestyles, farming, and stock raising began to disappear from Gay Head:* "Evidence for Proposed Finding," 37.

17 *A group of federal laws known as Termination Policy:* Treuer, *Heartbeat of Wounded Knee*, 250.

OFF-ISLAND

24 *Around 12 percent of Native Americans served in the US military:* Danielle DeSimone, "A History of Military Service: Native Americans in the U.S. Military Yesterday and Today," United Service Organizations, November 8, 2021, https://www.uso.org/stories/2914-a-history-of-military-service-native-americans-in-the-u-s-military-yesterday-and-today.

24 *In the middle of the twentieth century, less than 10 percent of Natives lived in cities:* "American Indian Urban Relocation," National Archives, Educator Resources, accessed August 20, 2024, https://www.archives.gov/education/lessons/indian-relocation.html.

26 *a picture book called* How My Parents Learned to Eat: Ina Friedman and Allen Say, *How My Parents Learned to Eat* (Clarion Books, 1987).

27 *In 1950, the Greater Tokyo Area:* The Portal Site of Official Statistics of Japan, "Population of Regions and Prefectures: Quinquennially, 1920 to 1950 and 1947," October 1, 1950, https://www.e-stat.go.jp/en/stat-search/files?page=1

&layout=datalist&toukei=00200521&tstat=000001036869&cycle=0&tclass1=000001037373&stat_infid=000007914588&tclass2val=0.

27 *Gay Head had a population of eighty-eight:* Final Field Count, Seventeenth Census of the United States: 1950, Massachusetts, Dukes County, Gay Head Town, https:/1950census.archives.gov/search/?county=Dukes&page=1&state=MA.

31 *The first Chinese immigrants to the US*: "Chinese Immigration and the Chinese Exclusion Acts," United States Department of State Office of the Historian, accessed August 20, 2024, https://history.state.gov/milestones/1866-1898/chinese-immigration.

31 *seventy Chinese "strikebreakers" from California:* Mary M. Cronin, "When the Chinese Came to Massachusetts: Representations of Race, Labor, Religion, and Citizenship in the 1870 Press," *Historical Journal of Massachusetts* 46, no. 2 (Summer 2018): 72–105, https://www.westfield.ma.edu/historical-journal/wp-content/uploads/2018/11/2018-Summer-Cronin-When-the-Chinese-Came-to-Massachusetts.pdf.

32 *These laws culminated in the Chinese Exclusion Act of 1882:* "Chinese Exclusion Act (1882)," National Archives, accessed August 20, 2024, https://www.archives.gov/milestone-documents/chinese-exclusion-act#:~:text=In%20the%20spring%20of%201882,immigrating%20to%20the%20United%20States.

33 *a nationwide effort that came to be called urban renewal:* Jack Spillane, "A New Bedford History Lesson: Building a Better City Can Be Tricky," *Standard-Times*, October 11, 2009, https://www.southcoasttoday.com/story/news/2009/10/11/jack-spillane-new-bedford-history/51857351007/; and Barry Richard, "New Bedford Neighborhoods Devastated by 1960s Urban Renewal," 1420 WBSM, February 28, 2023, https://wbsm.com/new-bedford-neighborhoods-devastated-1960s-urban-renewal/?utm_source=tsmclip&utm_medium=referral.

34 *a Fairfield Inn and Suites opened:* "Hotel in New Bedford Opens Ahead of Schedule," *The Standard-Times*, May 28, 2010, https://www.southcoasttoday.com/story/business/2010/05/28/hotel-in-new-bedford-opens/49616663007/.

35 *a steady flow of Native people from their homelands:* "World War II." Why We Serve, National Museum of the American Indian, accessed August 20, 2024, https://americanindian.si.edu/static/why-we-serve/topics/world-war-2/.

35 *about 75 percent of Native people live off their reservations:* "American Indian/Alaska Native Health," US Department of Health and Human Services, Office of Minority Health, accessed August 20, 2024, https://minorityhealth.hhs.gov/american-indianalaska-native-health#:~:text=22%20percent%20of%20American%20Indians,percentage%20of%20any%20minority%20population.

BRINGING OUR PEOPLE HOME

46 *Gay Head was a place in flux:* "When Gay Head Was Just Still a District," *Vineyard Gazette*, February 26, 1937, https://vineyardgazette.com/news/1937/02/26/when-gay-head-was-still-just-district.

47 *In 1792, Moses Howwassawee:* "Evidence for Proposed Finding against Federal Acknowledgment of the Wampanoag Tribal Council of Gay Head, Inc." (United States Department of the Interior, Office of Federal Acknowledgment, 1985), 21.

47 *The fledgling town government:* "When Gay Head Was Just Still a District."

49 *"More than half the tribe lives off-island":* Jeff McLaughlin, "Rebuilding Wampanoag Community New Housing Seen as Crucial to Saving Town's Tribal Heritage," *Boston Globe*, July 24, 1994.

50 *In 1993, the town's zoning board*: Ibid.

51 *the median home sale price on the island*: Kerry Lester Kasper, "Vineyard Real Estate Market Shows Signs of Cooling," *Vineyard Gazette*, July 7, 2022, https://vineyardgazette.com/news/2022/07/07/vineyard-real-estate-market-shows-signs-cooling.

THE SETTLEMENT

53 *an agreement that it would follow all town and state laws:* Michael F. Bamberger, "Gay Head Pact Makes History," *Vineyard Gazette,* November 23, 1983, https://vineyardgazette.com/news/1983/11/25/gay-head-pact-makes-history.

54 *a new era of self-determination was beginning:* "A Brief History of Civil Rights in the United States: The Self-Determination Era (1968–Present)," Howard University School of Law, accessed August 20, 2024, https://library.law.howard.edu/civilrightshistory/indigenous/selfdetermination#:~:text=Beginning%20in%20the%20late%201960s,of%20mistreatment%20toward%20Native%20Americans.

54 *operate as sovereign entities*: Vine Deloria Jr., *The Nations Within* (Pantheon, 2013), 215–31.

54 *a loophole in the 1790 federal Nonintercourse Act:* Brian Kevin, "Fifty Years Ago, Passamaquoddy v. Morton Launched a Pivotal Fight for the Return of Tribal Land," *Down East,* April 2022, https://downeast.com/history/passamaquoddy-v-morton/.

55 *Tureen began reaching out to more tribes:* Susan Chira, "Whose Vineyard?" *Harvard Crimson*, September 19, 1977, https://www.thecrimson.com/article/1977/9/19/whose-vineyard-pia-crowded-tour-bus/?page=.

55 *Using Tureen's strategy:* "Gay Head Council Sues to Recover Lands from Town," *Vineyard Gazette*, December 6, 1974, https://vineyardgazette.com/news/1974/12/06/gay-head-council-sues-recover-lands-town.

55 *the new banner of the Wampanoag Tribal Council of Gay Head, Incorporated*: "Wampanoag Council: Tribe Organizes to Protect Gay Head's Future," *Vineyard Gazette*, November 10, 1972, https://vineyardgazette.com/news/1972/11/10/wampanoag-council-tribe-organizes-protect-gay-heads-future.

55 *In 1978, the council elected Gladys Widdiss:* Phyllis Meras, "Gladys Widdiss Dies at 97, Was Widely Respected Tribal Elder," *Vineyard Gazette*, June 14, 2012,

https://vineyardgazette.com/news/2012/06/14/gladys-widdiss-dies-97-was-widely-respected-tribal-elder.

55 *Bob Stutz, a labor arbitrator who worked for the US Department of Labor:* Michael Stutz, "Arnold and My Dad, Bob Stutz. Growing Up with 'Uncle' Arnold," *Chronicle,* National Academy of Arbitrators, 2020, https://naarb.org/wp-content/uploads/2020/05/Spring-2020-Chronicle.pdf.

56 *This more radical group, led by my grandfather's cousin Thelma:* "Evidence for Proposed Finding Against Federal Acknowledgment of the Wampanoag Tribal Council of Gay Head, Inc." (United States Department of the Interior, Office of Federal Acknowledgment, 1985), 47–49.

56 *The settlement gave 238 acres of land to the tribe:* Elaine Lembo, "Historic Ruling Grants Gay Head Indians Federal Recognition," *Vineyard Gazette*, February 12, 1987, https://vineyardgazette.com/news/1987/02/12/historic-ruling-grants-gay-head-indians-federal-recognition.

57 *the tribe also received federal recognition as a sovereign nation:* Ibid.

57 *national celebrities like Walter Cronkite:* Mary Breslauer, "All About Bill," *Martha's Vineyard Magazine*, July 22, 2023, https://mvmagazine.com/news/2023/07/22/all-about-bill.

57 *The enormous popularity of the 1975 blockbuster film* Jaws*:* Kate Erbland, "How 'Jaws' Forever Changed the Modern Day Blockbuster—and What Today's Examples Could Learn from It," *IndieWire*, June 18, 2024, https://www.indiewire.com/features/general/jaws-modern-blockbuster-steven-spielberg-1201844390/.

57 *rumors flew across the island that former First Lady Jacqueline Kennedy Onassis:* Richard Reston, "Mrs. Onassis Is Purchaser of 375-Acre Gay Head Tract," *Vineyard Gazette*, August 18, 1978, https://vineyardgazette.com/news/1978/08/18/mrs-onassis-purchaser-375-acre-gay-head-tract.

59 *By the 1970s, less than two hundred Wampanoags remained in Gay Head:* "Gay Head Council Sues to Recover Lands from Town," *Vineyard Gazette*, December 6, 1974, https://vineyardgazette.com/news/1974/12/06/gay-head-council-sues-recover-lands-town.

59 *"If they're killing Kennedys, then my children are targets":* Katharine Q. Seelye, "John F. Kennedy Jr., Heir to a Formidable Dynasty," *New York Times*, July 19, 1999, https://www.nytimes.com/1999/07/19/us/john-f-kennedy-jr-heir-to-a-formidable-dynasty.html?pagewanted=all.

59 *controversial photographer Ron Galella:* Karen Matthews, "Photographer Ron Galella, Sued by Jackie Onassis, Dead at 91," Associated Press, May 3, 2022, https://apnews.com/article/entertainment-arts-and-new-york-celebrity-lady-gaga-0f856b91db1a065ba43e0328922400a0.

59 *Alexander Forger, the attorney, bought a share of Lot 615:* Richard Reston, "Mrs. Onassis Breaks Silence; Says She Owns Gay Head Tract," *Vineyard Gazette*, August 22, 1978, https://vineyardgazette.com/news/1978/08/22/mrs-onassis-breaks-silence-says-she-owns-gay-head-tract; and "Onassis Battles with

Indian Legend," United Press International archives, January 19, 1989, https://www.upi.com/Archives/1989/01/19/Onassis-battles-with-Indian-legend/8624601189200/.

60 *Forger offered to swap another piece of land for Lot 615:* "Jackie Sues Indians in Martha's Vineyard Over a Beach," *Chicago Tribune*, https://www.chicagotribune.com/1989/01/23/jackie-sues-indians-in-marthas-vineyard-over-a-beach/; and Dana Kennedy, "Indians Stood by Ancient Creed in Fight with Onassis," *Tampa Bay Times*, March 11, 1990, https://www.tampabay.com/archive/1990/03/11/indians-stood-by-ancient-creed-in-fight-with-onassis/.

62 *During a 1986 Senate hearing on the settlement:* Indian Land Claims in the Town of Gay Head, MA, Before the Select Committee on Indian Affairs of the U.S. Senate, April 9, 1986, 99th Congress.

63 *Finally the two sides came to an agreement:* Kennedy, "Indians Stood by Ancient Creed."

64 *the Kennedy-Schlossberg family put over three hundred acres:* Julia Wells, "Kennedy Property, One of Last Unspoiled Tracts on Martha's Vineyard, Goes on the Market," *Vineyard Gazette*, June 27, 2019, https://vineyardgazette.com/news/2019/06/27/ending-era-kennedy-family-property-aquinnah-goes-market.

64 *the Martha's Vineyard Land Bank Commission bought 350 acres of land:* "Red Gate Farm Purchased by Land Bank," *Martha's Vineyard Times,* September 15, 2021, https://www.mvtimes.com/2021/09/15/red-gate-farm-purchased-land-bank/.

HATMARCHA GIFTS

69 *Shearer Cottage:* Nicholas Som, "Shearer Cottage and the Rich African American Heritage of Martha's Vineyard," National Trust for Historic Preservation, January 29, 2019, https://savingplaces.org/stories/shearer-cottage-and-the-rich-african-american-heritage-of-marthas-vineyard.

69 *Senator Ted Kennedy drove off a bridge on Chappaquiddick:* "50 Years Later, the Kennedy Accident Still Lures People to Chappaquiddick," *WGBH*, July 16, 2019, https://www.wgbh.org/news/local/2019-07-16/50-years-later-the-kennedy-accident-still-lures-people-to-chappaquiddick.

70 *the Nantucket Sound Island Trust bill*: Laurence Michie, "Island Trust Bill 25 Years Ago Foreshadowed Debate Over Land Use," May 23, 1995, https://vineyardgazette.com/news/1997/05/23/island-trust-bill-25-years-ago-foreshadowed-debate-over-land-use.

70 *Despite Senator Kennedy's efforts*: Ibid. and Richard Reston, "Islands Trust Bill Dies in House Subcommittee, *Vineyard Gazette*, September 24, 1976, https://vineyardgazette.com/news/1976/09/24/islands-trust-bill-dies-house-subcommittee.

70 *In June 1975, Steven Spielberg's* Jaws: Kate Erbland, "How 'Jaws' Forever Changed the Modern Day Blockbuster—and What Today's Examples Could Learn from It," *IndieWire*, June 18, 2024, https://www.indiewire.com/features/general/jaws-modern-blockbuster-steven-spielberg-1201844390/.

71 *It was the first major movie to be filmed on the ocean*: "Jaws—The Monster That Ate Hollywood," *WGBH,* accessed August 20, 2024, https://www.pbs.org/wgbh/pages/frontline/shows/hollywood/business/jaws.html.

71 *relatively shallow beaches*: Debby Wolfinson, "The Real-Life Locations Where Jaws Was Filmed," *Entertainment Weekly*, August 28, 2023, https://ew.com/movies/jaws-filming-locations/.

72 *In September 2022, Florida Governor Ron DeSantis:* Brooke Kushwaha, "Vineyard Community Rallies Relief Efforts to Assist Stranded Migrants," *Vineyard Gazette*, September 15, 2022, https://vineyardgazette.com/news/2022/09/15/vineyard-community-rallies-relief-efforts-assist-stranded-migrants; and Brooke Kushwaha, "Planeloads of Venezuelan Migrants Arrive at Martha's Vineyard Airport," *Vineyard Gazette*, September 14, 2022, https://vineyardgazette.com/news/2022/09/14/planeload-venezuelan-refugees-arrive-marthas-vineyard-airport.

73 *"their virtue-signaling is a fraud":* Snejana Farberov, "DeSantis Slams 'Virtue Signaling' Dems Going 'Berserk' Over Martha's Vineyard Migrants," *New York Post*, September 16, 2022, https://nypost.com/2022/09/16/desantis-slams-liberals-over-marthas-vineyard-migrant-move-outrage/.

74 *An op-ed in the* Los Angeles Times: Bob Drogin, "Op-Ed: Ron DeSantis' Cruel Political Theater Falls Flat on Martha's Vineyard," *Los Angeles Times*, September 15, 2022, https://www.latimes.com/opinion/story/2022-09-15/marthas-vineyard-migrants-ron-desantis.

86 *a UNESCO report on Maasai presence in the park:* "Report on the Joint WHC/ICOMOS/IUCN Mission to Ngorongoro Conservation Area, United Republic of Tanzania," United Nations Educational, Scientific and Cultural Organization, World Heritage Committee, 43rd Session, June 30–July 10, 2019, https://www.oaklandinstitute.org/sites/oaklandinstitute.org/files/pdfpreview/unesco-nca-report.pdf.

86 *The government is also trying to compel the Maasai*: "Broken Promises: Relocation Sites for Maasai Facing Evictions Remain Critically Flawed with Risk of Conflict Escalating," *The Oakland Institute,* December 1, 2022, https://www.oaklandinstitute.org/relocation-sites-maasai-evictions-critically-flawed.

86 *a Belgian report*: Raf de Bont, "'Primitives' and Protected Areas: International Conservation and the 'Naturalization' of Indigenous People, ca. 1910–1975," *Journal of the History of Ideas* 76, no. 2 (April 2015): 215–36, https://www.jstor.org/stable/43948735.

87 *a novel about a young Indigenous Sámi woman*: Ann-Helen Laestadius, *Stolen* (Scribner, 2023).

THE PEOPLE AND THE PANDEMIC

99 *the US passed the Indian Reorganization Act*: Vine Deloria Jr., *The Nations Within* (Pantheon, 2013), 140–53.

99 *Nearly two hundred tribes across the country voted in favor of the IRA*: Eric Lemont, "Developing Effective Processes of American Indian Constitutional and Governmental Reform: Lessons from the Cherokee Nation of Oklahoma, Hualapai Nation, Navajo Nation, and Northern Cheyenne Tribe," *American Indian Law Review* 26, no. 2 (2002): 147–76, https://digitalcommons.law.ou.edu/ailr/vol26/iss2/1.

99 *"a unique reflection of the country's traditions"*: Ibid.

RECOGNITION

104 *The treaties were approved by Congress*: "American Indian Treaties," Nation Archives, accessed August 20, 2024, https://www.archives.gov/research/native-americans/treaties#:~:text=The%20form%20of%20these%20agreements,to%20cross%20sovereign%20Indian%20lands.

104 *After the Civil War:* "Termination Era, the 1950s, Public Law 280," *Tribal Governance,* University of Alaska Fairbanks, accessed August 20, 2024, https://www.uaf.edu/tribal/academics/112/unit-2/terminationerathe1950spubliclaw280.php#:~:text=Over%20100%20tribes%20were%20terminated,the%20Menominee%20Tribe%20in%20Wisconsin.

104 *the Office of Federal Acknowledgment:* "How Is Federal Recognition Status Conferred?" Bureau of Indian Affairs, US Department of the Interior, November 8, 2017, https://www.bia.gov/faqs/how-federal-recognition-status-conferred.

105 *specific criteria for federal recognition*: Testimony of R. Lee Fleming, Director, Office of Federal Acknowledgment, for the Hearing Before the Committee on Indian Affairs, United States Senate, on the Federal Acknowledgment Process, 109th Congress, May 11, 2005.

WE CANNOT WAIT FOR OTHERS

113 *Countries like Ecuador had gone even further:* Audrey Carbonell, "The Legal Protection of Pachamama: The Implications of Environmental Personhood in Ecuador," *Columbia Undergraduate Law Review*, May 9, 2024, https://www.culawreview.org/journal/the-legal-protection-of-pachamama-the-implications-of-environmental-personhood-in-ecuador.

113 *a law codifying the rights of salmon*: Joseph Lee, "Do Salmon Have Rights?" *Grist*, March 1, 2022, https://grist.org/indigenous/do-salmon-have-rights/.

117 *representatives from dozens of communities in the Peruvian Amazon:* "The Wampis Nation—the First Indigenous Autonomous Government in Peru," International Work Group for Indigenous Affairs, June 25, 2018, https://www.iwgia.org/en/peru/3265-wampis-nation-peru.

117 *fifteen thousand people spread across 1.3 million hectares:* Ibid.

117 *Petroperu, Peru's national oil company:* Andrew E. Miller, "New Oil Company Enters Failed Block 64, Again," Amazon Watch, February 8, 2022, https://

amazonwatch.org/news/2022/0208-new-oil-company-enters-failed-block-64-again.

118 *Decades of spills and shoddy infrastructure:* "Assessing Petroperú's Financial, Legal, Environmental, and Social Risks," Amazon Watch, April 2024, https://amazonwatch.org/assets/files/2024-04-petroperu-risk-alert.pdf.

118 *Major financial institutions in the US and abroad:* Roshan Krishnan, "Vanguard Funds Indigenous Rights Violations in Peru's Amazon," Amazon Watch, September 9, 2022, https://amazonwatch.org/news/2022/0909-vanguard-funds-indigenous-rights-violations-in-perus-amazon; and "BlackRock, Vanguard Among Financiers That Poured $14.8 Billion into Mining Companies with Interests in Amazonian Indigenous Territories," Amazon Watch, February 22, 2022, https://amazonwatch.org/news/2022/0222-blackrock-vanguard-among-financiers-that-poured-14-8-billion-into-mining-companies-with-interests-in-amazonian-indigenous-territories.

121 *US military bases, which cover about 25 percent of the island:* "US Military Base Issues in Okinawa," Okinawa Prefectural Government, accessed August 20, 2024, https://dc-office.org/basedata.

121 *the Indigenous Ainu:* "Japan: New Ainu Law Becomes Effective," Library of Congress, August 5, 2019, https://www.loc.gov/item/global-legal-monitor/2019-08-05/japan-new-ainu-law-becomes-effective/#:~:text=(Aug.,People%20Is%20Respected%2C%20Act%20No.

122 *over $9 trillion in assets:* "BlackRock Reports Full Year 2023 Diluted EPS of $36.51, or $37.77 as adjusted Fourth Quarter 2023 Diluted EPS of $9.15, or $9.66 as adjusted," BlackRock, January 12, 2024, https://www.blackrock.com/corporate/newsroom/press-releases/article/corporate-one/press-releases/blackrock-reports-full-Year-2023-diluted; Peru, The World Bank, accessed August 20, 2024, https://data.worldbank.org/country/peru?_gl=1*7vcwhn*_gcl_au*MTg5ODMyNzQ0NS4xNzIzOTIwNzQ2; and GDP, The World Bank, accessed August 20, 2024, https://data.worldbank.org/indicator/NY.GDP.MKTP.CD?_gl=1%2A7vcwhn%2A_gcl_au%2AMTg5ODMyNzQ0NS4xNzIzOTIwNzQ2&most_recent_value_desc=true.

122 *a document written by Shapiom Noningo:* Shapiom Noningo, "Routes to Indigenous Autonomy: The Case of the Wampis Nation and Its Autonomous Territorial Government (GTANW)," January 2018.

TIME IS ON OUR SIDE

127 *the largest dam removal in US history:* Mia Estrada, "'The Evergreen': The Largest Dam Removal Project in the US," *Oregon Public Broadcasting*, March 11, 2024, https://www.opb.org/article/2024/03/11/the-evergreen-podcast-klamath-dam-removal-dams-native-tribes/#:~:text=On%20the%20Oregon%2DCalifornia%20border,returned%20to%20Native%20American%20tribes.

130 *gold was discovered in nearby Yreka, California:* "History of Yreka," City of Yreka, accessed August 20, 2024, https://ci.yreka.ca.us/302/History-of-Yreka.

130 *the six dams of the Klamath Hydroelectric Project:* Juliet Grable, "After a Century of Displacement, Shasta Indian Nation Sees Hope in Dam Removal," Jefferson Public Radio, October 15, 2023, https://www.ijpr.org/politics-government/2023-10-15/after-a-century-of-displacement-shasta-indian-nation-sees-hope-in-dam-removal.

131 *Peter Burnett, the state's first governor:* Peter Burnett, California State of the State Address, January 6, 1851, https://governors.library.ca.gov/addresses/s_01-Burnett2.html#:~:text=That%20a%20war%20of%20extermination,wisdom%20of%20man%20to%20avert.

137 *a wetland area stretching over one hundred thousand acres:* Robert Donnelly, "Tulelake, California," Oregon Historical Society, 2003, https://www.oregonhistoryproject.org/articles/historical-records/tulelake-california/; and "About Tulelake," City of Tulelake, accessed August 20, 2024, https://cityoftulelake.com/about-tulelake/.

140 *the 2002 fish kill:* Kristen Boyles, "The Legacy of the Klamath River Fish Kill," *Earthjustice*, May 9, 2006, https://earthjustice.org/feature/the-legacy-of-the-klamath-river-fish-kill.

THE WILL OF THE PEOPLE

143 *the first official Indian gaming operation in the country:* Eve Darian-Smith, "Indian gaming." Encyclopedia Britannica, May 22, 2016, https://www.britannica.com/topic/Indian-gaming; and "History," National Indian Gaming Commission, accessed August 20, 2024, https://www.nigc.gov/commission/history.

144 *the Indian Gaming Regulatory Act:* "History," National Indian Gaming Commission, accessed August 20, 2024, https://www.nigc.gov/commission/history.

144 *the Foxwoods Resort Casino:* Michael Sokolove, "Foxwoods Is Fighting for Its Life," *New York Times,* March 14, 2012, https://www.nytimes.com/2012/03/18/magazine/mike-sokolove-foxwood-casinos.html.

144 *over $5 billion in gross gaming revenue:* Growth of Tribal Gaming Revenue (in Billions), National Indian Gaming Commission, https://www.nigc.gov/images/uploads/reports/19962006revenues.pdf.

144 *the state would issue three gaming licenses:* "The Road to Casino Gambling," *Vineyard Gazette*, February 27, 2019, https://vineyardgazette.com/news/2019/02/27/road-gaming.

144 *a Class II gaming facility:* "News Update: Friday, April 13—Tribe Looks to Build Casino on Vineyard," *Vineyard Gazette*, April 13, 2012, https://vineyardgazette.com/news/2012/04/13/news-update-friday-april-13-tribe-looks-build-casino-vineyard.

145 *At the May 2011 general membership meeting:* Nelson Sigelman, "Aquinnah Wampanoag Tribe Approves Community Center Casino," *Martha's Vineyard Times*, May 7, 2012, https://www.mvtimes.com/2012/05/07/aquinnah-wampanoag-tribe-approves-community-center-casino-10579/.

145 *joined the town in a lawsuit:* "Judge Rules Town, Local Group Can Join Casino Lawsuit," *NECN,* August 6, 2014, https://www.necn.com/news/local/judge-rules-town-local-group-can-join-casino-lawsuit/173524/.

148 *the tribe did not exercise "sufficient governmental authority":* John H. Kennedy, "Court Denies Tribe Rights to Pursue Gambling on Martha's Vineyard," *Vineyard Gazette*, November 13, 2015, https://vineyardgazette.com/news/2015/11/13/court-denies-tribe-rights-pursue-gambling-marthas-vineyard.

149 *the First Circuit appellate panel ruled in favor of the tribe:* John H. Kennedy, "U.S. Appeals Court Rules Soundly for Wampanoag Tribe in Casino Case," *Vineyard Gazette*, April 11, 2017, https://vineyardgazette.com/news/2017/04/11/us-appeals-court-rules-soundly-wampanoag-tribe-casino-case.

BIG SLOW-MOVING THING

151 *The mine was being backed by Calista Corporation:* "Calista Corporation June 2024 Statement on Proposed Donlin Gold Project," Calista Corporation, June 24, 2024, https://www.calistacorp.com/news/june-2024-statement-on-proposed-donlin-gold-project/.

151 *one of the largest river deltas in the world:* "Yukon Delta, Alaska," Jet Propulsion Laboratory NASA, March 8, 2022, https://www.jpl.nasa.gov/images/pia25124-yukon-delta-alaska.

152 *a city of about six thousand:* "About the YK Delta," Yukon-Kuskokwim Health Corporation, accessed August 20, 2024, https://www.ykhc.org/story/about-yk/.

153 *one of thirteen Alaska Native Corporations:* "Our Region," Calista Corporation, accessed August 20, 2024, https://www.calistacorp.com/shareholders/our-region/.

SOVEREIGNTY ISN'T JUST "I'M GOING TO DO WHAT I WANT"

167 *the Cherokee Nation had enslaved about four thousand people: Treaty with the Cherokee 1866*, July 19, 1866, https://treaties.okstate.edu/treaties/treaty-with-the-cherokee-1866-0942; and "Slave Revolt of 1842," *The Encyclopedia of Oklahoma History and Culture*, accessed August 20, 2024, https://www.okhistory.org/publications/enc/entry?entry=SL002#:~:text=Of%20the%20Five%20Tribes%2C%20the,as%20English%20interpreters%20and%20translators.

168 *eligible for Cherokee enrollment:* Kat Chow, "Judge Rules That Cherokee Freedmen Have Right to Tribal Citizenship," NPR, August 31, 2021, https://www

.npr.org/sections/thetwo-way/2017/08/31/547705829/judge-rules-that-cherokee-freedmen-have-right-to-tribal-citizenship.

168 *the Cherokee Nation removed the phrase "Cherokee by blood":* Mary Louise Kelly and Farah Eltohamy, "Cherokee Nation Strikes Down Language That Limits Citizenship Rights 'By Blood,' " NPR, February 25, 2021, https://www.npr.org/2021/02/25/971084455/cherokee-nation-strikes-down-language-that-limits-citizenship-rights-by-blood.

169 *Over ten thousand people have been disenrolled:* Jamie Dunaway, "The Fight Over Who's a Real Indian," *Slate*, June 12, 2018, https://slate.com/news-and-politics/2018/06/native-american-disenrollments-are-waning-after-decades-of-tribes-stripping-citizenship-from-members.html.

169 *Since the Picayune Rancheria of the Chukchansi Indians built a successful casino:* Carmen Kohlruss, "California Tribe Looks to Oust Members on Election Eve as Casino Profits Soar," *Modesto Bee*, September 30, 2022, https://www.modbee.com/news/california/article266621041.html.

170 *hanged by the US army:* Chuck Williams, "Kalliah Tumulth (Indian Mary) (1854–1906)," Oregon Encyclopedia, June 11, 2024, https://www.oregonencyclopedia.org/articles/indian_mary/#:~:text=In%20April%201856%2C%20Tumulth%20and,nonlocal%20Yakama%20and%20Klickitat%20people.

170 *the Grand Ronde enrollment committee notified sixty-six citizens:* Amanda Preacher, "Tribal Court Reverses Grand Ronde Disenrollment Decision," *Oregon Public Broadcasting,* August 8, 2016, https://www.opb.org/news/article/grand-ronde-disenrollment-decision-reversed-chief-tumulth/#:~:text=A%20tribal%20appeals%20court%20has,recognized%20as%20official%20tribal%20members.

180 *appointed to the tribe's Environmental Protection Commission:* B. Toastie Oaster, "Marilyn Vann Becomes the First Person of Freedmen Status in Cherokee Nation Government," *High Country News*, September 28, 2021, https://www.hcn.org/articles/indigenous-affairs-interview-marilyn-vann-becomes-the-first-freedmen-in-cherokee-nation-government/.

WE KNOW WE ARE NOT ALONE

187 *one of the first major international studies of Indigenous peoples:* José R. Martínez Cobo, "Study of the Problem of Discrimination Against Indigenous Populations," United Nations, July 30, 1981, https://www.un.org/development/desa/indigenouspeoples/publications/2014/09/martinez-cobo-study/.

194 *Tommy Orange's novel* There There: Tommy Orange, *There There* (Knopf, 2019).

195 *The Gisborne area is about 50 percent Māori:* Matai O'Connor, "Gisborne Leads NZ with Highest Māori Population Proportion," *Te Ao Māori News,* June 6, 2024, https://www.teaonews.co.nz/2024/06/02/gisborne-leads-nz-with-highest-maori-population-proportion/.

WHOLLY AND ALWAYS AND FOREVER—INDIAN

199 *an 1869 quote from William Claflin:* "Evidence for Proposed Finding Against Federal Acknowledgment of the Wampanoag Tribal Council of Gay Head, Inc." (United States Department of the Interior, Office of Federal Acknowledgment, 1985), 28.

201 *"wholly and always and forever—Indian":* Ibid., 28.

204 *the first member of a federally recognized tribe to ride in the Tour de France:* James Raia, "Neilson Powless Is the First Tribally Recognized Native North American to Race the Tour de France," *Velo*, May 31, 2023, https://velo.outsideonline.com/road/road-racing/neilson-powless-is-the-first-tribally-recognized-native-american-to-race-the-tour-de-france/.

CONCLUSION: OUR OWN MAP

214 *"An Indian place should have an Indian name":* "Gay Head Journal; A Town with History, but Whose?" *New York Times,* April 20, 1991, https://www.nytimes.com/1991/04/20/us/gay-head-journal-a-town-with-history-but-whose.html.

214 *Carl and others brought the name change to a vote again:* The Associated Press, "Gay Head or Aquinnah? Change Comes to a Vote," *Standard-Times*, May 14, 1997, https://www.southcoasttoday.com/story/news/state/1997/05/14/gay-head-aquinnah-change-comes/50614223007/.

215 *Joy Harjo's "A Map to the Next World":* Joy Harjo, "A Map to the Next World," in *How We Became Human: New and Selected Poems: 1975–2001* (W. W. Norton & Company Inc., 2002), https://www.poetryfoundation.org/poems/49621/a-map-to-the-next-world.

ABOUT THE AUTHOR

Joseph Lee is an award-winning Aquinnah Wampanoag writer and teacher in New York City. He has an MFA from Columbia University. His work has appeared in *The New York Times*, *The Nation*, *The Guardian*, and others. Learn more at josephvlee.com or on Instagram @joseph.v.lee.

ATRIA BOOKS, an imprint of Simon & Schuster, fosters an open environment where ideas flourish, bestselling authors soar to new heights, and tomorrow's finest voices are discovered and nurtured. Since its launch in 2002, Atria has published hundreds of bestsellers and extraXordinary books, which would not have been possible without the invaluable support and expertise of its team and publishing partners. Thank you to the Atria Books colleagues who collaborated on *Nothing More of This Land* as well as to the hundreds of professionals in the Simon & Schuster advertising, audio, communications, design, ebook, finance, human resources, legal, marketing, operations, production, sales, supply chain, subsidiary rights, and warehouse departments who help Atria bring great books to light.

Editorial
Alessandra Bastagli
Rola Harb

Jacket Design
James Iacobelli
Kelli McAdams

Marketing
Erin Kibby
Annie Probert

Managing Editorial
Paige Lytle
Shelby Pumphrey
Lacee Burr
Sofia Echeverry

Production
Fausto Bozza
Jill Putorti

Publicity
Joanna Pinsker

Publishing Office
Suzanne Donahue
Abby Velasco

Subsidiary Rights
Nicole Bond
Sara Bowne
Rebecca Justiniano